HOLY RESILIENCE

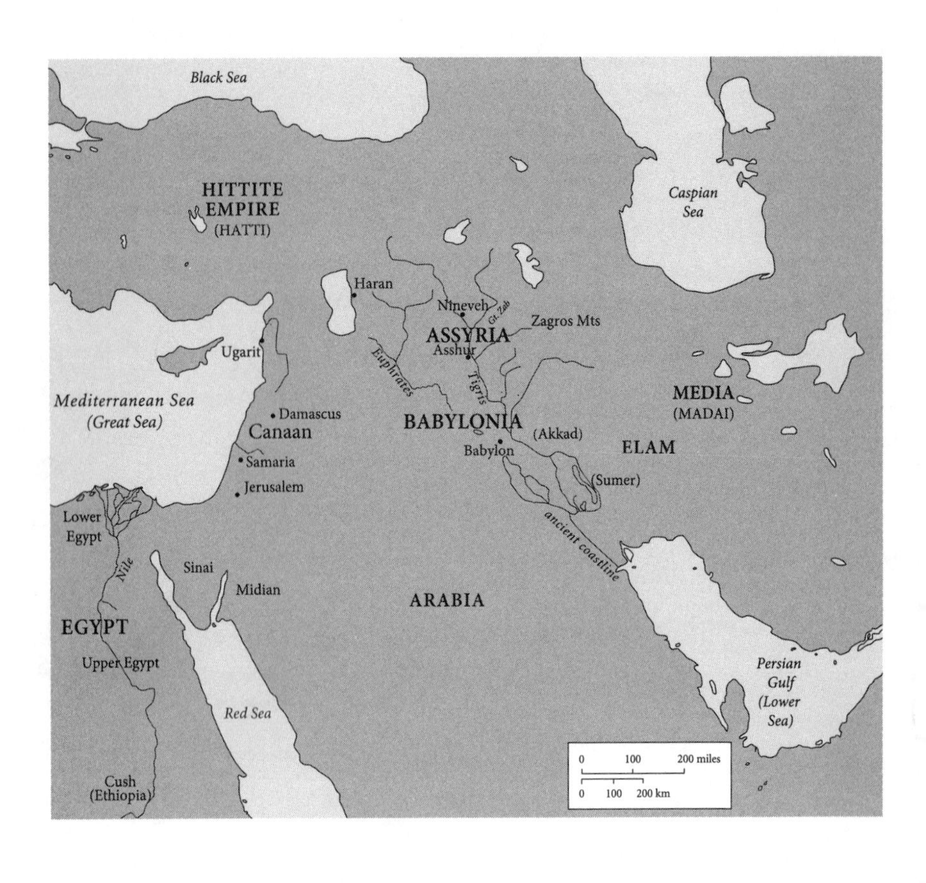
Black Sea
HITTITE EMPIRE
(HATTI)
Caspian Sea
Haran
Nineveh
Gt. Zab
Zagros Mts
ASSYRIA
Asshur
Ugarit
Euphrates
Tigris
Mediterranean Sea
(Great Sea)
Damascus
Canaan
BABYLONIA
MEDIA
(MADAI)
(Akkad)
Babylon
ELAM
Samaria
Jerusalem
(Sumer)
Lower Egypt
ancient coastline
Nile
Sinai
Midian
ARABIA
EGYPT
Upper Egypt
Persian Gulf
(Lower Sea)
Red Sea
0 100 200 miles
0 100 200 km
Cush
(Ethiopia)

HOLY RESILIENCE

The Bible's Traumatic Origins

David M. Carr

Yale UNIVERSITY PRESS

New Haven & London

Published with assistance from the foundation established in memory of Philip Hamilton McMillan of the Class of 1894, Yale College.

Frontispiece: The ancient Near East, significantly adapted from "Israel and Ancient Trade Routes," in Oxford Bible Atlas, 4th ed., ed. Adrian Curtis (Oxford: Oxford University Press, 2007), 67.

Yale University Press books may be purchased in quantity for educational, business, or promotional use. For information, please e-mail sales.press@yale.edu (U.S. office) or sales@yaleup.co.uk (U.K. office).

Designed by James Johnson.
Set in Walbaum Roman type by IDS Infotech, Ltd.
Printed in the United States of America.

Library of Congress Cataloging-in-Publication Data
Carr, David McLain, 1961–. Holy resilience: the Bible's traumatic origins/David M. Carr.
pages cm
Includes bibliographical references and index.
ISBN 978-0-300-20456-8 (hardback)
1. Bible—History. 2. Suffering—Biblical teaching. 3. Suffering—Religious aspects—Judaism. 4. Suffering—Religious aspects—Christianity.
I. Title.
BS445.C37 2014
220.6—dc23
2014009144

A catalogue record for this book is available from the British Library.

This paper meets the requirements of ANSI/NISO Z39.48-1992 (Permanence of Paper).

10 9 8 7 6 5 4 3 2 1

This book is dedicated to all haunted by suffering,
especially those haunted by experiences
of war

The spaces which are unwritten are anything but empty. They are the places where deeper power lives, where the "more" of living experience refuses to be ruled by the "less" of what can be written. ... These unwritten spaces pull with the power of a star's gravity, drawing everything into orbit around themselves. It is around the unwritten spaces that the "texts" rotate. ... The lived world is stronger than the authorized world. It is around the lived world that the texts of authorization revolve as lesser satellites, although a Ptolemaic imagination believes otherwise.

—DOW EDGERTON,
The Passion of Interpretation

CONTENTS

PREFACE

I OFFER THIS BOOK as a synthesis of research on the Bible and an experiment in supplementing such scholarship with research on trauma and memory. Though I could have added qualifiers to many more sentences in the book, readers should just take note that the whole represents my considered judgment on issues of continuing discussion. The translations of Hebrew texts throughout are my own, while translations of the Greek are drawn or adapted from the New Revised Standard Version unless otherwise noted.

Writing this book, I felt surrounded by a cloud of witnesses of people, near and far, who have been traumatized. Some such traumas are named and known, while many others are not. As a Quaker, I am especially conscious of those who have suffered and are now suffering in war—the war on terror, the war on drugs, and more conventional wars in Iraq, Afghanistan, and many other places. Others may read this book with their own cloud of witnesses or personal experiences of trauma. Though I write here about ancient trauma, I dedicate this book to those who have experienced trauma more recently.

HOLY RESILIENCE

Introduction

WHEN MY WIFE and I rolled out on a spectacular Columbus Day weekend, 2010, thoughts of biblical research were far from my mind. It was our tenth anniversary, and we were meeting some friends for a bike ride in the Catskill Mountains of New York. Just a half-hour into our ride my bicycle fell apart on a downhill. The impact on pavement left me with ten broken ribs, a broken collarbone, a collapsed lung, and months of healing and rehabilitation ahead. I lived, barely. The thoracic surgeon who eventually rebuilt my chest with six platinum plates said that I was the only patient he knew who had survived the level of chest trauma he saw. He speculated that this was due to conditioning I'd built up as an amateur bike racer. In the months to come I remained haunted with images of what life might have been like for my family and friends if I had died.

This experience of personal suffering meshed in an unexpected way with a research initiative on trauma and the Bible that I had started just a year before. I am a biblical scholar who specializes in what academics often term the Hebrew Bible, usually called the Old Testament by Christians and the Tanach by Jews; I shall use the first of these terms in this book. A year before my bicycle accident I had presented a paper at my professional association that focused on the study of trauma and the biblical prophets.[1] My thesis was that contemporary studies of trauma could explain characteristics of prophetic books written in the context of the exile of Jews in Babylon. As a biblical scholar, I was acutely aware, of course, of differences between ancient Israelite experiences of suffering and contemporary experiences labeled traumatic. Still, humans started experiencing trauma a long time before trauma studies began. The more I read psychological, anthropological, and other studies of trauma, the more I have come to believe that they can teach me and others about how this ancient Israelite people suffered and how their experiences live on with us through the Bible.

The accident, combined with my reading on trauma, allowed me to see the Bible with fresh eyes. It sensitized me to ways that both the Jewish and Christian scriptures were formed in the context of centuries of catastrophic suffering.

Here I tell the story of how the Jewish and Christian Bibles both emerged as responses to suffering, particularly group suffering. Both Judaism and Christianity offer visions of religious life that emphasize religious community, whether the people of Israel or the church.[2] Moreover, the Jewish and Christian scriptures define these communities in ways that have helped these communities endure catastrophe, rather than be devastated by it. Perhaps most important, the scriptures of Judaism and Christianity, written in part as a response to communal suffering, present suffering as part of a broader story of redemption. In complicated ways, each tradition depicts catastrophe as a path forward. This is the kind of religious perspective, for example, that can include the exhortation by Jesus, "If any want to become my followers, let them take up their cross and follow me" (Mark 8:34; parallels in Matt 16:24; Luke 9:23).

The cross of Jesus, of course, is just one of many painful episodes that fed into the Bible, some better known than others. First, the Assyrians, an efficient and terrifying empire based in what is now northern Iraq, destroyed the Northern Kingdom of Israel and almost destroyed the kingdom of Judah to the south. The Assyrians then dominated Judah for almost a century. Next, another Mesopotamian empire, the Babylonians, destroyed Jerusalem and deported its population to remote parts of Babylon. A few decades later the Persian Empire defeated the Babylonians and allowed a few Judean exiles to trickle back home to Jerusalem. These returnees, however, never regained their Davidic kings or statehood. Instead, they formed a Temple-centered community shaped by lessons learned while in exile in Babylon. Centuries later a Hellenistic king, Antiochus the fourth, gained control of Judah, rededicated the temple to a Greek god, and enforced the death penalty for anyone practicing Judaism. Though his rule was eventually ended by the Maccabean revolt, Judah soon fell under the power of Rome. And this set the stage for the crucifixion of Jesus and other Jews convicted of rebellion, the eventual destruction of Jerusalem, and Roman criminalization of the emergent Jesus movement.

Before all this suffering, ancient Israel had a set of scriptures much like that of other nations—some hymns celebrating the royal dynasty and its capital, royal instructions, love songs, some myths of creation and flood. These were Israel's "pretrauma" scriptures. After centuries of crisis, ancient Israel had transformed its scriptures so they focused instead on landless ancestors and life in the wilderness. The later Christian church then built its scriptures around stories of a crucified savior. The Bible's distinctive themes and emphases can be traced back to century after century of crisis. It certainly contains texts about other aspects of human experience—joy, gratitude, love, wonder, and the like. Nevertheless, it was during periods of crisis that the overall shape and emphases of the scriptures were shaped the most.

Thus suffering, and survival of it, was written into the Bible. This helps explain why these scriptures survived into the present when many other ancient texts did not. The once-famous texts of ancient empires in Egypt and Mesopotamia perished. They died with the empires they celebrated. Only in the past two centuries have archaeologists rediscovered these texts and deciphered them. Even the great texts of the Roman Empire—now studied in universities and some upper-level schools—have not enjoyed the impact and circulation of the New Testament texts that were written in their shadow. The embedding of survival of trauma into the Bible provides a partial answer to why Jewish and Christian scriptures flourished when such imperial scriptures did not. The Jewish and Christian scriptures arose out of and speak to catastrophic human trauma.[3]

This does not, of course, reduce the message of the Bible to ancient experiences that shaped it. Rather, experiences of suffering can teach forms of wisdom that transcend their original contexts. Sometimes it can take a painful experience to learn difficult truths. That does not mean, however, that such truths learned in pain are mere reflections of life's difficulties. Instead, in at least some situations, trauma can strip away one's illusions. It can reveal life's transitory and often random character. The story that one learns to tell after trauma must encompass that experience and transcend it. The chorus in Aeschylus's *Agamemnon* describes Zeus's intention for suffering in this way:

> He [Zeus] leads mortals to understand
> that knowledge comes through suffering—
> he has established this as law . . .
> wisdom comes unwillingly.
> It is a violent gift, I suppose,
> from the gods on the awesome rowing bench.[4]

Survivors of this "violent gift" can never leave their suffering completely behind. Some, however, find that they grow from it. They develop a deeper resilience and grow in unforeseen ways.[5]

The Bibles, both of Judaism and of Christianity, are a written deposit of centuries of survival of suffering, communal resilience. Where the myths of other nations focused on triumph and died with them, the Bible speaks of survival of total catastrophe. Other scriptures pictured gods who sponsored empires in their domination of others. The Jewish and Christian scriptures envision a God who brought suffering on God's own people and yet carried them through it. The contemporary cultural scene seems to favor politicians and religious leaders who affirm their constituents and their lives without much question. The scriptures of Judaism and Christianity offer pictures of a God who is still present when life shatters to pieces. Life can shatter us into pieces. That, I suggest, is a big reason why we still have the Jewish and Christian Bibles with us now.

So far I have used a variety of terms to describe human affliction—"catastrophe," "suffering," "trauma." Before turning to the story at hand, let me say more about the concept of trauma and why I find it useful for this discussion. After all, the word "trauma" has been increasingly trivialized in recent years, and most studies of trauma have focused on contemporary experiences distant from those of ancient Israel and the church. I have heard the word "trauma" applied to experiences as diverse as genocide and frustration over a bad grade. Some people with whom I have discussed this project even suggested leaving the concept of trauma to the side in this study, focusing only on the story of how historical catastrophes contributed to the writing of the Bible.

I share some of these reservations, but I still find contemporary research on trauma helpful in study of the Bible. Here is why: such trauma studies highlight how overwhelming suffering often affects memory and behavior in *indirect* ways. My definition of trauma is implicit in this statement. As I understand it, trauma is an overwhelming, haunting experience of disaster so explosive in its impact that it cannot be directly encountered and influences an individual/group's behavior and memory in indirect ways.

This definition builds on characterizations of trauma by others. For example, Judith Herman writes in her classic *Trauma and Recovery* that "traumatic events overwhelm the ordinary systems of care that give people a sense of control, connection, and meaning." A leading literary theorist of trauma, Cathy Caruth, states that "trauma is the confrontation with an event that, in its unexpectedness or horror, cannot be placed within the schemes of prior knowledge." Later she adds, it is "history that *has no place*." It is "speechless terror." Finally, in a less well-known article on the metapsychology of trauma, Carole Beebe Tarantelli describes trauma as an "explosion" of the psyche, so catastrophic that there is no "I" that can experience it. It temporarily annihilates the "I" of the psyche, batters down every frame for experience. The psyche's templates cannot comprehend it.[6]

In this book I am primarily focused on trauma that affected ancient *groups*, not the explosion of individual psyches. Nevertheless, I find Tarantelli's metaphor of explosion a helpful corrective to the use of "trauma" as a virtual synonym for "suffering." Groups, of course, can experience all kinds of deeply painful experiences. In some cases, modern groups even choose to focus on such painful experiences in their past, coming to define themselves by shared "chosen traumas" (as psychoanalyst Vamik Volkan terms them): the 1620 disaster at Bilá Bora for Czechs, the massacre at wounded knee in 1890 for the Lakota people, the Nazi genocide for Jews. In these cases a profoundly painful experience comes to be integrated by a group into its master narrative about itself, helping to define that group's identity and often grounding that group's claims for redress. Though the Bible does describe events akin to modern "shared traumas"—such as accounts of the destruction of Jerusalem in the Old Testament or Jesus' crucifixion in the New Testament—I am even more interested here in places where these traumas and others were so explosive that their impact on the Bible was indirect. Contrary to our contemporary world, which often valorizes trauma, the world of ancient Israel and the early church tended to see suffering as clear evidence of an individual or group's cursedness.[7]

In this book I examine how ancient Israel, early Judaism, and the early church did not just suffer but faced catastrophic disasters that shredded their existing group identity. I will describe how the original "Israel" was destroyed by the Assyrians, how a Judah centered on Jerusalem took on the identity of destroyed Israel, how the inhabitants of Jerusalem reshaped their identity when Jerusalem was destroyed and they were sent into exile, how the Hebrew Bible we now have was fixed in response to a sustained Greek attempt to obliterate Judaism, and how Judaism and Christianity both emerged out of Roman attempts to use terrorizing violence to suppress Jewish nationalism and Christian missionary monotheism. These crises did not just produce pain and suffering for individuals. They shattered the identities of whole groups, requiring them to come to new understandings of themselves, understandings now inscribed and fixed in the Jewish and Christian scriptures.

The concept of trauma helps us understand how Western culture remains haunted by these catastrophes, even as many in this culture know little about them. For example, one might not initially think of monotheism as a response to suffering, but Israel's development of monotheism arguably was prompted at every turn by communal disasters.[8] Christianity conveyed this monotheism beyond the bounds of Israel. Indeed, central aspects of the Christian tradition, including the very name *Christian*, owe their origins to the suffering of early Jesus followers as they spread their form of monotheism across the Roman Empire.

Western culture inherits this monotheistic legacy, even parts of Western culture that are relentlessly secular. For the core innovation of ancient monotheism was not some kind of pure belief in only one God, but the rejection of other gods. Ancient Israel came to be distinguished from its neighbors by an increasingly disenchanted world, where a person was expected to worship only the national God (a deity called Yahweh, but translated as LORD in most English translations). Worship of any other spirit or divinity was forbidden—not ancestral spirits, not God's spouse (Yahweh did once have one), not local deities or flashy foreign ones. No god but Yahweh. The peoples around Israel and early Judaism generally recognized and even worshiped a diverse variety of spirits and divinities, even if some saw one deity as supreme over all. Their world was infused with divine spirits, spirits who could be interacted with through use of vivid pictures and sculptures. The crises of ancient Israel, however, birthed a form of piety that allowed devotion to only one deity, who could not be given a worldly image. All others were rejected. Yet further crises led Israel to deny that any other deities than Yahweh even existed. Their world became disenchanted. Contemporary secular Western views of the world continue that tradition of a disenchanted world, only now without recognition of even the one deity endorsed by Judaism and Christianity.

A disenchanted world. Rejection of others' deities. Religious communities built around common scriptures and concepts of God rather than land- and state-based political structures. These are just some of the elements of the contemporary world connected to ancient Israelite and Christian experiences of suffering. We turn now to ancient texts and communities that preceded such experiences: Israel, Judah, and the writing of their pretrauma scriptures.

CHAPTER ONE

Israel, Judah, and the Birth of Scripture

Ancient Israel suffered, but its scriptures did not *begin* with trauma. The most ancient Israel did not even have written texts. Its oral traditions, if anything, celebrated victory rather than mourning defeat.

"Israel" first appears in the record of the Ancient Near East about three thousand years ago in 1250 BCE (BCE=BC). The land of Canaan was dominated by Egypt, an empire built around the Nile River about four hundred miles to the west. The ruler of Egypt, Pharaoh Mernephtah, sent an expedition to Canaan to assert his dominance over the area. In an inscription celebrating his campaign, he boasts of having "decimated the people of Israel and put their children to death."[1] This is the first clearly datable reference to "Israel" in world literature, and it records the suffering of the tribal people of Israel at the hands of an invading Egyptian army.

This Israelite people, however, was not completely helpless before its foes. One of the earliest poems preserved in the Bible, the song of Deborah in Judges 5, describes the joining of Israelite tribes to repel the attack of an army from the major Canaanite city of Hazor. The singer is Deborah, a female leader who led the tribes in battle. Using a particularly ancient form of Hebrew, Deborah lists tribes that answered the call to battle (the tribal names are in **bold**):

> From **Ephraim** they set out in the valley.
> After you, **Benjamin** is in your ranks.
> Commanders have come down from **Machir**,
> those who wield the marshal's staff, from **Zebulun**.
> The chiefs of **Issachar** are with Deborah;
> **Issachar** following Barak, sent in the valley hot on his heels. (Judges 5:14–15)

After listing these tribes that answered the call, Deborah chastises those tribes that failed to come when called:

> In the clans of **Reuben**
> there were great searchings of heart.
> Why did you stay among the sheep,
> listening for the shepherd's whistle among the flocks?
> (In the clans of **Reuben**,
> there were great searchings of heart.)
> **Gilead** stayed away across the Jordan,
> and why did **Dan** have stay by the ships?
> **Asher** stayed away on the seacoast,
> dwelling secure within his ports. (5:14–17)

Deborah concludes by affirming the help of the tribes of Zebulun and Naphtali: "**Zebulun** is a people that mocked death, also **Naphtali** on the heights of the field" (5:18). In sum, six tribes came to the battle: Ephraim, Benjamin, Machir, Zebulun, Issachar, and Naphtali. Four did not: Reuben, Gilead, Dan, and Asher.

These names may be foreign and unfamiliar to some readers. What is important is this: the tribal name of Judah, so central in the rest of the Bible, is never mentioned in this early survey of "Israel." Though Deborah lists many tribal groups who did or did not help, the southern tribes of Judah and Simeon are not even on her radar. And we see a similar pattern across other stories about tribes in the biblical book of Judges. With the exception of an initial Judean "judge" added as a prologue to the book (Othniel in Judges 3:7–11), *all* of the judges and tribes mentioned in the rest of Judges come from the central and northern highland regions of Canaan. These were the regions first inhabited by tribal groups when "Israel" first appears in the archaeological record around 1225 BCE. These are the "Israel" mentioned by Mernephtah.

Our story starts with this tribal Israel, an early Israel formed only of these highland tribes. We have no written texts from these tribal groups. Like most other tribal groups of the ancient Near East, these tribes were nonliterate. At most a clan leader in Israel might hire a scribe to label a particularly valuable dagger or bowl. Otherwise, the people of Israel sang songs of victory like the song of Deborah. They told tales of ancestors, such as Jacob, also known as Israel, their namesake.

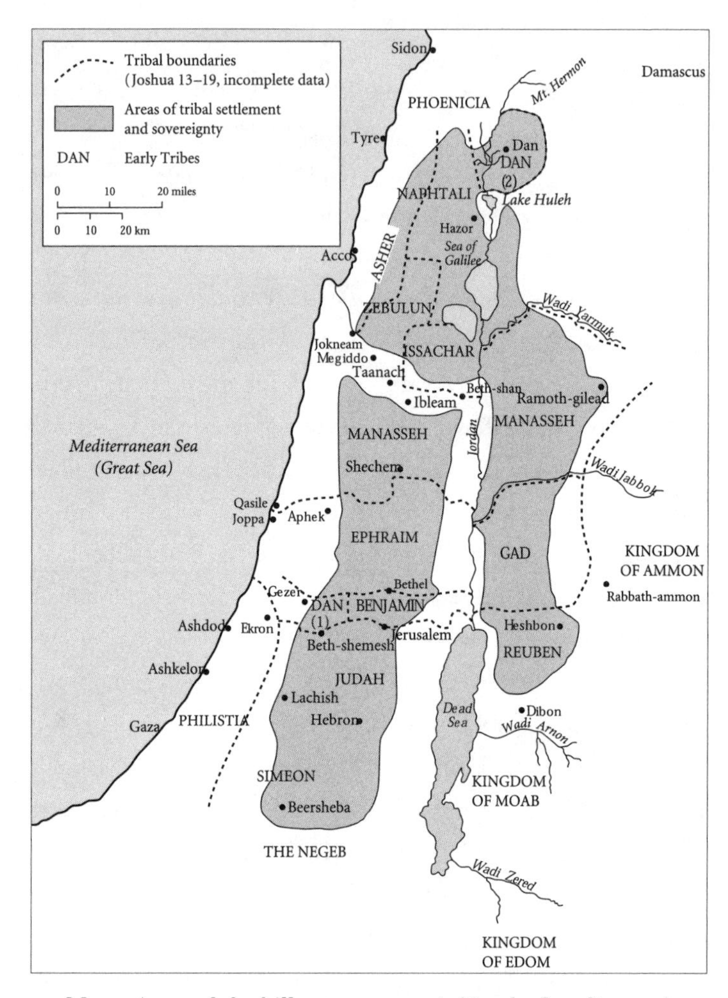

Map 1: Areas of the hill country occupied by the Israelites and Judeans, and where the tribes are said to have been located in the prestate period. Redrawn from Norman Gottwald, *The Hebrew Bible: A Socio-Literary Introduction* (Philadelphia: Fortress, 1985).

And they probably also told stories about how their parents, enslaved in Egypt, enjoyed an early victory over the Egyptian pharaoh and his army, back then under the leadership of "Moses." These Israelite oral tales stand behind the biblical books of the Pentateuch (Genesis–Deuteronomy), but they are hardly identical with them. Despite claims to the contrary, exclusively oral cultures like tribal Israel do not precisely preserve their traditions from generation to generation.[2]

Meanwhile, writing was the sort of thing that the urban enemies of Israel, enemies like Hazor or Egypt, did. The great empires like Egypt or Mesopotamia used literary texts—royal psalms and epics, myths, wisdom instructions, and love songs—to educate their elite leaders. Nearby cities in Canaan imitated those cultures, using writing to claim the prestige of those great cultures for themselves.[3] Writing was a thing for enemy city-state monarchies. The tribes of Israel had little use for it.

THE BIRTH OF THE BIBLE IN ISRAEL'S FIRST MONARCHY

Little use for writing, that is, until the Israelites adopted a city-state monarchy for themselves. There came a time when alliances like the one formed by Deborah did not suffice to repel Israel's enemies. The result was that Israel adopted a centralized political system, a monarchy, like that of its enemies. With this came writing, indeed a set of written scriptures like those of neighboring nations. These early scriptures form the pretraumatic core of the Old Testament.

The crisis occurred about 1000 BCE. The Israelite tribes were attacked by an alliance of five cities on the Canaanite coastland, the "Philistines." This Philistine attack proved harder to repel than earlier ones, and it shocked the Israelite tribes to the core. The tribes rallied first around a figure named Saul, who achieved initial success against the chariots and professional soldiers of Philistia. Nevertheless, Saul's success proved temporary. The organized military power of the Philistines was too much for the voluntary army of Israelites to handle. The future existence of "Israel" was in question.

When Saul was killed in battle, the Israelite tribes took radical action. They chose a leader from outside Israel. His name was David, and he was a mercenary from the tribe of Judah who had even worked for a Philistine king for a time. David accepted leadership of the Israelite tribes, defeated his former Philistine allies, and went on to military victories over other neighboring peoples. But David did more than achieve temporary military success for Israel. He set up a kingship over Israel that resembled the urban monarchies that tribal Israel once had fought. He started by conquering a walled city possessed by Jebusites, Jerusalem, and made it the capital of his new kingdom. Jerusalem was well situated for this function, since it was located safely in a remote part of the Canaanite hill country on the border between Judah and Israel.

Little by little David's Jerusalem-based kingdom acquired the trappings of a city monarchy. It had not only a walled base in Jerusalem but a standing army, a royal court modeled on the Egyptian court, and even a scribe bearing a name resembling the Egyptian word for scribe—a name variously given in the Bible as Shavsha, Seriyah, Shisha, and Sheva.[4] Later Hebrew scribes seemed unsure how to render the foreign name, but this "Shisha" may well have been an Egyptian scribe appointed by David to his fledgling court. When Solomon, a young son of David's, succeeded to David's throne, he further built up David's kingdom over several decades of rule. He even installed two of Shisha's sons as official scribes, one of whom, Elihoreph, had a name—meaning "my god is Horeph"—honoring an Egyptian deity (1 Kings 4:13).

Shisha, Elihoreph, and other scribes of David and Solomon's court wrote the first scriptures of this "Israelite" kingdom based in Jerusalem, and they modeled them on the scriptures of the great cultures that surrounded them. The book of Psalms contains royal hymns (for example, Psalms 2, 72, 110) that imitate the royal traditions of other monarchies. Proverbs includes a whole section—Proverbs 22:17–23:11—that is an adaptation of the Egyptian Instruction of Amenemope. And the oldest stories of creation and flood embedded in Genesis are adaptations of analogous myths seen in the ancient Mesopotamian Atrahasis and Gilgamesh epics. We may even have further echoes of ancient literatures in other "Solomonic" books of the Bible, including the erotic love poetry of Song of Songs and the skeptical wisdom of Ecclesiastes.[5]

If we can say anything about Israel's oldest "Bible," the bible of David and Solomon's kingdom, it is this: it was profoundly different from the Hebrew Bible/Old Testament we now have. Though God is present, the focus in these texts is not on God's history with Israel. Instead, these texts educate students about social life, the structure of the cosmos, and the role of kingship in it. In addition, such educational texts were a "Bible" or "scripture" in only the most qualified of senses. Though seen as numinous and even divine, most of these texts were and are not pitched as "words of God." Rather, they were remarkably "secular" from a modern perspective. These ancient texts form the first written part, a nontraumatic part, of the Old Testament.

THE OTHER PRETRAUMATIC CORE OF THE OLD TESTAMENT

The Old Testament, however, contains another block of pretraumatic scriptures. It was written when the northern "Israelite" tribes had had enough of being dominated by David and Solomon's Judah. When Solomon died, the Israelite tribes split off from his successor, King Rehoboam. The story about this split, found in 1 Kings 12, describes how the new Israelite leader, Jeroboam, set up his royal sanctuary at Bethel, installed a golden calf there, and reminded his people of the tradition of exodus from Egypt: "Here are your gods, oh Israel, who brought you up out of the land of Egypt" (1 Kings 12:28). This is our first clue that Jeroboam's new Israelite monarchy claimed roots quite different from David's Judean monarchy to the south. Where David and Solomon had their royal hymns, wisdom instructions, and myths, Jeroboam called Israel back to its older traditions about ancestors and exodus.

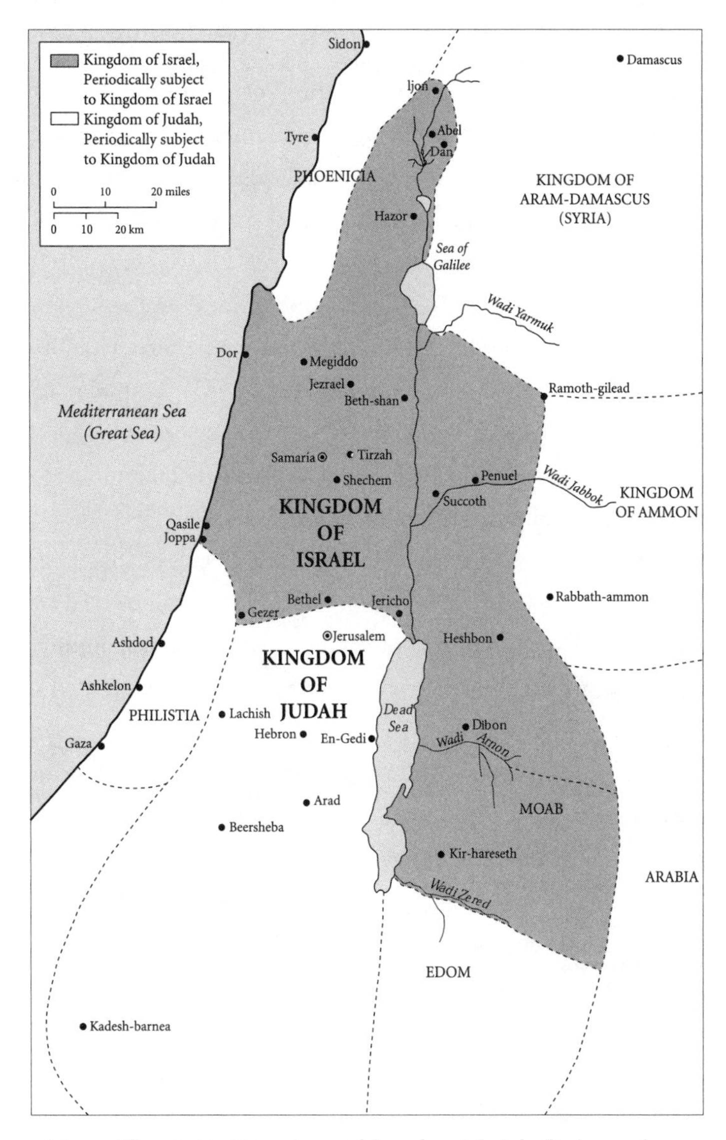

Map 2: The divided kingdoms of Israel and Judah. Redrawn from Norman Gottwald, *The Hebrew Bible: A Socio-Literary Introduction* (Philadelphia: Fortress, 1985).

Thus begins the history of the Northern Kingdom of Israel. We don't know as much as we'd like about this kingdom, especially because it was destroyed less than two centuries after it was founded. Nevertheless, scholars at least agree that there was a northern monarchy of Israel. Moreover, while it existed, this kingdom of Israel became more prominent than the Davidic kingdom in Jerusalem. The northern Israelite kingdom controlled more land than the tiny kingdom of Judah. Where major trade routes ran through Israel, Judah was remote. Over time, Israel grew more powerful and dominated the surrounding area, including Judah.

As we will see in the next chapter, the success of this great Israelite kingdom proved its undoing, and it was destroyed by an empire, the Assyrians, based in northern Mesopotamia. Less prominent and out-of-the-way Judah survived the Assyrian onslaught, and our only records of Israel come through them. The Old Testament/Hebrew Bible as a Judean document tells the history of the Israelite monarchy with a slant. From the Judean perspective, Jeroboam's revolution was an insurrection, and his founding of sanctuaries outside Jerusalem was apostasy.

Even so, Judean scribes preserved major chunks of ancient Israelite scriptures. We see a sign of this in Exodus 32, a golden-calf story with multiple connections to the story of Israel's founding in 1 Kings 12. As in 1 Kings 12, we have a golden calf in Exodus 32. Where Jeroboam proclaims, "Here are your gods, oh Israel, who brought you up out of the land of Egypt" in 1 Kings 12:28, the people as a whole in Exodus 32 say, "Here are your gods, Oh Israel, who led you out of Egypt." But where 1 Kings 12 had Jeroboam founding sanctuaries at Bethel and Dan, Exodus 32 has Aaron, a figure later associated with Bethel's priesthood, establishing a sanctuary in the wilderness. Scholars have not succeeded in unraveling the relationship between these stories. But together 1 Kings 12 and Exodus 32 suggest that the new royal sanctuary that Jeroboam founded at Bethel had an exodus cult with an Aaronide priesthood.[6] More surprising: this would be a place where parts of Israelite royal memory of that fact—both an account of Jeroboam's founding of golden-calf sanctuaries (in 1 Kings 12) and a retrojection of that founding back into the exodus story (in Exodus 32)—are now embedded in *Judah's* texts, the Old Testament. The Judean authors of Exodus depict Aaron's building of the golden calf at Sinai as a great sin, but they preserve the account in some form.

This is just one sign that the monarchy founded by Jeroboam in Israel developed its own set of written scriptures, texts now partially preserved in the Old Testament. Another example can be found in Genesis. There the story of Jacob contains a protest, probably authored by Jeroboam's scribes, against the claims of David's monarchy in Jerusalem. Where the royal psalms of David proclaim that Yahweh dwells in Jerusalem (Psalms 9:11, 135:21), the Genesis Jacob story insists that Yahweh lives in Israelite Bethel instead (Genesis 31:13). Earlier, the Genesis Jacob story describes how Jacob saw a ladder to heaven at Bethel and dedicated a temple to God there (Genesis 28:10–22). Later, Genesis describes how Jacob wrestled God and was renamed Israel at Penuel, one of the first capitals of Jeroboam's Israel (Genesis 32:22–32; see 1 Kings 12:25). These clues suggest that the Jacob story found in Genesis, like parts of the biblical story of Moses, originated as specifically Israelite counterscriptures to the texts developed in Jerusalem. Jeroboam's scribes created such counterscriptures by writing down Israel's older oral traditions. Along the way, they added a special focus on the Israelite monarchy's royal sanctuary (Bethel) and capital (Penuel).

TWO KINGDOMS, TWO SCRIPTURES BEFORE IMPERIAL TRAUMA

We now have the cast of characters for the next part of the story of the Bible—not individual characters but peoples, kingdoms, and their cherished texts. On the one hand, we have the kingdom of Israel, founded by Jeroboam, ruling most of ancient Israel's tribal territory, and built around written versions of Israel's ancient Jacob and Moses traditions. On the other hand, we have the kingdom of Judah ruled by David's heirs in Jerusalem. This Davidic kingdom was focused on ancient scriptures more like those of surrounding nations: myths of creation and flood, Davidic psalms celebrating Jerusalem and its kingship, and wisdom attributed to Solomon.

These differences between Judean and Israelite scriptures persisted for centuries in the separate Judean and Israelite kingdoms. Even prophets speaking more than a century later, in the 700s BCE, reflect this basic division. The Judean prophecies of Micah and Isaiah mention Jacob only in passing and focus on traditions that celebrate the Davidic kingship and Jerusalem's special status as God's "Zion." These early Judean prophets say nothing about the exodus or wilderness.[7]

Not so with Hosea, the only truly Israelite prophet whose words are collected in the Bible. He alludes to Genesis's stories of Jacob founding the sanctuary at Bethel and wrestling God at Penuel (Hosea 12:3–4, 12). Hosea also knows traditions now in Exodus and Numbers about Moses leading Israel out of Egypt (Hosea 12:13), and about Israel wandering in the wilderness (Hosea 9:10, 12:9). These Hoseanic references to stories found in Genesis, Exodus and Numbers are the earliest datable references to those traditions anywhere in the Bible. Moreover, Hosea's early witness to these early Torah writings is *northern*, it is *Israelite*.

These distinctions between Judah and Israel, and between their texts, are important because they form the pretrauma background of the Bible. Both Judean and Israelite scriptures were linked with the monarchies that created them. It is in this sense that I describe these scriptures as pretraumatic. People did suffer, of course, during this period of biblical formation. Nevertheless, both bodies of scripture—both Judean and Israelite—supported existing royal political structures. If they had not developed beyond this stage, they probably would have been forgotten. They could not have survived the eventual destruction of both Israel and Judah.

CHAPTER TWO

The Birth of Monotheism

Sometime in the 700s BCE the nation of Israel was attacked and fell under the domination of the greatest superpower of its time, Assyria. The Assyrian empire was based in Mesopotamia, in what is now northern Iraq. Starting in the early 700s the Assyrians began conquering kingdoms to their west, gradually gaining control of the plains and other country separating them from the Mediterranean and important trade routes. Scholars debate their motivation, but the impact was clear: kingdom after kingdom across a vast realm became subject to Assyrian rule. Sometimes a group of small kingdoms would band together to resist Assyrian might for a time. The nation of Israel was even part of some of these coalitions. But eventually Assyria conquered Israel and Judah, and even dominated Egypt for a period. The Assyrian military machine was unparalleled.

And the Assyrians carefully cultivated a reputation for brutal punishment of all who defied them. An appropriate dose of terror could accomplish things more cheaply than a large dose of military might.[1]

From 745 BCE onward, the Assyrian army, the most efficient and effective military machine on earth, repeatedly destroyed the armies of Israel and its allies. The equivalent loss of life in the United States would equal millions of soldiers and civilians. The survivors of such attacks suffered from famine caused by the devastation of croplands that Assyrians left in their wake. They also had to pay heavy tribute and swear loyalty to their Assyrian conquerors through a "covenant" that required the whole population to pronounce curses on themselves if they stopped being loyal to Assyria. The Assyrians did not invent such oath covenants, but they perfected them as a way to enforce loyalty on the nations they dominated. From king to commoner, all were expected to show "love" for the Assyrian king by being loyal to him alone and rejecting any alliance with another country. Foreign alliances, after all, were the only way a small nation like Israel could hope to gain freedom from Assyria. Not surprisingly, they sometimes tried to form such alliances anyway, during throne transitions in Assyria and other times when the Assyrian empire might be vulnerable. But Israel's rebellions were never successful. Initially the attacking Assyrian armies just punished the kingdom of Israel by killing more people, reducing its size, and installing supposedly pro-Assyrian leaders. Finally, in 722 BCE, the Assyrians wiped northern

Israel off the map. They permanently destroyed the kingdom Samaria. They dismantled the monarchy of Israel. And they permanently removed thousands of surviving Israelites, anyone who could conceivably lead a rebellion, and moved in peoples from other parts of their empire to take over the exiles' homes and fields. There have been rumors ever since about the lost tribes of Israel, but little else survived of the specifically northern alliance that bore the name Israel.

HOSEA'S PROPHECY OF HOPE AND JUDGMENT TO A TRAUMATIZED ISRAEL

This is the traumatic situation in which Hosea, the prophet whose name means "Yahweh saves," delivered a message of hope. He proclaimed that Yahweh was the people's parent, a parent who could never give up on God's people. Calling his people by the name of its most central tribe, Ephraim as well as by the more common name, Israel, Hosea's God cries:

> When Israel was a child I loved him,
> and from Egypt I called him to be my son.
> But the more I called,
> the more they went away their own way;
> they offered sacrifice to Baal gods
> and burnt incense to carved images.
> I myself taught Ephraim to walk,
> I myself took them by the arm,
> but they did not know that I was the one who healed them,
> I led them with bonds of human kindness,
> with bands of love,

I was with them like someone lifting an infant to his cheek,
 and I bent down to feed him . . .
How can I part with you, Ephraim?
 How could I give you up, oh Israel?
How could I make you like Admah
 How can I treat you like Zeboiim?
My heart is changing.
 My tender thoughts for you burn hot within me.
 (Hosea 11:1–4, 8)

As a father myself, I can't imagine a more powerful image of unconditional compassion. From the moment I saw my first child born, my daughter, I was overcome with a deep emotion I'd never felt before. I had a sense that there was nothing, at any time, that would cause me to stop loving her. That is the kind of love that Hosea says God had for Israel, an Israel being traumatized by Assyria.

Yet there is a harsher side to Hosea's message as well. He insists that the things his people are doing to end Assyrian domination are actually making it worse. When his people try to gain divine support through worshiping Baal, it is like they are "playing the whore" (Hosea 5:3). The very altars Israelites build to atone for their sin only aggravate it. Hosea preaches, "Ephraim keeps building altars for his sins, these very altars are themselves a sin" (Hosea 8:11). He even proclaims that Israel's golden calf and other divine symbols incur God's wrath and will be destroyed. In Hosea's view, Israel's unfaithfulness to God, its worship of Baal and devotion to divine images, are precisely why it suffers under Assyrian oppression:

When Ephraim used to speak, all trembled.
He was powerful in Israel;
but when he became guilty through Baal, he died.
And now they keep sinning
and make a cast image for themselves.
false gods of their own invention, made out of silver
all of it work of mere craftsmen.
"Sacrifice to them," they say.
Humans even kiss calves!
Therefore, they will be like morning mist,
like quickly disappearing dew,
Like chaff whirled from the threshing-floor,
like smoke through a window. (Hosea 13:1–3)

To a typical polytheistic Israelite, such words must have sounded like nothing short of blasphemy. Golden calves were an ancient Israelite symbol, and Hosea's people had worshiped Yahweh alongside other deities, like El, for as long as anyone could remember. Though Hosea imagines a time, many centuries ago in the time of Moses, when Israel was faithful to only Yahweh, Hosea's contemporaries would not have known such a time. Indeed, scholars are increasingly skeptical that early Israel was ever monotheistic. Hosea's prophecy was revolutionary. Hosea's fellow Israelites would have needed a lot of persuading to give up the help of gods like Baal and Asherah, along with ancient spiritual symbols like the golden calf, especially in their hour of need.

Hosea got their attention with a radical act and an even more radical idea. He married a prostitute. He then built his prophecy on the revolutionary idea that this marriage was a symbol of God's relationship to Israel. Yahweh was married not to Asherah, but to God's people Israel. This was new. We know ancient myths about gods marrying goddesses, and there were even rituals by which ancient kings entered into "sacred marriage" with priestesses representing goddesses. Never before, however, had a prophet reimagined the relationship between God and an entire people as that between man and wife.

Ancient marriage involved many things—love, procreation, and raising of children, often a partnership in producing food and goods as part of a small-scale farm. It also involved reciprocal obligations of husband and wife: the husband was to protect and provide for his wife, while his wife was expected to be sexual with her husband and her husband alone. Ancient laws prescribed harsh penalties for adulterous wives and the men who had sex with them. A married woman who had sex outside her marriage faced possible death, or at least stripping, humiliation, and shaming if discovered by her jealous husband.

In one of his most famous prophecies, Hosea depicts Yahweh as just such a jealous husband, a husband of Israel. At the beginning of the prophecy God speaks to Israel's children, proclaiming to them, "To court, take your mother to court! For she is no longer my wife nor am I her husband" (Hosea 2:2). Ancient husbands could divorce their wives by merely proclaiming such words, and this first sentence suggests that Yahweh is divorcing Israel. But Yahweh then goes on to offer the people an alternative:

> Either she [Israel] must remove her whoring ways from her face
> and her adulterous offspring from between her breasts,

or I shall strip her naked
  and expose her like the day she was born;
I shall make her as bare as the desert,
  I shall make her as dry as barren lands,
  and let her die of thirst. (Hosea 2:2–3)

With these words Hosea informs his audience that the religious practices they thought were sacred are as repugnant as a wife's infidelity. Yahweh is about to withdraw from them his husbandly protection. If the people of Israel want to avoid being stripped, humiliated in front their false lovers, and left to die of thirst, they must renounce their worship of Baal and use of divine images. God's ultimate hope is that Israel, his wife, will return to him. After all her suffering she will say, "I shall go back to my first husband, it was better for me back then than now" (Hosea 2:7). But Hosea proclaims a God who uses violence, including Assyrian domination, to bring his wayward wife back to him.

For many modern readers, particularly women or anyone who has been subjected to abuse, these images are repugnant. Even if a woman has been unfaithful to her marriage, most people today would not condone her husband stripping, beating, or starving her. An entire movement has developed in recent decades to offer shelter to battered women and improve legal protection for vulnerable wives. How, one might ask, can one imagine Yahweh as such an angry, jealous, violent, out-of-control husband? And Hosea's image of redemption—Yahweh promising to take her back—can look like the cycle of abuse sometimes seen in human partnerships. In marriage, this cycle involves the husband wooing his battered wife back with promises of love, only to subject her to violence later when his wrath rises again. In Hosea's prophecy Israel might be subject to a cosmic, theological version of this abusive cycle. Israel is Yahweh's battered wife. When Israel suffers Yahweh's punishment, what reassurance does it have that God's violence will not recur after God takes her back in?

This prophetic picture of divine-human marriage was an attempt to process imperial trauma. Hosea's people faced an impossible situation. Their lives were falling apart. Every few years the Assyrian army removed yet another rebellious Israelite monarch and ravaged the countryside. In between such rebellions the people struggled to recover while paying huge tribute payments to their Assyrian lord, whom they were supposed to "love" with their whole heart. Eventually the monarchy of Israel and its magnificent capital Samaria would be obliterated, thousands of people resettled permanently in other parts of the Assyrian empire, and the northern state of Israel consigned to the dust heap of history. The crisis that Hosea addressed involved a situation of truly explosive disintegration of the Israelite communal self.

Within this explosive, traumatic situation, this metaphor of marriage was a shock intended to produce a radical change in Hosea's people. The majority of them thought the Assyrian crisis could be managed by tactics that had worked in the past: a treaty here or a prayer there to the right deity. Yet Hosea believed something deeper was really wrong. Israel was not suffering because of poor strategic decisions. Israel was suffering because it had failed to be exclusively loyal to its god, Yahweh. In other words, Israel was suffering because it had sinned. Assyria was not the real agent causing Israel's suffering. God was. God was allowing, even sending, Assyrian armies to ravage Israel, closing off every means of escape in order to punish Israel for her sins of unfaithfulness.

This prophetic blame of Israel for Assyrian oppression offered a sense of control amidst an overwhelming experience. As Kai Erikson has observed, groups that are traumatized often feel as if their world has suddenly proven to be dominated by randomness and chaotic violence. "They come to feel that something awful is *bound* to happen."[2] In response, trauma survivors often seek some reason for their trauma in their own behavior. They escape this sense of a terrorizing world by attributing at least part of their trauma to behavior that they can control. People who suffer regain a sense of power by drawing some kind of lesson from their experience. To feel that they could have avoided suffering by acting otherwise can be more bearable than facing the reality of total helplessness.[3]

Such self-blame offered Israel a way to see itself as empowered in an otherwise helpless situation. My colleague and the president of my seminary, Serene Jones, put it well when she said to one of my classes: "For many who suffer deeply, the only thing that frightens them more than the idea that God is punishing them is the idea that God is not in charge at all."[4] For some, such self-blame can be corrosive, undermining their faith. But for others the idea of a powerful God, even a judging God, can be reassuring. At least there is a chance to change one's behavior and be saved. Things can look quite different if the world is totally devoid of God. Then one is truly subject to its most powerful forces, even if they are brutally tyrannical like the Assyrian king.

Hosea offered the Israelites an interpretation of their experience, one in which Yahweh had not lost to the Assyrians but was working through them. Yahweh was using the Assyrians as mere puppets as he temporarily chastised his wayward people. Assyrian texts and art depicted the Assyrian army as feminizing and raping their victims, but in Hosea's prophecy it was Yahweh and only Yahweh who terrorized Israel. But this also meant that Israel could change its behavior and regain control over its situation. In this way, Hosea offered a way of self-empowerment to his traumatized people.

The revolutionary import of Hosea's message, however, was not in attributing Israel's suffering to God, but in the particular explanation that he offered. Throughout the ancient world, including in Israel, the assumption often was that suffering could be caused by not worshiping the full range of gods enough. Sin was offending this or that deity through neglect, sometimes even deities that one had not known before.[5]

Hosea's marriage metaphor turned this all around. According to Hosea, Israel had worshiped other gods and images too much. It was this worship of other gods that made

God jealous and explained God's rage. Where Hosea's contemporaries saw the royal golden calf and a gods like Asherah and Baal as treasured religious resources, Hosea saw signs of profound, divine-rage-producing adultery. Where they were inclined to seek help from any divine source that they could, Hosea insisted that their worship of multiple deities was precisely the problem.

By so depicting his people's worship of other gods and images as adultery, Hosea tried to shock his traumatized audience into giving up some of its most cherished religious practices, and at a time when the people felt most vulnerable. As renowned Egyptologist Jan Assmann has argued, Hosea's critique of gods and images was the innovative core of the so-called monotheistic religions of Judaism, Christianity, and Islam. Such religions are defined not by affirmation of one god but by a prohibition, like Hosea's, from worship of many.[6]

Hosea's contemporaries must have been stupefied at his ideas. Why, they may have asked, should we abandon any strategy to fight the Assyrian menace? If Baal or Asherah might help, why not give them a try? And trying to secure some kind of help from Egypt probably seemed a far more effective deterrent to Assyria than simply relying on Yahweh alone. They still had some strategies that they thought might work.

What would lead Hosea to propose such a radical idea, and at such a difficult time? If it was such an innovation, why did it come to Israel as it was ground under the heel of the Assyrian covenant? Many, of course, believe the answer is simple: God told Hosea to present this prophecy and he did. But I believe deeper forces of communal trauma were at work.

Put briefly, Hosea saw God's face in the catastrophes his Israelite people endured, and God's face looked a lot like that of the Assyrian king. It was not just that Hosea offered his people a way of understanding and feeling in control of their suffering. Hosea's particular explanation of what Israel had done wrong derived its central metaphors from Assyrian royal propaganda. According to Assyrian propaganda, Israel was experiencing death and destruction as a consequence of its disobedience of the Assyrian king. Hosea likewise thought that this suffering came from disloyalty and disobedience. But Hosea thought the real king punishing Israel's disobedience was Yahweh. Hosea described Yahweh as demanding absolute loyalty, much like the Assyrian king required his vassals to "love" him alone. And like the Assyrian king, Hosea's Yahweh punishes the people of Israel for allying themselves with others. In this way Hosea did a remarkable thing that would shape the course of subsequent religious history: he redescribed Israel's God, Yahweh, as a (partial) reflection of the world-dominating, subordination-demanding Assyrian emperor, an emperor who would settle for nothing less than absolute allegiance.

Hosea even has this emperor-Yahweh promise destruction on Israel for violating a divine covenant: "Put a trumpet to your lips! One like a vulture hovers over Yahweh's home! Because they have violated my covenant and transgressed my law" (Hosea 8:1). This sounds like an Assyrian threat of punishment for violation of an Assyrian vassal covenant. But in Hosea his threat is put in God's mouth and refers to God's covenant with Israel. Where his audience might think it is suffering because it disobeyed a covenant with the Assyrian king, Hosea prophesies that the real covenant broken by Israel was its covenant with Yahweh. This stands as our earliest datable reference to a "covenant" between God and Israel.[7]

There is a good chance that Hosea invented the God-people covenant idea. The covenant imposed by the Assyrian king was his model for Yahweh's covenant with Israel. We have other references to covenant, to be sure, even in biblical stories whose setting is long before the prophet Hosea, but it is not clear exactly when these other stories were written. Hosea's prophecy about Israel's covenant with God, however, is explicitly attributed to a prophet living in the time when Assyria dominated Israel.

Finally, Hosea's picture of the people of Israel as a terrorized woman had parallels in Assyrian propaganda. Assyrian kings presented themselves as the most masculine of men, brutalizing and feminizing every opponent. For the Assyrians, the foreign peoples and their kings were like "women" when compared to the hypermasculine and brutal Assyrian king. Some royal texts even threaten that disobedient subjects will be turned into women. Other texts tell of the king's army penetrating a foreign land, violating it like a man raping a woman. Royal art complemented such descriptions, depicting the king as a huge male figure standing over the tiny, feminized figures of his foes, often equipped with a massive royal bow, itself a symbol of masculine potency.[8] In these and other ways, Assyrian royal propaganda treated Assyrian subjects like Israel as equivalent to dominated women. By the time of Hosea, his people of Israel and its king had long endured being treated like women by Assyria and faced threats of further emasculation. In this way, even Hosea's picture of Israel as Yahweh's wife had a parallel in Israel's Assyrian-imposed trauma.

SUFFERING'S WISDOM

Hosea's images of God as an Assyrian-like monarch punishing a disobedient people are disturbing for many readers, and rightly so. It is hard to know how to redeem Hosea's depiction of God as an abusive husband in particular. Yet judgment prophecies like Hosea's born in trauma may offer difficult truths as well. As trauma researcher Ronnie Janoff-Bulman has observed, people often go through life with inaccurately positive pictures of the world and their role in it. At least temporarily, they are protected from reality by rosy assumptions easily shattered by life's random tragedies. Other studies have shown that depressed or pessimistic people actually were more on target in assessing their future prospects than those who were optimistic.[9]

Perhaps there is some virtue in living with somewhat optimistic and rosy assumptions. This is no plea for depression or despair. But life can show the limits of a worldview and/or theology that is relentlessly upbeat. And this is when biblical texts formed in catastrophe deserve another look. It is tempting in the contemporary, ever more secular context to dismiss biblical images of judgment and hope as outmoded and uncomfortable. But sometimes, when one's back is against the wall, these images of broken love and restoration, perhaps even images originally modeled on Assyrian propaganda, can have a new attraction. I am reminded of a friend who said: "We make plans according to our ideas, but obey our pain." Israel and Judah had many pretrauma "ideas," ideas that would be shattered by centuries of Assyrian and Babylonian domination. The survivors of that domination found ways to "obey their pain."

I have given away the end of the story: Hosea's Israel did not survive. The rulers of Israel kept vacillating between negotiations with Assyria and scheming against Assyria with Egypt and other nations. Its people kept worshiping Yahweh alongside others gods at shrines featuring calves, Asherah trees, and other divine images. Eventually, the Assyrian army came through, destroyed what was left of Israel and its capital Samaria, exiled many survivors to distant parts of the Assyrian empire, and resettled much of Israel with peoples from elsewhere. Israel was no more.

But Hosea's prophecies were written down by disciples and survived. This is unusual. Most ancient Near Eastern prophecy was exclusively oral, presented live to the audiences it concerned. At the most some prophecies were recorded in archives by scribes. But the book of Hosea is a full literary composition, starting with the image of Yahweh's marriage to Israel and ending in Hosea 14 with a vision of hope saturated with love poem images. This kind of broader composition is a prophetic teaching. It is no scribal record, but more like the oral-written wisdom teachings used in ancient Near Eastern education. Perhaps that is why the book concludes by saying, "Let the one who is wise understand these words, and those who are discerning will grasp their meaning" (Hosea 14:9). The current generation, the Israelite audience that Hosea personally spoke to, did not have ears to hear his radical new teaching, but the medium of writing was used to preserve his message for another generation to come. Initially, perhaps only Hosea's children or other disciples had any interest in writing his prophecies on the tablets of their hearts. There is no way to know.

What we do know, however, is this: somehow Hosea's prophecies, probably already written down, found their way south to Judah. It was there, in Judah, that these prophecies of Hosea became the seeds of later Old Testament theology. It was there that Hosea's vision of faithfulness was eventually accepted as a way to engage Judah's communal trauma. With time his prophecy and his broader monotheistic vision transcended its original context and helped later generations deal with their traumas.

Hosea's monotheistic message was to be extended well beyond anything he could have imagined. He interpreted a specific historical crisis, the Assyrian onslaught, as the result of his people's attachment to Baal, Asherah, and other gods rather than Yahweh. But in time, his message was reapplied by later generations to explain very different situations: wars and other disasters and losses, individual and communal.

In this way, normal human life—all too frequently characterized by experiences of trauma—became a god-shredder, at least among peoples who inherited this monotheistic message. Future generations of Jews, Christians, and Muslims would suffer trauma, whether as individuals or groups. Like others undergoing trauma, they would look for an explanation for their suffering, something to give them a fragile sense of control. Monotheism provided that explanation. Understood in the frame of the monotheistic impulse, suffering of all kinds could be explained by one's insufficient zeal to give up old gods. Violence, disease, famine, and other calamities would come in waves, each standing as a potential argument for increased devotion to the one true God and abandonment of false ones. "Are you suffering beyond what you think you can bear?" the monotheistic faiths asked traumatized individuals and groups. "Repent of your idolatry and be free."

CHAPTER THREE

Judah's Survival

ISRAEL WAS DESTROYED, but Judah survived. Judah's survival came to be symbolized in an event never fully understood: Jerusalem's mysterious escape from the armies of Sennacherib that besieged it in 701 BCE during the reign of Hezekiah, king of Judah. The Bible contains no fewer than four divergent accounts of this event, and we even have an account by the Assyrians themselves of attacking and then withdrawing from Hezekiah's Jerusalem. These accounts disagree on why the Assyrians pulled back, but one thing is clear: Jerusalem survived virtually certain destruction where Israel and other opponents of Assyria had fallen. For the Judeans this survival was deemed miraculous. Sennacherib's withdrawal, to be sure, did not mean the end of Assyrian rule. We know the Judeans endured Assyrian domination for decades to come, gaining freedom only in the

620s BCE. But they survived, where their northern sibling, Israel, did not. Why?

Judean answers, diverse as they were, emphasized the specialness of Jerusalem. Of course, ideas about Jerusalem's specialness were not new. From the founding of the Davidic monarchy onward, kings had insisted that God dwelled in and would protect the royal city, often termed Zion in hymns still preserved in the Psalter. But this ancient "Zion theology" took a new turn during the reign of King Hezekiah. It became the main way Judeans explained the mysterious fact of their survival.

The destruction of its neighbor Israel primed Judah to be traumatized by Assyrian domination in a way Israel itself was not. Israel moved through its Assyrian crisis with an illusion of invulnerability, dismissing prophetic warnings and seeing its usual strategies for survival fail. Not so for Judah. When Judah came under the covenantal yoke of Assyria, its people could recall how things ended up when Israel came under the same yoke.

Israel's destruction by the Assyrians hit close to home. The two peoples had been linked for centuries in complicated ways. Judah and Israel both inhabited the hills of Canaan, sharing a common lifestyle, culture, and religion. In addition, the Judean and Israelite peoples had been linked politically. David and Solomon ruled both during the tenth century, and a powerful dynasty in later Israel—Kings Omri and Ahab—temporarily controlled Judah and its armies (1 Kings 22:4, 44; 2 Kings 3:7). In these and other ways, Judah was not one tribe of Israel but a sibling nation to Israel. These two nations,

Israel and Judah, were complexly related, bound together by culture and a braided history.

We see this common bond expressed in two Judean prophets who spoke during the Assyrian crisis, Micah and Isaiah. They preached during the reigns of Ahaz, a Judean king who brought Judah under Assyrian control, and his son Hezekiah, who tried to gain freedom from Assyria. Both Micah and Isaiah emphasized that the Assyrian devastation of Israel would hit Judah too. For example, Micah proclaimed the terrifying arrival of God in the following way:

> The mountains will melt under him
> And the valleys burst open,
> Like wax before a fire,
> like waters pouring down a steep slope.
> All this is for the crime of Jacob
> and for the sins of the house of Israel
> What is the crime of Jacob?
> Is it not Samaria?
> And what is the illicit sanctuary of Judah?
> Is it not Jerusalem? (Micah 1:4–5)

Micah's contemporary, the prophet Isaiah, proclaimed a similar message, insisting that Judah and Jerusalem were not immune from the devastation they had seen in the north. Modeling his prophecy on Amos's earlier prediction of Israel's ultimate demise (Amos 4:6–12), Isaiah insisted that the Assyrian devastation of Israel was only the beginning of God's judgment. The God that had destroyed Israel was not finished. Instead, Isaiah intoned again and again, "In all this Yahweh's anger does not turn back; God's [attacking] hand is still outstretched" (Isaiah 5:25, 9:8–21, 10:1–4). Judah would face Israel's judgment.

These prophecies during the Assyrian crisis were not popular, but they touched a nerve. Micah quoted people telling him, "Do not preach, stop preaching these things" (Micah 2:6). Isaiah faced so much rejection that he felt called to write his prophecy down for a more receptive future generation (Isaiah 8:16–18). Micah's and Isaiah's contemporaries preferred to believe that Judah's fate would be different from Israel's. And for a time, it seemed they might be right.

Judah's temporary turn for the better began in 715 BCE, when Hezekiah succeeded his father, King Ahaz. The country had been under Assyrian control for about a decade. Seven years before, in 722 BCE, Judah had witnessed the final stages of the Assyrian destruction of Israel. The Assyrian army then suppressed revolts in cities along the coast of Palestine. Meanwhile, the Assyrians resettled peoples from other parts of their empire, from Babylon and Syria, into the former lands of Israel. These peoples brought their foreign gods with them, and we have business documents that show the new economic domination of these foreign settlers over native Israelites.[1] All around it, to the north and west, Judah could behold the effects of failed rebellions against Assyrian might.

Yet hopes were high when Hezekiah took the throne, and his capital city, Jerusalem, was on the rise. Jerusalem of the period of David and Solomon was the size of about five city blocks. In contrast, Hezekiah's Jerusalem encompassed about twenty city blocks, and its population grew to around thirty thousand inhabitants. Some believe a major factor for this expansion was the destruction of the Northern Kingdom of Israel and the flight of Israelite refugees south.[2] The Assyrian army had devastated the Israelite countryside, killed thousands of Israelites, and exiled many more. Jerusalem was a likely refuge for some who survived this catastrophe.

Another king might have expelled the refugees or forced them to live outside the city wall, but Hezekiah appears to have done otherwise. In the process of expanding Jerusalem's fortifications to resist possible Assyrian attack, he encompassed the city's larger population. In addition Hezekiah integrated formerly Israelite lands into his Judean kingdom. Evidence of Hezekiah's royal administrative system has been found not only in Judah but also at northern Israelite sites. He even named his son and royal heir Manasseh, after one of the two central northern tribes of Israel.[3] It appears that Hezekiah aimed to revive David and Solomon's glorious reign from Jerusalem over both Judah and Israel.

But first Hezekiah had to end Assyrian rule over Judah. When the Assyrian king, Sargon, died in 705 BCE, Hezekiah saw his chance. He enlisted the help of Egypt and other neighboring nations, forming an international coalition to end Assyrian control of the area. For four years the alliance appeared successful. Contenders for the Assyrian throne fought among themselves, and no Assyrian armies appeared at the gates. Meanwhile, Hezekiah engaged in an unprecedented building project in Jerusalem. Not only did he enlarge the city walls, but he constructed a protected tunnel to Jerusalem's water supply.

Many dreamed that Judah had achieved a freedom that had escaped Israel.

A reckoning came in 701 BCE in the form of a massive Assyrian army under the command of the new Assyrian king, Sennacherib. Within weeks he laid waste to the whole country of Judah. The relief shown here is a vivid Assyrian depiction of the destruction of Lachish, Judah's largest town outside Jerusalem. In this part of the relief an Assyrian battering

Figure 1: The Siege at Lachish. Photo: akg-images/Werner Forman.

ram is about to penetrate a tower. Meanwhile, other parts of the relief depict Assyrian archers and stone throwers on the attack, Judean soldiers impaled around Lachish, and later scenes of people being led from the defeated city into exile. This image represents the kind of destruction visited on scores of Judean towns and villages. According to archaeological surveys, the Assyrians decimated virtually all of the countryside outside Jerusalem.

The Assyrians also laid siege to Jerusalem, but, unaccountably, they withdrew. A tale doubly recorded in 2 Kings 19 and Isaiah 37 claims that an "angel of Yahweh set out and struck down one hundred eighty-five thousand in the camp of the Assyrians," causing them to leave (2 Kings 19:35–36//Isaiah 37:36–37). But, as mentioned at the outset of this chapter, there are other accounts as well. A tiny note found only in 2 Kings 18:14–16 (no parallel in Isaiah 36) speaks of Hezekiah paying off the Assyrian king by stripping the temple of its gold, and Sennacherib's own archives record that Hezekiah sent him a gift of much gold and other precious metals and stones.

In the end, Jerusalem survived while Samaria and other nations did not. This became the touchstone for the biblical writings about the Assyrian crisis found in 2 Kings 18–19 and the virtually identical chapters in Isaiah 36–37. These parallel accounts of the Assyrian attack on Hezekiah's Jerusalem describe Assyrian officials mocking the faith of Jerusalemites in their city's invulnerability. The Assyrian Rabshakeh, a high official ("head cup bearer") in the Assyrian army, taunts those on Jerusalem's wall, warning them, "Don't let Hezekiah trick you into relying on Yahweh by saying, Yahweh will surely deliver us." The Rabshakeh continued, "Has any of the gods of the nations ever delivered its land out of the hand of the king of Assyria? Where are the gods of Hamath and Arpad? Where are the gods of Sepharvaim? Have they delivered Samaria out of my hand?" (Isaiah 36:18–19//2 Kings 18:30, 33–34).[4] We don't know for sure about Sepharvaim, but Hamath was destroyed by the Assyrians in 720 BCE, and Arpad was destroyed twice, once in 738 and then again in 720 BCE. Together with Samaria, destroyed by Assyria in 722, these nearby cities seemed to represent the wreckage of hopes in failed gods. The Assyrian Rabshakeh challenges Judeans to believe that their god Yahweh will prove any better for them.

The taunts of the Rabshakeh do not go unanswered. The rest of the story tells of Yahweh's decisive refutation of his challenges. Yahweh saved Jerusalem for the sake of the Davidic monarchy within it. God tells Isaiah to announce the following message regarding the king of Assyria:

> He shall not enter this city, shoot an arrow there, march before it with a shield, nor cast a siege ramp against it. He shall return by the way he came. He shall not enter this city, says Yahweh. For I will defend this city to save it, for my own sake and for the sake of David, my servant. (2 Kings 19:32–34//Isaiah 37:33–35)

The following narrative describes the fulfillment of this promise. An angel of death visits the Assyrian camp, and Sennacherib himself is assassinated when he and his army returned home (2 Kings 19:35–37, Isaiah 37:36–38). According to these stories in 2 Kings 18–19//Isaiah 36–37, Zion was special in a way that Samaria, Arpad, Hamath, and other places were not. Yahweh delivered it from Assyrian destruction. Why? For God's own sake and the sake of the dynasty of David, whom Yahweh had promised to protect forever.

Scholars now doubt the historical veracity of many details of 2 Kings 18–19//Isaiah 36–37. Though the story is set in 701 BCE, it refers to events—such as the assassination of Sennacherib—that occurred in a time distant from the Jerusalem siege, and the triumphant tone of this story of miraculous deliverance contrasts with both Sennacherib's own accounts and the Bible's own version of the story in 2 Kings 18:14–16. Sennacherib claims to have trapped Hezekiah and exacted tribute, while Hezekiah claims to have provided tribute to the besieging Assyrians on his own initiative. Either way, the combination of Assyrian and biblical sources seem to point to an unusual Assyrian withdrawal from the siege of Jerusalem, one more likely prompted by some kind of tribute payment than by a miraculous plague.

All that said, the parallel stories found in 2 Kings 18–19 and Isaiah 36–37 are valuable memorials of how Judah came to process and understand its survival of the Assyrian crisis. The biblical story of the Assyrian siege of Jerusalem integrates the story of Jerusalem's siege and survival into a longer account of Israel and Judah. That account begins with God's choice of David and Jerusalem and includes a description of Samaria's destruction (2 Kings 17). As one final part of this broader history, the account of Jerusalem's deliverance in 2

Kings 18–19, just after the destruction of Israelite Samaria in 2 Kings 17, became a crucial way for Judah to embrace and explain its survival. Where Assyrian accounts (and the biblical account in 2 Kings 18:14–16) attribute Assyrian withdrawal to a large tribute payment by Hezekiah, the broader narrative in 2 Kings//Isaiah answers instead with this theological assertion: Jerusalem survived because it was the seat of Yahweh's chosen, Davidic kings.

The Bible features multiple mentions of a covenant that God made with David to protect his royal line forever, starting with Nathan's prophecy in 2 Samuel 7, where God promises David that "your house and your kingdom shall be made secure forever before me, and your throne will be established forever" (2 Samuel 7:12–16).[5] In addition, ancient "Zion psalms" still in the Bible insist that Jerusalem is the holy and invulnerable royal city of Yahweh. For example, Psalm 46 proclaims that "God is in the midst of the city, it shall not be moved" (Psalm 46:5).[6] Those ancient traditions about Zion (=Jerusalem) and its kingship gained new importance in the wake of Jerusalem's survival of Sennacherib's siege. Jerusalem's escape seemed to prove that even the might of Assyria, which had destroyed so many other nations, could not overcome Yahweh's will to defend Jerusalem/Zion. Judah held fast to Zion theology as a profound way to explain its ongoing survival: why it lived while Israel died.

The word "survival" here, however, needs to be qualified. Hezekiah's realm was in tatters and remained so under

Assyrian domination. I have already mentioned the widespread depopulation of areas outside Jerusalem. The attack of the Assyrian army must have resulted in much loss of life, and Sennacherib reports having deported thousands of Judeans. Even though the number of deportees that he gives (200,150) is exaggerated, the end result is clear. The Judeans lost approximately 70 percent of their population and 85 percent of their towns and villages. In addition, the Assyrians gave parts of Hezekiah's devastated kingdom to more loyal subjects and drastically increased Hezekiah's annual tribute payment. The following poem by Isaiah sums up the picture of post-Sennacherib Judah. In it Judeans exclaim over how close they came to being totally destroyed, like the legendary cities of Sodom and Gomorrah (see Genesis 19):

> Your country is devastated,
>   Your cities have been burned with fire;
> Your own fields, in your very presence
>   foreigners devour them!
>   it is desolate, as overthrown by strangers.
> And the daughter of Zion [Jerusalem] is left
>   like a booth in a vineyard,
> like a shelter in a cucumber field,
>   like a besieged city. (Isaiah 1:7–8)

Then Isaiah quotes what the people around him are saying as they behold this devastation.

> "If Yahweh of armies[7]
>   had not left us a few survivors,
> We would have been like Sodom,
>   We would be like Gomorrah." (Isaiah 1:9)

Sodom and Gomorrah were legendary examples of total destruction. Isaiah's contemporaries felt that falling just short of that destruction constituted "survival."

Judah endured for more than six decades as a rump kingdom paying heavy tribute. Year after year, the Judean king or his representatives made annual visits to Niniveh to pay tribute and see an eighty-by-eight-foot depiction of Lachish's destruction in the king's throne room. The people were subject to the demands of an Assyrian covenant requiring absolute devotion to the Assyrian king. To secure this loyalty, the upper classes had to send their sons to Assyria, where they were educated in Assyrian royal propaganda, writing Assyrian royal ideology on the tablets of their hearts, becoming loyal, pro-Assyrian Judeans before they returned home.

JOSIAH'S POST-ASSYRIAN REFORM

Eventually, however, the Assyrians' story ended. In the late 600s the Assyrian king Ashurbanipal lost control of Egypt, and Egypt gradually began to assert control over the Canaanite region, particularly the strategic coastal highways that led past Judah and Israel to the north and east. Nevertheless, even though the Assyrians were preoccupied with other parts of their empire, Judah remained a loyal Assyrian vassal across the long reign of Hezekiah's successor, Manasseh, and the following short reign of his son Amon. The latter king reigned only two years before being killed in a palace coup. At this point the "people of the land" in Judah saw a chance to make a change. They executed those responsible for the king's assassination and appointed the assassinated king's eight-year-old son Josiah to the throne (2 Kings 21:24, 22:1).

If Josiah or his regents made any immediate changes, they are not recorded. Nevertheless, eighteen years into his reign, the twenty-six-year-old Josiah instituted a reform that would have profound implications for later Judaism. One prompt for this reform appears to have been the discovery, during temple renovations, of an ancient law book. At first the law book needed to be certified by a prophet as authentic, because its contents were so revolutionary (2 Kings 22:13–20). Once this was done, the Bible says that King Josiah led the "elders of Judah and Jerusalem" in a "covenant" based on the newly found book of the law, a covenant under which the king and people swore to love and be loyal to Yahweh in a way analogous to the love and loyalty previously required by Assyrian kings. They pledged "to follow Yahweh, keeping his commandments, decrees, and statutes, with all his heart and all his life strength, to perform the words of this covenant that were written in this book" (2 Kings 23:3).

Josiah then proceeded to purify the Jerusalem Temple and destroy all other local sanctuaries throughout the land of Judah. He is said to have destroyed the sanctuaries in Israel as well, including and especially the ancient sanctuary of Israel at Bethel. Finally, he capped it all off by commanding that the people of both Israel and Judah come to Jerusalem to celebrate Passover. The Josiah narrative concludes by emphasizing that Josiah brought all Judah and Israel to Jerusalem for a centralized Passover that "had not been kept since the days of the judges who judged Israel, even during all the days of the kings of Israel and Judah" (2 Kings 23:22).

In this way Josiah fulfilled commandments in the law book that had been found, enacting a religious purge only dreamed of by Hosea. The Bible celebrates his obedience, exclaiming that no king before or after him "turned to Yahweh with all his heart, with all his life strength, and all his might." This reform, however, must have come as an immense shock to many of the people he ruled. Judah, like Israel, had worshiped Asherah (Yahweh's consort, mentioned in chapter 1), Baal, and other gods for centuries. The people of Judah, like those of Israel, were accustomed to relating to a diverse divine world at home and at different ancient sanctuaries across the land. We even find in the biblical book of Exodus instructions from before Josiah's time on how one should build an altar wherever one is (Exodus 20:24–25). Now Josiah demanded that all must come to Jerusalem and Jerusalem alone to celebrate holidays and offer sacrifice. Now all must worship Yahweh alone, loving Yahweh "with all your heart, all your life strength, and all your might," as is called for in Deuteronomy (6:5).

Scholars debate the motives of Josiah's reform and its extent, but we should pause to consider its impact. This shift was certainly difficult for the local priests who were deprived of their livelihood by Josiah's reforms. It was catastrophic for those who were killed. In addition, Josiah required his people to turn from a whole world of spirituality to which they had been devoted. Both older goddesses like Asherah and newer ones like the Babylonian Ishtar were prohibited. Baal and astral gods were off limits. Even ancient and familiar local sanctuaries, where clans had celebrated Passover and other holidays for centuries, were defiled and prohibited. It was as if the mayor of New York City suddenly decreed the destruction of every church and non-Christian worship place in the entire region, requiring all to worship at one and only one cathedral located somewhere in Manhattan.

Historian of religion Jan Assmann argues that this reform represented a traumatic break from prior forms of worldly worship. Premonotheistic piety, whether in Israel, Judah, or elsewhere, helps people imagine themselves as related, in a direct and personal way, with the forces that dominate their world: weather, war, love, and so on. Assmann terms this piety "cosmotheism" rather than "polytheism," to indicate how such belief connects people with the world around them. Subject to multiple forces in that world, the ancients understood that world as governed by multiple "gods" and fashioned concrete images to visualize such gods and beseech their favor. They even understood powerful parts of their world—the sun, moon, ocean, human monarchs—as vivid images of broader cosmic powers they were at the mercy of. Political figures and natural forces did not just have their own godlike impact on the lives of ancient people, they served as natural icons of overwhelming divine power, symbols as tactile and real to ancient believers as small-scale statues of deities might be. As a result, the world of the ancients, including early Israel and Judah, was enchanted by worldly gods and tangible symbols of divinity. Josiah asked his people to renounce such gods and symbols as idols, leave behind the evidence of their everyday senses, and strip the world of its magical nature. In its place, he gave them a religion centered in Jerusalem and focused on an imageless God separate from the world that God cared for.[8]

When Assmann terms Josiah's reform "traumatic," he points to later generations haunted by the "cosmotheism" that Josiah repressed. A much earlier Egyptian reformer, the pharaoh Akhenaton, had attempted a similar monotheistic reform in the fourteenth century BCE, only to have Egypt revert to its older cosmotheism after his death and try to erase any memory of his rule. Josiah's reform proved more successful in the long run, but only because future catastrophes led Judeans to see his reforms as correct and their suffering as caused by reversion to idolatry after Josiah's death. And Assmann suggests that Western culture, twenty-five hundred years later, remains haunted by the repression of ancient cosmotheistic religion that Josiah represents. The continuing emergence of cosmotheistic movements in Western culture—Neoplatonism, alchemy, Deism, pantheism, New Age spirituality—represent a "return of the repressed," that is, forms of worldly spirituality widespread in the ancient world. Josiah's reform was not and could not be finished. It was so radical, so traumatic, that both his own people and later generations would remain tempted toward devotion to the world before their eyes, in its diversity and rich imagery.[9]

THE ORIGINS OF JOSIAH'S REFORM

What could have caused Josiah to enact such a traumatic break with earlier religious practice? The story about the reform in 2 Kings attributes it to one main factor: the discovery of "a scroll of Torah" in the process of Temple renovations and Josiah's decision to lead the people in making a covenant with Yahweh based on this rediscovered scroll, also called "the scroll of the covenant":

> Then the king sent and gathered to himself all the elders of Judah and Jerusalem. The king went up to the house of Yahweh, and with him went all the people of Judah, all the inhabitants of Jerusalem, the priests, the prophets, and all the people, from small to great; he read aloud in their hearing all the words of the scroll of the covenant that had been found in the house of Yahweh. The king stood by the pillar and made [Hebrew *karat*, cut] a covenant before Yahweh, to follow Yahweh, keeping his commandments, his laws, and his decrees, with all his heart and all his life strength, to establish the words of this covenant that were written in this book. All the people joined in the covenant. (2 Kings 23:1–3)

This is what sets in motion Josiah's massive purification project, removing the Asherah pillar and other ancient symbols from the Jerusalem temple and destroying local sanctuaries in Judah and parts of Israel as well: a "scroll of the covenant" found in the house of Yahweh, "this book."

A closer look at the wording of this story of Josiah's reform reveals the identity of the law book at its foundation. The story in 2 Kings 23 describes Josiah as making a covenant "to follow Yahweh . . . with all his heart and life strength," which echoes a command found in the biblical book of Deuteronomy, "love Yahweh your God with all your heart, all your life strength, and all your might" (Deuteronomy 6:5). Deuteronomy is the fifth and final book of the Pentateuch or Torah, and presents itself as Moses's final address to the Israelites just before they cross the Jordan to enter the land of Israel and conquer it. In the book Moses gives the people legal instructions on what they must do to please God when God brings them into the land promised to their ancestors. Josiah's campaign to eliminate local sanctuaries outside Jerusalem appears to be an execution of laws found in Deuteronomy 12 that call for elimination of non-Yahwistic worship objects and local sanctuaries, requiring worship at the one and only place that God will choose. And Josiah's leading of Judah and Israel in a centralized Passover celebration in Jerusalem is a fulfillment of the law in Deuteronomy 16 that requires Israel to celebrate all such pilgrimage feasts at the one place God will choose. These and other clues suggest that Josiah based his reform on an early form of the biblical book of Deuteronomy. It was this proto-Deuteronomy that was the "scroll of the Torah" or "scroll of the covenant" that guided his covenant and purification program.

It might be tempting to see Deuteronomy as a mere pseudo-Mosaic prop created by Josiah's scribes to support his reform, but the book contains clues that it did not begin this way. For example, Deuteronomy calls for worship of Yahweh at only one place, and that place is not Jerusalem. Instead, toward the end of the earliest manuscripts of Deuteronomy, Moses tells Israel to build an altar on the northern sanctuary of Mount Gerizim and make sacrifices there.[10] Mount Gerizim is in the heartland of ancient Israel, not Judah; Mount Gerizim represents an ancient Israelite holy place. This is hardly something that Josiah's Judean scribes would have invented. Instead, the original book of Deuteronomy, perhaps the scroll found by Josiah's officials, probably was a northern law scroll calling for worship at one place, Mount Gerizim. Most scholars agree it was not written by Moses, but neither was it created from scratch by Josiah's supporters.

That said, Josiah's scribes almost certainly expanded and revised this ancient law book when they made it the center of Josiah's covenant and reform. And when we look at Deuteronomy, Josiah's "covenant" law book, we find the deep impact of Assyrian trauma on the Judean soul. In the chapter on Hosea, I discussed how countries like Judah were required to engage in, or at least learn, covenants with Assyrian kings. For example, just a few decades before Josiah, the peoples of the whole Assyrian empire had been required in a "succession treaty" to swear curses on themselves if they failed to "love" and obey the Assyrian king's successor "as you do your own lives." In Deuteronomy this Assyrian call for exclusive loyalty to a king is redirected: "Love Yahweh with all your heart, life strength, and might."

In this and other ways, Deuteronomy—presented as an ancient speech of Moses—actually reflects the impact of Assyrian trauma that long postdates Moses. It is an ancient, post-Mosaic northern law book that was then modified by Josiah's scribes into an Assyrian-styled covenant between the people and their god, Yahweh. The major parts of Deuteronomy—historical prologue, calls for allegiance, laws, and provisions for enforcement of law through curses, blessings, and ongoing reading of the law—correspond to the major parts of "vassal treaties" imposed on the nations the Assyrians dominated. And certain parts of Deuteronomy, such as the prohibition of treason in Deuteronomy 13, specifically echo parts of the Assyrian succession treaty mentioned above.[11]

In the past, Judeans, especially elite Judeans, had been required to learn and even act out Assyrian vassal treaties requiring their allegiance and love. Memorizing such treaties had carved the way of imperial loyalty into their hearts. But Josiah redirected that loyalty through turning an ancient, northern, law book into an Assyrian-styled treaty with Yahweh. Imperial trauma thus powered and shaped religious trauma. Judeans had been terrorized over the years into renouncing alliances with foreigners. Now the same cultural form used to enforce that renunciation, the imperial covenant, was used by Josiah to require renunciation of gods and ancient sanctuaries.

To be sure, Josiah's law book, Deuteronomy, is presented by his scribes as a speech of Moses, but that is probably their attempt to gain ancient authority for their Assyrian-influenced covenant text. Once we look at the content of the biblical Deuteronomy—now reshaped by Josiah's and later scribes—it closely parallels Hosea's earlier prophecies to Israel. Hosea had called for an Assyrian-like love of Yahweh alone; Josiah enforced it. Hosea denounced worship of other gods; Josiah destroyed their symbols and local sanctuaries outside Jerusalem. Hosea briefly mentions a covenant that Israel has broken; Josiah turns the ancient northern law book found in the temple into a theological version of the Assyrian covenant and leads the people to "cut" that covenant with Yahweh. Where Hosea was an Israelite prophet who influenced Judeans, Josiah was a Judean king who enacted Hosea-like ideas, using a document originally from the north.

JUDAH'S ADOPTION OF "ISRAELITE" IDENTITY

This Judean appropriation of northern, Israelite tradition was a crucial step in a remarkable transformation of collective identity. Remember that, before this point, Judah and Israel were separate peoples joined by complex relations of similar lifestyle and occasional shared rule. They shared the state god, Yahweh, and numerous other cultural elements, but their traditions were distinct. As I have discussed, Judah's Davidic monarchy was centered on Jerusalem. Its scriptures featured royal hymns and wisdom, Zion psalms, and myths. It was northern Israel's distinctively different scriptures, written down when Israel split off from the Davidic, Jerusalem monarchy, that had focused on Moses and the exodus. Israel was the first home of the type of iconoclastic, anti-"idolatrous," monotheistic fervor that we saw in Hosea and the northern law book (early Deuteronomy) found and adapted for Josiah's reform.

Josiah's reform joined these two streams. He maintained the Judean focus on Jerusalem, understanding early-Deuteronomy's call for centralized worship to apply to

Jerusalem and not to Mount Gerizim or another northern sanctuary. This was no small thing. Yet in making Deuteronomy the basis of his reform, Josiah imported not just a northern document (early Deuteronomy) but northern ideas and even northern identity into Judah. For Deuteronomy presents itself as Yahweh's covenant with Israel. Its laws appear in the context of Yahweh's past acts on behalf of God's people Israel. In leading his people to enact this covenant, Josiah led them to take on Israel's identity as their own. The Bible says, "The king directed that all the elders of Judah and Jerusalem be gathered to him" to enact the covenant (2 Kings 23:1), but they emerged from this covenant as "Israel." They became the Israel who must love Yahweh and observe the laws given in Deuteronomy. They took onto themselves, as Israel, the curses for disobeying the covenant and blessings for following it.

In describing Josiah's purging of Israelite sanctuaries as well as Judean ones, the biblical narrative about Josiah suggests that this transformation was no simple transfer of Israelite identity from Israel to Judah. Instead, in purifying Israelite sanctuaries, Josiah implied a claim to be the rightful ruler of northern Israel along with Judah. The books of 1–2 Kings, probably drafted initially by Josiah's scribes, attribute the downfall of northern Israel to the failure of that nation to observe the calls to religious purity seen in Hosea and Deuteronomy. From the perspective of the (Josianic) authors of Kings, the big mistake of the north was its failure to listen to these ancient calls to reject other gods and love Yahweh alone.[12]

Now, just coming free of Assyrian domination, Josiah's Judean people saw themselves faced with a choice. They could continue "as is" and risk being destroyed like Israel was. Or they could revise an older northern law with a covenant format learned from Assyria. They chose the latter option, and the speeches of "Moses" in Deuteronomy are the result of Judean labors. Using newly rewritten Deuteronomy as the "scroll of the covenant," Josiah, his scribes, and the rest of the people offered a more exclusive commitment to Yahweh than anything they had ever offered to an Assyrian king. Josiah's Judah became the "Israel" that obeyed the Deuteronomic covenant.[13]

This move by Josiah's Judah parallels the phenomenon of the "replacement child" seen in families traumatized by the loss of an older sibling. In such families the parents unconsciously transfer onto a younger sibling the hopes and expectations that they once had for the child that was lost. Sometimes even the name is transferred, and the surviving child takes on the identity of the lost brother or sister. In this case, we have two sibling nations, Israel and Judah, only one of which survived the Assyrian onslaught. "Judah" took on the name and identity of its sibling, "Israel," who didn't make it. Moreover, in enacting the Deuteronomic covenant, this new "Israel" led by Josiah worked to fulfill divine expectations that the original Israel had fallen short of. With Josiah's adoption of this covenant, based as it was on a previous northern law code, his people Judah saw themselves ever more in terms of the stories, legal traditions, and even the identity of Israel.

Indeed, Judah became a Jerusalem-based Israel that could survive, where the Samaria-based Israel had not.

To some extent the northern traditions seen in Deuteronomy reinforced the older focus by Judeans on Jerusalem. Josiah and his people read Deuteronomy's call for centralized worship at a northern sanctuary as a mere prelude to God's ultimate choice of Jerusalem. Meanwhile, the northern traditions also brought major changes to Judah's scriptures, changes prompted by Assyrian trauma. Josiah began a shift from a typical Near Eastern focus on royal traditions to a new Judean focus on nonroyal legal traditions, particularly Deuteronomy, now functioning as the "scroll of the covenant." Even the biblical books of 1–2 Kings, focused as they are on the kings of Israel and Judah, were shaped by Josiah's scribes so they evaluated the kings of Israel and Judah on one criterion: whether they did or did not fulfill the Deuteronomic call for centralization of the cult in Jerusalem. Indeed, an earlier edition of those books probably concluded well before the current end of 2 Kings. That Josianic edition ended with a verse saying that Josiah did a better job than any other king at obeying the law of Deuteronomy (2 Kings 23:25; compare Deuteronomy 17:14–20).

In taking on this Deuteronomic covenant with Yahweh, Josiah's Judah tried to justify and secure its ongoing existence. As we have seen, this covenant involved a radical, even traumatic denial of older piety: abandonment of familiar deities, destruction of cult objects associated with them, defilement of ancient sanctuaries, and the demotion or elimination of the priesthoods associated with them. This was the new order, shaped in response to Assyrian trauma, that Josiah believed would solve the problems that led to decades of Assyrian domination. This was the new order that would ensure the eternal future of Zion and its kingship. He was horribly wrong.

EPILOGUE

Josiah and his officers may have believed they had secured the eternal future of Judah, but they did not survive even a chance encounter with the Egyptian army. We do not know why Josiah went to meet the Egyptians. They were not attacking or threatening Judah. Instead, they were traveling past Judah on the coastal road, on their way to help the Assyrians as they battled a new upstart empire, the Neo-Babylonian empire of the Chaldean people.

The details of the story are murky. The terse report in 2 Kings says only that Pharaoh Necho went up against the Assyrian king, that Josiah went out to meet him, and that Pharaoh Necho "killed him when he saw him" (2 Kings 23:29). A burial report follows, and then the anointing of the next Davidic king. The report of the event in 2 Chronicles gives a more extended account of the interaction between Necho and Josiah. In that account Josiah insists on donning armor to fight Necho, is mortally wounded by Egyptian archers when he goes out to battle, and dies in Jerusalem after being carried there (2 Chronicles 35:20–24). Yet this report is later and appears to be an attempt to dress up what appeared at the time to be an inexplicable, senseless death of one of Judah's greatest monarchs.

Yet the inexplicability and senselessness of Josiah's death pales in comparison with what it presaged: the eventual destruction of Jerusalem/Zion, the ending of its supposedly eternal Davidic kingship, and the exile to Babylon of much of the surviving population of Jerusalem and Judah. I turn to that story now.

CHAPTER FOUR

Jerusalem's Destruction and Babylonian Exile

The Egyptians who killed Josiah in 609 BCE controlled Judah only for a few years. A new "Chaldean" empire arose, based in ancient Babylon. In 604, five years after Josiah's death, this Chaldean "Neo-Babylonian" empire seized power over lands once controlled by Assyria, including Judah. We do not know much about the background of these Chaldeans who took over rule of Babylon, but they generally had a less bloodthirsty reputation than the Assyrians.

At first the Chaldean-Babylonians allowed the existing king of Judah, Jehoiakim, to remain. But he had been appointed to power by Egypt and was pro-Egyptian. After only three years of submission to Babylonia, Jehoiakim seized the opportunity to declare independence from Babylonian rule. At first, this bold act may have seemed successful. The

Babylonians were preoccupied with subduing other parts of their restive empire, and they left Jehoiakim's Judah alone. But by 596 BCE the Babylonians returned. Even though Jehoiakim had died shortly before their attack, the Babylonians exacted a punishment. They plundered the Temple and effectively depopulated Jerusalem, resettling the elite population of Jerusalem along with some inhabitants of surrounding Judah in remote parts of Babylon. Jehoiakim's successor, King Jehoiachin, and the rest of the royal family were among these thousands of Jerusalemite and Judean exiles, as was the priest, Ezekiel, whose prophecy will be discussed shortly.

Jerusalem, however, remained standing, and the Babylonians even allowed the Davidic kingship to continue, after a fashion. They tried to ensure Judean submission through handpicking a son of Josiah, Zedekiah, to be the new king of Jerusalem-Judah. Apparently Jerusalem revived somewhat, since several thousand lived there when Zedekiah eventually rebelled against Babylon himself. About nine years after being appointed by the Babylonians to his throne, Zedekiah stopped sending tribute to Babylonia and began preparing for the inevitable attack.

Within months the Babylonian army was back, and it laid siege to Jerusalem for almost two years. When the starved city eventually fell in 587 BCE, the Babylonians were ruthless. The last thing that Zedekiah saw before the Babylonians blinded him was the killing of each of his children in front of him. Then the Babylonians took blind Zedekiah and most of the surviving population of Jerusalem into exile, thousands of people. Weeks later the Babylonians systematically destroyed Jerusalem, pulling down its wall and burning the Temple, the palace, and other buildings. Supposedly invulnerable "Zion" was nothing but rubble, its inhabitants dead or in exile. Now two waves of exiled Judeans lived in Babylon, those who had been exiled during the first Babylonian attack in 596 BCE and this later group, who had witnessed the total destruction of Jerusalem in 587. They represented a collection of virtually all elite leaders and craftspeople of Jerusalem and Judah that might stir up some kind of rebellion against Babylon. The Bible records that the "poor of the land" were left to live in Judah, but the top had been skimmed off Judean society in 596, and then it was skimmed again in 587 (2 Kings 25:12).[1]

It is hard to imagine that such events could fail to traumatize a people. Thousands had died in battle. Yet more had starved in besieged cities. By the end, Jerusalem and much of Judah was in ruins, with its urban population dead or in exile. Rural settlements continued to the north and south of Jerusalem, and the Babylonians used older administrative centers to keep collecting taxes. But Judah had lost both its monarchy and its holy city, and the authors of the Bible found themselves in exile.[2]

These events severely undermined two core beliefs of the Judeans: that Jerusalem was the invulnerable city of God and that God would make sure that an heir of David would always be king in Jerusalem.[3] These beliefs in Jerusalem and its invulnerability became so powerful in the years leading up to exile that the prophet Jeremiah was almost executed when he declared during this time that the Jerusalem Temple would be destroyed. He was saved only when someone remembered that the prophet Micah had prophesied something similar a century before.

In the end, as mentioned, Jeremiah turned out to be right. Jerusalem was destroyed. The Davidic king, Jehoiachin, was imprisoned. The leadership of Judah was removed to distant Babylon, possibly never to return. Prior foundations of Judean communal identity were broken.

VOICES OF PAIN IN THE WAKE OF DESTRUCTION

The Bible preserves the cries of those who faced this catastrophe. An entire biblical book, called Lamentations, mourns the destruction of Jerusalem. The book starts with an exclamation over how the city, personified as a woman, has fallen:

> How deserted she sits,
>   the city once full of people!
> Now like a widow,
>   Is she who once was greatest of nations
> Once the princess of states,
>   she now faces forced labor. (Lamentations 1:1)

The rest of the book alternates descriptions of devastated Jerusalem with poems in which Jerusalem herself, personified as a woman, cries out about her suffering.

> Look, Yahweh. I am in distress!
>   My guts boil over.

My heart turns over inside me.
For I have been such a rebel.
Outside, the sword bereaves;
inside it is like death. (Lamentations 1:20)

Her exclamation "I have been such a rebel" is just one of numerous places where texts written at this time manifest self-blame so typical of survivors of trauma. Much like Hosea blamed Israel for Assyrian attacks and Josiah and his scribes blamed Judah for years of Assyrian oppression, so also Judeans in the wake of Jerusalem's destruction blamed themselves for their disaster.

Lamentations has no happy ending. It is one of the few books in the Bible to conclude with a question: "Why have you forgotten us forever? Why have you forsaken us so long? Restore us to yourself, Yahweh. Unless you have totally rejected us and are angry beyond limit?" (Lamentations 5:20–22).

We find similar cries in the book of Psalms, this time over the loss of the Davidic kingship. A Judean author concluded an early collection of psalms with a lament about this loss in Psalm 89. The psalm starts hopefully, with a review of God's past promises to David to preserve his line: "I will establish your descendants forever, and build your throne for all generations" (Psalm 89:4). But the rest of Psalm 89 then shows how the Babylonian attack has shattered this trust in God's protection of David's line. The psalmist cries to God, "you have stripped him [the Davidic heir] of his great scepter, and hurled his throne to the ground. You have cut short the days of his youth; and enveloped him in shame" (89:44–45). The exiled psalmist then confronts God with more questions: "How long, O Yahweh, will you hide yourself forever? How long will your anger burn like fire?" (89:46). The psalm concludes by speaking directly of God's broken promises: "Where is your past steadfast love, my lord, which you swore to David in truth?" (89:49).

The Judeans' collective trust in God's protective relationships with them had been broken. Exile also provided them with new challenges as it severed their sense of connection with their land and city. These thousands of upper-class Judeans taken into exile had never lived anywhere by Judah. Most had spent their entire lives within a few miles of Jerusalem. Now they found themselves resettled in depopulated parts of Babylon, scattered among settlements of exiled Judeans such as "Tel-Aviv" and "the city of Judah."[4] Previously these exiles had been priests, officers, and other privileged leaders in Judah. That is why they were removed by the Babylonians. Now they were foreigners in a strange land, trying to survive and enduring taunts by their Babylonian captors. These exiles had undergone the same things—destroyed capital, ended monarchy, exile—that permanently terminated their sibling nation, Israel, a century before, and there was no clear sign for these Judeans in Babylon that their fate would be any different.

We hear their cry in a psalm (Psalm 137), popularized in the 1970 reggae song "Rivers of Babylon" by the Melodians. In it a group of exiles voice their confusion and rage as they endure taunts by their Babylonian captors:

By the rivers of Babylon
There we sat and we wept
at our memory of Zion.
On the poplars there
We hung our harps.
For our captors there had asked us to sing them songs,
Our tormentors looking for amusement.
"Sing for us
one of the songs of Zion."
How could we sing a song of Yahweh
on foreign soil?
If I forget you, Jerusalem,
may my right hand wither!
May my tongue remain stuck to the roof of my mouth
if I do not remember you,
if I do not count Jerusalem
my greatest joy. (Psalm 137:1–6)

Such memory of Jerusalem was one thing that bound Judean exiles together, even as they lived in disparate towns across central Babylon. Most such exiles never returned, dying on foreign soil. In a world where the average life expectancy for adults averaged around thirty years, the fifty-year period of forced exile in Babylon lasted more than a generation. As a result only a handful of people taken into exile got the chance to return. By the time Babylon fell, the "sons of the exile" (as they called themselves) were mostly children of those who had once lived in Judah. They were "exiles" who had never seen their homeland. Their only bond to one another was the memory—often only through their parents' memories—of Jerusalem and the land of Israel.

WRITING IN BUT NOT ABOUT BABYLON EXILE

We have seen some of the cries of Judeans in the wake of Jerusalem's destruction. Yet the Bible contains a striking gap when it comes to narratives about what life was like during exile. The books of Kings conclude with stories about Jerusalem's destruction and the initial exile of Judeans to Babylon. And the story does not resume again until the Babylonians are defeated and the Persian king, Cyrus, proclaims that Judeans may return and start rebuilding Jerusalem (Ezra 1:2–3//2 Chronicles 36:23). The only exilic event reported is a three-verse fragment about the end of imprisonment of the exiled king, Jehoiachin (2 Kings 25:27–29). The exile remains a black hole in the biblical tradition. Only hundreds of years later did Jews start to write stories about exilic figures like Daniel (Daniel 1–6). Otherwise, the exile is a gap in the middle of biblical history.

This gap may be an index of what was truly traumatic about the Babylonian onslaught. Of course, the destruction of Jerusalem was devastating. The book of Lamentations is just one testimony to that. And the loss of Davidic rule was painful too, though there remained hope that it might be restored. Yet neither of these events was so traumatic that it could not be written about. The Bible describes Jerusalem's fall. It chronicles the gradual dissolution of the Davidic kingship. These are things ancient Judeans could describe. Painful as these events were, they could be talked about by Judean authors using genres of lament that were available to them. In contrast, actual life in Babylonian exile was truly traumatic "speechless terror." It was "history that has no place." As a result, those nonassimilated Judean exiles in Judah who still wept "at the memory of Zion" did not speak of life in Babylon.[5]

Nevertheless, despite this striking lack of history about exile, the Old Testament is, in large part, a collection of writings by these Judean exiles and their descendants. After all, the leaders that the Babylonians removed in wave after wave from Judah were exactly the sorts of people who would have been literate in the ancient world: priests, officers, bureaucrats, and royalty. Previously, only a small minority of the population of pre-exilic Judah was literate. In exile, however, literacy levels were far higher among the educated Judean elites deported to Babylon in 597 and 586 BCE. In a stroke, King Nebuchadnezzar of Babylon had created an unusually highly literate exiled Judean community.

Little did Nebuchadnezzar know, but this tiny community of Judean exiles would be the incubator for a set of scriptures that would long outlast his empire. Over the coming decades Babylon successfully extended its imperial reach to Egypt in the west and Persia to the east. Babylon's Ishtar temple became a wonder talked about for centuries, and Babylon's texts were the jewels of the Mesopotamian library. Yet less than fifty years after Jerusalem fell, Babylon was conquered by Cyrus the Persian (538 BCE). Within a few centuries, the tablets of Babylon's libraries were buried in sand, their script and language forgotten.

Meanwhile, like many people affected by trauma, the Judean exiles were coming to a fundamentally new understanding of themselves, one that would ultimately outlast empires like Babylon and its successors. The Hebrew Bible contains the deposit of their work. Virtually every book shows the impact of the Babylonian exile. This was the time, for example, when older prophecies of judgment, such as those by Amos, Micah, and Hosea, became the common focus of an exiled people trying to understand what had happened to them. Seized by the self-blame endemic to trauma, the exiles took to heart such previously marginalized judgment prophets and saw the exile as God's promised judgment for their sins. In addition, Judah's story of Israel's destruction and Judah's survival up through the reign of Josiah had to be modified in light of Jerusalem's subsequent destruction. It would no longer do to have the books of Kings end, as they probably originally did, with Josiah's covenant with God, purification of Jerusalem and land surrounding, and celebration of Passover. So Judean authors in exile added onto the end of the books of Kings to provide an answer. They argued that, in the end, even Josiah's great faithfulness was not enough to outweigh the disobedient acts of his father, Manasseh, before him.[6]

EZEKIEL, EXILED PRIEST AND PROPHET

Judean exiles, however, did not just modify earlier prophetic collections and histories. They also created new texts that reflected their struggle with self-blame. We see this particularly in the biblical book devoted to Ezekiel, a priest taken into Babylon in the first wave of exiles, ten years before Jerusalem was destroyed. In chapter after chapter, the prophet proclaims the sins of his people, vividly describing the sins of the city and its exiles. For example, Ezekiel prophesies, "I shall spare some of you from the sword among the nations and be scattered among the lands. . . . They [the exiles] will loathe themselves for the evils they have committed, for all their abominations. And they shall know that I am Yahweh; I was not speaking lightly when I said I would bring this disaster upon them" (Ezekiel 6:8–10). The self-blame seen in this and other texts must have been difficult for exiled Judeans to hear. At the same time, Ezekiel offered his contemporaries a way to make sense of what had happened to them. It allowed them to interpret Jerusalem's destruction and the exile in a way that left Yahweh in control, a way that did not assume Yahweh was powerless or did not care.

Yet exile is not just reflected in Ezekiel's words. Its impact is also manifest in his strange actions. Over the years scholars have been quick to diagnose Ezekiel with the mental ailments of their day, mainly because Ezekiel's behavior and visions seem so bizarre: lying on his side for 390 days (Ezekiel 4:1–17), shaving his hair with a sword and burning it (5:1–4), spiritual "travels" back to the Jerusalem from which he'd been exiled (8–11), and pornographic images of hypersexual "Samaria" and "Jerusalem" (16 and 23). Each generation of biblical scholars has seen a different illness in Ezekiel—hysteria, schizophrenia, and (more recently) PTSD.[7]

There is no way to know, of course, what Ezekiel himself suffered from. But it is clear that his actions came to symbolize the broader trauma that Babylonian exiles suffered. For instance, just after Ezekiel has heard of the Babylonian attack on Jerusalem, he prophesies about Jerusalem's impending destruction and then quickly jumps to another topic: the death of his own wife. He speaks of God announcing to him that his wife, "the delight of [his] eyes," would soon die and commanding Ezekiel not to mourn her. She dies, Ezekiel does not mourn her, and the people around him ask why he is behaving so strangely: "Can't you tell us what all this means for us, that you are so acting [in this strange way]?" He proceeds to tell them that they are about to lose Jerusalem, "the pride of your strength, the delight of your eyes and your heart's desire," along with their children (Ezekiel 24:20–21). And Ezekiel tells them that when this happens they will not mourn either. Instead, they'll be struck dumb by the depth of their misdeeds. The prophecy concludes with God telling Ezekiel that he, personally, shall be a "sign" to his people, a sign in his numb response to his wife's death.

Centuries of interpreters have been disturbed by Ezekiel's failure to mourn his wife, but this story vividly images the exiles' psychic numbing.[8] When Jerusalem is in ashes and the Judeans are in Babylon, they "do not cover their upper lip or eat the bread of mourners, they keep their turbans on and sandals on their feet, they do not mourn or weep." (Ezekiel 24:22–23). These exiles find themselves, like the Ezekiel described in his book, experiencing a kind of "death in life" typical of people experiencing trauma.[9] As an individual, Ezekiel embodies the psychic numbing that his people experienced in the wake of Jerusalem's destruction. This narrative about Ezekiel, an individual person, became a way for Judean exiles in Babylon to depict their own collective struggle to mourn. Like many who suffer, they dissociated from their own experience. Not able to depict their experience directly, exiled Judeans found their traumatized communal self in Ezekiel. This served as a "sign" for them of God's role in their world.

JEREMIAH AND THE DAUGHTER OF ZION IN LAMENTATIONS

The other major prophet who worked during the early exile was Ezekiel's contemporary Jeremiah. Though he remained in Jerusalem, he too served as a symbol of the unspeakable suffering of his people. Where Ezekiel suffered the loss of his wife, Jeremiah suffered a long career of rejection and isolation because of his harsh prophecies. In the years leading up to Babylonian destruction, Jeremiah's was a lone and unpopular voice that criticized the anti-Babylonian, pro-Egyptian strategies of the last kings of Judah. He was mocked, imprisoned in a pit, and almost executed. In one of his prophecies he speaks of how he tried to stop speaking his unpopular message, but that "there is within me a burning fire, shut up in my bones; I am tired of holding it in, I cannot" (Jeremiah 20:9).

Jeremiah's once marginalized prophecies found their way into scripture, perhaps partly because his unpopular words of destruction came true. But that may not be all. The level of biographical description of Jeremiah in the book and the focus on laments about his painful experience are unusual. His laments are so prominent that Jeremiah has been labeled "the weeping prophet." Yet like Ezekiel's numbness in the wake of losing "the delight of his eyes," Jeremiah's suffering mirrored that of his people. Exiles read and added to Jeremiah's book because he personally embodied their collective suffering self. Like Ezekiel, he gave them a way to dissociate from their own pain, to speak of it in the third person. Through not just focusing on prophetic words, but also focusing on suffering prophetic persons like Jeremiah and Ezekiel, the Babylonian exiles found a way to speak of their traumatized self/selves in a safe and separate form.

We see a similar phenomenon in the above-mentioned book of Lamentations. It includes a focus on "the daughter of Zion" who personifies the suffering of exiled Judah and Jerusalem. Though earlier prophecy like Isaiah had mentioned the "daughter of Zion" in passing (Isaiah 1:8), she becomes a major character in Lamentations. There she laments over her lost children and repeatedly cries out to God. In contrast to the examples of Ezekiel and Jeremiah, this figure of suffering "Daughter Zion" is gendered female. Insofar as women were more vulnerable to trauma in the ancient world (as in the contemporary one), the feminine gender of the Daughter Zion image made that image a particularly powerful expression of the suffering, dissociated "self" of the Babylonian exiles.

COMFORT FOR EXILES IN "SECOND ISAIAH"

So far we have seen cries out of exile, symbols of exilic suffering in prophets and the "daughter of Zion,"' and despair. Yet the exiles needed something more than this. The self-blame often accompanying suffering needed to be accompanied by hope.[10] We see such hope in exilic additions of comforting prophecies to older collections of prophecies of judgment.

One of the best examples of this can be found in the extension of an older collection of Isaiah's prophecies (contained in Isaiah 1–32) with new prophecies written during the last years of exile—Isaiah 40–55. Already two centuries ago scholars recognized that these chapters were not written by the eighth-century prophet "Isaiah" but instead by an anonymous prophet in exile. This "second Isaiah" looked back on God's judgment of Judah, encouraged the exiles to trust God's plan to rescue them, and mentioned Persian Cyrus by name as their deliverer (Isaiah 45:1–5). His prophecy, coming on the eve of Cyrus's defeat of the Babylonians, is an invaluable key to how the exiles came to understand themselves after decades of life away from home. Speaking to an exiled Judean people in despair, he reassured them. His prophecy opens with God's commission to "comfort my people, comfort them" (40:1), and it closes with a promise to exiles that "you shall go out [of Babylon] in joy and be led back in peace" (55:12). These and many other words of hope in Isaiah 40–55 focused on restoring the trust in God and the world that exile had undermined.[11]

Such texts of comfort were crucial in the wake of Babylonian destruction of Jerusalem and exile of its surviving inhabitants. The exiled prophet Ezekiel had quoted the exiles as saying, "Our bones are dry, our hope has gone; we are done for" (Ezekiel 37:11) and "Our crimes and sins weigh heavily on us; we are wasting away because of them. How are we to go on living?" (Ezekiel 33:10). And the exiles did not doubt just themselves. They were not sure God still cared about them. The book of Lamentations ends with Zion's cry about Yahweh forsaking her (Lamentations 5:20), and Ezekiel quotes elders saying, "Yahweh has abandoned the land. Yahweh cannot see" (Ezekiel 9:9). Even the images of divine love that Hosea once used to give hope to Israelites facing the Assyrians turn into terrorizing images of pure, divine gender violence. Ezekiel, for example, includes two long chapters extensively depicting Yahweh's violent punishment of female Jerusalem for her wanton sexuality (Ezekiel 16 and 23). Among the most difficult texts in the entire Hebrew Bible, these prophecies in Ezekiel depict Yahweh as a terrorizing, misogynist despot, and God's once beloved people as a worthless "whore."

Yet the later prophecy of Second Isaiah offered exiles a comforting counterpoint to such texts of terror. The God we find there tells Zion, "Do not fear, for you will not be ashamed," and insists that she will "forget the shame of [her] youth" (Isaiah 54:4). The God prophesied there recognizes the despair of earlier exile—"for a brief time I abandoned you"—but promises better times ahead—"with great compassion I will gather you back." Or again, "in an outburst of anger, for a brief time, I hid my face from you, but now, with everlasting love, I will have compassion on you" (Isaiah 54:7–8). Such promises of restoration sound like Hosea again, and this picture of divine rage and remorse in Isaiah 54 sounds eerily like the abuse cycle many women past and present have faced in their lives. Yet by now, in contrast to the time of Hosea, the exiled Judeans felt that they had much in common with such battered women. They lived, it seemed, in a cosmos dominated by an abusing God. Such images helped exiles make sense of their world.

This belief in God's control of world history led to another development that happened during exile: the emergence of a purer form of monotheism than had previously existed. Hosea's and Josiah's monotheism required only that Israel worship Yahweh alone. It said nothing about whether other gods were real. Second Isaiah, in contrast, is the first datable biblical text to deny that other gods even exist. Yahweh is the one and only God to have punished Judah with Babylon, and Yahweh and only Yahweh is the one who has called the Persian ruler, Cyrus, to rescue Yahweh's exiled people (Isaiah 45:1–5). All other gods are a sham. Second Isaiah ridicules Babylonian image worship, making fun of the craftsman who takes a log, uses half of the log as fuel for his fire, and carves the other half of the log into a divine statue that he then prays to, saying, "Save me, for you are my god!" (Isaiah 44:13–17). For Second Isaiah, there is no true god in the entire world but

Yahweh, and the world of non-Judean divine statues and images is false.[12]

Finally, Second Isaiah offers comforting divine prophecies to not one but two figures who symbolize exilic suffering. To start, this anonymous prophet speaks, like Lamentations, of "Daughter Zion" as a personified figure. It even quotes parts of Lamentations in the process of offering comforting words of hope to Judeans who had been in Babylonia for decades by this point. Where "Daughter Zion" in Lamentations cried out that she had "no comforter" (Lamentations 1:2, 9, 16), Second Isaiah's prophecy describes God's call to "comfort" and "speak to the heart" of Jerusalem (Isaiah 40:1–2). And where "Daughter Zion" complained of having been abandoned by God (Lamentations 5:20), Second Isaiah quotes this lament and responds with a vision of God as loving mother who could never forget her children (Isaiah 49:14–21).

Second Isaiah still focuses on "Daughter Zion" as a figure representing exilic suffering and despair. But in comparison with Lamentations, this "Daughter Zion" figure is no longer completely dissociated from the people she symbolizes. Instead, the speech to Daughter Zion in Isaiah 49 subtly shifts into an address to the exiles themselves (50:1–3), and the same happens soon again in a shift from address to Daughter Zion (52:1–9) to the exilic community (52:10–12). Written toward the end of the forced life of exile in Babylon, Second Isaiah's prophecy thus represents a step toward recovery for the Judeans there. By this point, the metaphor of "Daughter Zion" is starting to be associated with the exiles it is meant for.

This shift in Second Isaiah away from pure use of the third person for "Daughter Zion" represents a form of healing.[13] The exiles now can see themselves as "Daughter Zion."

In addition, Second Isaiah's prophecy features another important figure, a "servant of Yahweh" that symbolizes both the suffering and the hope of the Babylonian exiles. As in the case of "Daughter Zion," this enigmatic "servant" figure is an individual who symbolizes the community. Early in Second Isaiah, God even addresses the community of Jacob/"Israel" as God's servant, saying, "You, Israel, my servant, Jacob, whom I have chosen, the offspring of Abraham, my friend, . . . saying to you 'You are my servant, I have chosen you and not cast you off' " (Isaiah 41:8–9).

As the exilic prophecy continues, however, we hear of a "servant" that sometimes seems to be an individual within the community. Isaiah 42:1–4 is the first of several "servant songs" in Isaiah, and in it God introduces a servant apparently unknown to the text's audience: "Here is my servant whom I support, my chosen one in whom I delight. I have put my spirit on him. He'll bring the nations justice" (Isaiah 42:1). Later in Second Isaiah, this servant himself speaks of his mission, "God said to me, 'you are my servant, Israel in whom I will be glorified"' (Isaiah 49:3). This seems to identify the servant again with the community of Israel, but soon he implies that his individual mission is to restore Israel: "And now Yahweh says, who formed me in the womb to be his servant, to bring Jacob back to him, and that Israel might be gathered to him" (49:5). Just verses later we hear that this servant suffered much of the same rejection the prophets once had. He says, "I gave my back to those who struck me, and my cheeks to those who pulled out my beard. I did not hide my face from insult and spitting" (50:6). Yet he also insists on his ultimate redemption: "I know that I shall not be put to shame, the one who declares me innocent is close. . . . See the lord Yahweh will help me" (50:8–9).

Finally, the last "servant song," found in Isaiah 52:13–53:12, describes others' amazement at how God has restored this suffering servant. It starts with God's exclamation that "my servant shall succeed," with his success surprising "kings" and "nations" (52:13–15). Then the poem turns to quote a group, perhaps these "kings" and "nations," as they marvel at what has happened to this "servant."

> Who has believed what we have heard?
> And to whom has the arm of Yahweh been revealed? . . .
> He was despised and rejected by humans,
> a man of suffering, and well acquainted with grief;
> and like one from whom people avert their gaze,
> he was despised, and we did not regard him as anything.
> [50:1, 3]

Yet this group comes to the striking belief that this suffering person, the one they thought was cursed by God, actually was bearing the punishment of their own sins:

> Yet, surely ours were the sicknesses that he has bore
> our pains were what he carried;
> yet we thought he had been struck down,
> struck by God, and oppressed.

But he was wounded by our crimes,
he was crushed by our bloodguilt;
the discipline that restored us was laid on him,
and with his wounds we have been healed.
All of us have lost our way like sheep;
we have turned every one to his own way;
and Yahweh has put on him
the bloodguilt belonging to all of us. (53:4–6)

The text goes on to describe concrete things this "servant" suffered quietly, he was "taken away" by a "perversion of justice," "cut off from the land of the living" and placed in a grave "for the wicked," though he had done no violence or engaged in any deceit (53:7–9). The poem concludes by asserting that God will restore this servant, and quoting a promise from God to make the servant's suffering atone for others' sins, much like a temple sacrifice:

But Yahweh wanted to crush him with sickness.
when you make his lifestrength an offering for sin,
he shall see his children grow up, he shall prolong his days;
the will of Yahweh shall prosper in his hand;
... the righteous one, my servant, shall make many others righteous
and their bloodguilt he shall bear.
Therefore I will give him a portion with the many,
and with the mighty he shall divide spoil;
because he poured out his life strength unto death,
and was counted as among criminals;
yet he bore the sin of many,
and sought mercy for law breakers. (53:10–12)

This suffering servant song stands as one of the most famous poems in the Bible, and also one of the most controversial. Early Christians took it to be a prophecy of Jesus' crucifixion, telling of how he "bore the sin of many" and that his death was a "sacrifice for sin." Jews have understood the poem to be about a collective "servant," the whole people of Israel. Recent historical scholarship has failed to resolve the problem. Just when one scholar has identified reasons to see the "servant" as an individual, another argues that the servant is really the community. On the one hand, the "servant" in Second Isaiah speaks for himself (49:1–6, 50:4–9) and seems to have specific experiences of suffering as an individual—being insulted for his message, rejected for his appearance, and subjected to unfair judicial processes. On the other hand, Second Isaiah repeatedly identifies the "servant" with the whole community of Israel (41:8–9, 49:3).

How might we explain this mix of data, some favoring the idea of an individual suffering servant, and other supporting the idea that the suffering servant is the people? Following the suggestion of one of my students, Caroline Perry, I suggest that we might use trauma theory to affirm both alternatives.[14] Yes, on one level, Isaiah 40–55 talks of a suffering individual, probably a prophet like Jeremiah who suffered for his message and was rejected by those around him. This figure, like other prophets in the Hebrew Bible, spoke of being commissioned by God (Isaiah 42:1–9, 49:1–6), and like many other prophets his message was initially unpopular. Yet, as in the cases of Jeremiah and Ezekiel, the exiles came to see their own suffering in that of this anonymous exilic prophet. Speaking of his suffering provided a manageable, safe way to speak of their own suffering. So the suffering servant was also a suffering community, the exiles. He embodied their pain and their hoped-for restoration. As we have seen, the exiles did not easily describe their experience of suffering and often described it via figures like Daughter Zion or suffering prophets. The "servant" found in the exilic prophecy of Isaiah 40–55 is a vivid example of such reflection on communal suffering by way of poems about a suffering exiled prophet, one whose name we'll never know.

Histories of religion often focus on the momentous shift represented by Second Isaiah's demonstrable monotheism: the shredding of belief in any real deity besides Yahweh in the entire cosmos, even those worshiped by other peoples. And indeed, this development is an important step toward the worldview found in much of the contemporary West, including the denial in many quarters of any cosmic deity whatsoever.

Nevertheless, Second Isaiah is the culmination of another major development amidst exilic trauma: the processing of unspeakable trauma using individual figures like "Daughter Zion" and "the servant of Yahweh." Lamentations already started with lengthy quotations of the cries of "Daughter Zion" out of the ruins of Jerusalem. The books of Ezekiel and Jeremiah each feature depictions of prophetic personalities whose suffering mirrored that of the exiles.

In the long run, however, it was the "servant of Yahweh" figure in Second Isaiah that resonated most with later communities facing their own forms of unspeakable suffering. As mentioned, Jews saw the suffering servant in Isaiah 53 as a symbol of the pain and eventual redemption of the Jewish people. Christians saw the same poem as a description of the suffering and resurrection of Jesus Christ, who in turn mirrored their suffering. Individuals and communities each found an echo of their otherwise unrecognized distress in the anonymous figure in Isaiah, the servant who was "a man of suffering, and well acquainted with grief" (53:3). Though they might "be despised," later readers of Isaiah hoped that they, like him, might be restored. Like the exiles, later readers of Isaiah might not always speak of or even remember their deepest pain. Nevertheless, they found a companion in Isaiah's suffering servant who symbolized their deepest suffering, rejection, and hopes for restoration.

Together, the suffering servant, daughter of Zion, Ezekiel, and Jeremiah stand as examples of the processing of exilic trauma through depictions of individual figures to whom exiles could relate. Next we will see how exiles also reshaped stories about ancient figures like Abraham and Moses so that these ancient individuals represented their suffering and hope as well.

CHAPTER FIVE

Abraham and Exile

WHEN ASKED TO SING "songs of Zion," the exiles asked, "How can we sing the song of Yahweh in a foreign land?" (Psalm 137:4). Some exiles, unable to see a future as Judeans, assimilated into Babylonian culture. We may even have written records of such assimilated Jews in recently discovered legal contracts written by exiled Judeans in Babylon. The people in these contracts bear Judean names, but their legal documents are otherwise indistinguishable from the documents composed by native Babylonians. These records show how thoroughly some exiles had adapted to their Babylonian cultural context.

Yet the Hebrew Bible is a testimony to the idea that some exiled Judeans resisted assimilation. They survived profoundly changed. Where earlier generations focused particularly on the king and holy Jerusalem/Zion, Psalm 137 attests to the fact that the exiles now found "songs of Zion" (Jerusalem) difficult to sing in Babylon. They still collected such songs and other pre-exilic texts, but the center of gravity in the Hebrew scriptures shifted. In the end, the exiled scribes focused more and more on texts about ancient ancestors (Abraham and Sarah, for example) and the generation of Moses (thus exodus)—texts that never mention Jerusalem explicitly.[1] Their work helped make the stories we now find in the Pentateuch into the heart of the Hebrew Bible, the Torah.

During the exile the Judeans came to focus more than before on stories of their distant past. The Torah focuses on figures in Israel's earliest history—Abraham and Sarah, Isaac and Rebecca, Jacob and his offspring, and the whole generation of Moses and Aaron that left Egypt and spent forty years in the wilderness. If these are historical figures, they lived long before the founding of the Israelite monarchy around 1000 BCE.[2] Thus these figures—whether Moses or the ancestors before him—flourished in a time (1200 BCE or before) when Israel was an oral culture. There were no scribes at the time to write long literary texts about them.[3]

The Hebrew Bible contains lots of written texts about these very ancient figures. Indeed, four whole books of the Torah cover the span of Moses' lifetime, 136 chapters in all, despite the fact that he lived centuries before written Hebrew literature began in Israel or Judah. This is more chapters than are spent talking about David or any other famous figure in Israelite history. Who wrote these chapters and when? Scholars have

Table 1. The Gap Between Historical Figures in the Pentateuch and the Babylonian Exile

c. 1550–1200 BCE	New Kingdom period in Egypt (most likely time of a historical Moses)
c. 1250	The people of "Israel" first appears in textual and archaeological record
c. 1000	Beginning of monarchies in land of Israel (probable beginning of Israelite literature)
c. 586–538	Exile in Babylon (exilic focus on Moses, Abraham, and other ancestors)

been debating this question for about three hundred years and have not found a definitive solution. Nevertheless, an increasing number, myself included, believe that the period of Babylonian exile and its aftermath were the crucial time when older oral and written traditions about these ancient ancestors—Abraham, Moses, and others—were revised into their present form. Even though the Judean exiles in Babylon were distant chronologically from the time of these ancient ancestors (see Table 1), these exiles found more comfort in stories about Abraham and Moses than they did in accounts of their more recent past.[4]

We can trace the development of this focus on ancient ancestors by contrasting two prophetic quotations about Abraham from the early and then the late exile. The first "before" quotation comes from just before the Babylonian destruction of Jerusalem, while the second "after" quotation comes toward the end of forced exile. In the quotation from before the destruction of Jerusalem, the prophet Ezekiel (again, part of the first wave of Judean exiles) berates people in the land who say that "Abraham was only one man, and he took possession of the land, but we are many, the land is given to us as an inheritance." Ezekiel then says that God promises that the people who so trust in Abraham's example will die by the sword if they are in the "wastelands," will be eaten by beasts if they are "in the open field," and will be claimed by plague if they hide in caves. "Then they will know that I am the LORD, when I have made the land a desolate waste" (Ezekiel 33:24–29). In this "before" quotation from Ezekiel it is wrong—at least for people remaining in the land—to look to Abraham as a beacon of hope.

The second quotation comes from "Second Isaiah" after forty to fifty years of exile, and it shows a much more positive attitude toward seeing hope in Abraham. Speaking to exiles, this anonymous prophet says:

> Look to the rock from which you were hewn,
> and to the quarry from which you were dug.
> Look to Abraham your father,
> and Sarah who bore you.
> He was only one man when I [Yahweh] called him,
> and I blessed him and multiplied him.
> For Yahweh will comfort Zion;
> he will comfort all her desolate places,
> and will make her wasteland like Eden,
> her desolate places like the garden of Yahweh. (Isaiah 51:1–3)

Both prophets speak of what it means to look to Abraham, who was "only one man." Both speak of the land being full of "waste places." But their messages could hardly be more different. Whereas Ezekiel rejects people who claim an inheritance through Abraham, Second Isaiah tells the exiles to take hope in "Abraham your father, Sarah who bore you." And whereas Ezekiel promises that the land will be a desolation, Second Isaiah promises that Yahweh is about to restore it. He even looks back to the Garden of Eden, described at the beginning of Genesis, as an image of this restoration: God "will make her wasteland like Eden, her desolate places like the garden of Yahweh."

In the time between the beginning and end of exile we have moved from Abraham as a false hope to Abraham as the rock on which hope should be based. Where current figures like "Daughter Zion" and the anonymous servant of Second Isaiah symbolized the exiles' suffering, ancestral figures like Abraham become a way for exiles to envision hope. And this hope is based on figures (like Abraham) who lived long ago. This is why Second Isaiah called on Judeans late in their experience of Babylonian exile to "Look to Abraham your father, Sarah who bore you."

THE PROMISE TO ABRAHAM AS ANTIDOTE TO THE CURSE OF EXILE

What led to this call to "look to" distant ancestors? On the one hand, the Judean exiles could relate to figures like Abraham and Sarah, who lived, like them, in a land not their own. More than earlier generations, the Judeans in exile saw themselves in Abraham, Jacob, Moses, and others who lived in foreign lands and were subject to foreign rule. On the other hand, these stories about Abraham and other figures were distinct enough from exilic experience to be safe. They thus served as a form of "screen memory" for Judean exiles disinclined to speak directly about their present condition. Caught in collective amnesia about their exilic present and past, these Judeans in Babylon focused instead on stories of ancient ancestors.[5] They "looked to" landless ancestors like Abraham and Sarah, related to their struggles, and found hope in their promise.

The stories about ancestors that the exiles "looked to" are a blend of old traditions and later adaptations to make the stories more closely parallel to diaspora life in Babylon. For example, the Abraham story begins at the end of chapter 11 of Genesis with his father, Terah, departing for Canaan, taking Abraham, his nephew Lot, and his wife Sarai "out of Ur of the Chaldeans" (Genesis 11:31). This reference to the Chaldeans is one of our first clues that the stories about Abraham were reshaped by later Jews living in Babylonian exile. As mentioned before, the "Chaldeans" were a Semitic people who took over Babylon in the mid-first millennium BCE, around 700 BCE. This biblical mention of the Chaldeans in relation to Abraham is a problem. Genesis places Abraham and the other ancestors of Genesis hundreds of years before the Chaldeans dominated Mesopotamia, before the Israelite exodus from Egypt and entry into the land in the 1200s and 1100s BCE. Scholars have many questions about how historically accurate the stories about Abraham are, but it is clear that the Chaldeans were not prominent in Mesopotamia at the time of Abraham. Instead,

"Ur of the Chaldeans" evokes the Mesopotamia that the Judean exiles knew. By including this brief mention of "Ur of the Chaldeans," the exilic authors of this Abraham story in Genesis made him into an indirect picture of themselves. Abraham in "Ur of the Chaldeans" is now a proto-exile whose story mirrors the hopes and fears of the Judean exiles.

The Abraham story continues then in chapter 12 of Genesis, each aspect of it crafted as a message to exiles. God gives Abraham a difficult command and a connected promise. He must leave his "land, kindred and ancestral home." In return, God says:

> I will make you a great nation, and I will bless you, and make your name great, and you will be a blessing, and I will bless those who bless you and curse anyone who even treats you lightly, and all the clans of the earth shall use you as an example in blessing themselves. [Genesis 12:2–3]

Again, each part of this brief promise rings with particular significance for Judean exiles, many of them born in Babylon. Like Abraham of this story, they must contemplate leaving Babylon and their kindred who remain in order to return to Judah/Jerusalem. Yet this ancestral Abraham of the story gives them hope. Where their nation has been destroyed, Abraham is promised future nationhood by God. They may feel small, but their ancestor Abraham is promised that his name will be great. Where they feel vulnerable, their father Abraham is offered special divine protection. The exiles writing and reading this story could claim Abraham's place in it and take comfort. Not only will God bless those who bless them, but God will curse those who even treat them lightly (a nuance often obscured in translation). In these ways, exiles could find hope in this story's Abraham that they too could receive such divine gifts.

Most important, this proto-exile Abraham is offered a blessing in chapter 12 of Genesis, and in multiple ways: I will bless you, . . . you will be a blessing . . . I will bless those who bless you . . . all the clans of the earth shall bless themselves by you." The repetition indicates that this is a crucial theme. Its repeated emphasis on the idea that God promised Abraham a blessing hints that someone might think otherwise—that Abraham, or his exiled descendants, are cursed.

In fact, we do have clues in the Bible that the exiles felt cursed as they went through exile. Psalm 79 speaks of becoming "an object of disgust by our neighbors, of mocking and derision by all who surround us" (Psalm 79:4). Jeremiah speaks of the people and of Jerusalem becoming an example among the nations of curse (Jeremiah 24:9, 25:18). And a postexilic prophet, Zechariah, looks back on exile as a time when the people was "a byword of cursing among the nations" (Zechariah 8:13).[6]

The Abraham story that we find in Genesis 12 responded to the exiles' belief that they were a worldwide example of curse. The last, often mistranslated part of the promise to Abraham speaks the most directly to this issue. Many translations have God conclude the promise in Genesis 12 by telling Abraham "in you all the families of the earth shall be blessed" (NRSV). This version, quoted in the New Testament by the apostle Paul (Galatians 3:8), well fits the church's theology of seeing non-Jews as receiving Abraham's blessing. But the famous Jewish commentator Rashi observed in the eleventh century CE, again CE=AD) that the verse is best translated instead as "all clans of the earth shall bless themselves by you." The idea is not that other nations will be blessed, but that they will bless themselves. Abraham will have become such a beacon of blessing that other nations will wish on themselves the kind of divine blessing that Abraham is famed to have.[7]

Understood this way, God's promise to Abraham in Genesis probably builds on the model provided by an older prayer for the king found in Psalms, one that prays that all nations will "bless themselves by" the Davidic king and "declare him happy" (Psalm 72:17). We see a similar idea later in Genesis, when Jacob blesses Joseph's sons, Ephraim and Manasseh, saying, "May Israel bless itself by you, saying 'May God make you like Ephraim and Manasseh' " (Genesis 48:20). The exilic storyteller who wrote Genesis 12 took these ideas and applied them to Abraham. Countering the perception of Judeans as cursed, he describes their forefather, Abraham, as receiving a promise that "all clans of the earth shall bless themselves by you." When the exiles "looked to" this "father Abraham" in Genesis, they found an answer to concerns about their supposed cursedness. As Abraham's children, they too were destined to be examples of blessing, not curse. And Genesis reinforces this message as this promise is repeated by God to Abraham's heirs. Jacob, for example, is told, "All clans of the earth shall bless themselves by you and your descendants" (Genesis 28:14). For the exiles, "and your descendants" meant them. This exilic story about ancient Abraham's divine blessing comforted and encouraged them.

The exiles would have been reassured as well by the other stories about Abraham that we find in the rest of Genesis. Like them, he lives as a foreigner everywhere he goes—Canaan, Egypt, Philistia, on the Mediterranean coast)—and finds himself vulnerable. But God protects and even enriches him while he lives in virtual exile. Like exiles, this biblical Abraham has doubts, repeatedly, about whether God will really follow through on God's promises of protection and blessing, asking, for example, "What will you give me, as I am now childless" (Genesis 15:2), and laughing when God later promises him a son (17:17). He goes so far as to pass his wife off as his sister in order to protect himself in Egypt and Philistia, but God rescues him and his family anyway (12:10–20; 20:1–18). Questioning whether God will provide him an heir, he and Sarai arrange for him to father a son, Ishmael, through a slave. Despite all this, God still gives him an heir (Isaac) through elderly Sarai, and gives his son through Hagar (Ishmael) a special destiny (16).

Later readers often have missed the ways that biblical Abraham doubts God's promises. In this, they've been influenced by later rabbinic and Christian traditions of "faithful Abraham." (Galatians 3:9).[8] But if you take a closer look at the actual biblical stories about him in Genesis, they depict a figure who does not quite trust that God really will keep God's promises. In Genesis 15 he even protests, "Look you did not give me seed, and the son of my house [a servant] will inherit from me" (15:3), and responds to God's promise of land by asking, "How will I know this?" (15:8). But God does not chide or judge him for such questions. Instead, God gives him a covenant that solemnly seals a commitment to give him the land (15:9–21). And God's covenant of circumcision found in Genesis 17 provides additional reassurance that God's promise is secure.

Judging from references to father Abraham in Second Isaiah (Isaiah 40–55), the exiles, doubting as they did, found hope in such stories. They, like Abraham, doubted, and yet they longed for God to protect them, make them into a nation, and give them the land of Canaan (again), just like Abraham. The Genesis stories about Abraham were a comfort for exiles every bit as real as Second Isaiah's prophecies of hope, perhaps more so. It was as if someone took Second Isaiah's prophecies of comfort and packaged them in story form.

Unable to tell stories about themselves, exiled Judeans "looked to" Abraham and retold stories about him. Taking up and reshaping Abraham's story as their own, they found hope in it. The promise-saturated Abraham story countered others' claims that Judeans were cursed. It was a healing form of group memory. It was Bible for exiles.

I have taken so much time with this first promise to Abraham because the divine promise to Abraham and his heirs, Isaac and Jacob, will prove so important, both in the Torah story and the way the whole story helps despairing exiles restore trust.[9] This is why the Abraham story proved crucial to later exiles. We can see it, as mentioned above, in how Second Isaiah invokes the Abraham story in a way that Ezekiel did not. Second Isaiah shows us that Abraham's story, and particularly the story of God's promises to Abraham, had become a touchstone to later exiles. Abraham in Ur of the

Chaldeans was them, and they could take comfort in God's promises of fame, protection, and blessing to Abraham.

PRESERVING THE ENDANGERED SECOND GENERATION

Yet one final episode in the Abraham story shows how exiles were not just comforted but found their deepest fears in Abraham's story as well. I'm thinking here of the haunting story in Genesis 22, where God tells Abraham, "Take your son, your only one, the one whom you love, Isaac, and go now to the land of Moriah, and offer him up as a burnt sacrifice on a mountain that I will show you." The text leaves no doubt about the awfulness of the command. As if any parent needed help in imagining how cruel such a divine command would be, the story stresses "your son, your only one, the one whom you love." How could God command such a thing? After everything that Abraham has gone through, God, without explanation or promise, now tells him to sacrifice his future. As if to stress the irony, God's command to Abraham here echoes the one God gave at the outset, when Abraham was leaving Ur of the Chaldeans for a land he'd never seen. There, in Genesis 12, God had told him to leave "your land, your kindred and the house of your father" for a land "that I will show you." Here God tells Abraham to sacrifice "your son, your only one, the one whom you love" on a mountain "that I will show you." But there is a crucial difference. In the beginning, in Genesis 12, God had promised Abraham blessing and protection for leaving his family of the past, and God soon adds, "I will give this land to your descendants" (12:2–3, 7). Here, in Genesis 22:2, God tells him to sacrifice his one remaining descendent, "your only son," and no promise is given whatsoever. It is as if this story in Genesis 22 puts the entire promise given in Genesis 12 at risk.[10]

Perhaps more than any other story in Genesis, this one would have resonated with the exiles' deepest fears. Anyone who has experienced or studied exile understands this fear. It is the fear among exiles about what will happen to their children in the new, foreign land. As the children of exiles mature, the child can become a foreigner in her or his own family, and the parent-child bond, already tested by teenage dynamics, can be strained. To be sure, that bond can and often does survive, but for all too long a time the outcome is painfully uncertain. These Judean exiles too faced the possibility that "their child, their only one, their beloved" would be lost to them forever in the foreign land. And there was no more powerful way to evoke that challenge than through this story in Genesis 22 where Abraham, the proto-exile, is commanded by God to sacrifice his own son, his only remaining hope for the future.

This story of the almost-sacrifice of Isaac, more than anywhere else in Genesis, is where we encounter the "faithful Abraham" spoken of in later tradition. Perhaps worn down by all the other places where he made protests or overcame doubts, he just moves right ahead with preparations to sacrifice his son. We never hear what crosses his mind. Instead, we get a matter-of-fact report of his travel preparations: get up early in morning, saddle donkey, take Isaac and two servants, grab wood for burning Isaac as a sacrifice, and go (Genesis 22:3). How could he do this? The rabbis noticed that this Abraham does not seem to really believe that Isaac will be lost to him. When they reach the place of sacrifice, Abraham tells his servants to wait with the donkeys, and "I and the boy will go there, worship, and we will return to you" (22:5). *We* will return to you? This implies that Isaac will not be sacrificed, but will return with Abraham after they both have worshiped God. Abraham then loads Isaac with the wood for the burnt offering and moves on. The attentive reader picks up another hint of Abraham's trust in a good outcome in a poignant scene where he has to answer Isaac's query, "I see the fire and the wood, but where is the animal?" To this Abraham enigmatically replies, "God will provide the animal for himself" (22:7–8).

But the precise resolution of the crisis remains unclear for a bit longer in the story. When Abraham and Isaac arrive at the spot designated for his sacrifice, the story moves into agonizing slow motion, describing six separate actions leading up to the very point of Isaac's death: Abraham builds an altar, arranges wood on it, ties Isaac up, places him on the altar on top of the wood to burn him, draws out his hand, and takes the knife to sacrifice his son. Only at this very last point does a "messenger of Yahweh" call out from heaven and stay his hand. "Do not send forth your hand to the boy and do not do anything to him, because I know that you are a God-fearer and would not with-hold your son, your only one, from me." Only then does Abraham look up and see the animal that he had trusted God would provide, a ram caught in a thicket. Then he can offer the ram as a burnt offering on the altar he has built. And that is when he receives a reaffirmation of God's promises, found in Genesis 22:15–18, that had been missing from the initial command at the outset of the chapter. Because he would not withhold "your son, your only one," God now will bless Abraham, and multiply his offspring, and once again "all nations of the earth will bless themselves by you because you obeyed my voice."

If Abraham ever doubted that God would follow through on God's promises, if the exiles doubted this too, they receive their reassurance here. The text here stresses, in contrast to the promise in Genesis 12, that Abraham's obedience at Moriah ensured God's promises both for him and for subsequent generations, "his seed." Because Abraham was obedient, because he "listened to [God's] voice," both he and his descendants (including Judean exiles) could trust that God would multiply and bless them.[11] Having left their homeland, the exiles understood all too well the possibility that they might lose their children. Yet Genesis tells here of how Abraham faced and overcame just such a challenge. In the process he ensured that God would bless and protect every future generation of his heirs.

The message has not been lost on later generations of Jews, who likewise often have found themselves living among hostile foreigners. Time and time again, other Jews have faced persecution, whether in the medieval Europe of the Crusades, eastern European pogroms, the Nazi genocide, or numerous other communal traumas. Amidst all those, even as Jews sometimes have seen their children, their beloved ones, killed by their persecutors, they have found themselves drawn back to this story. For example, this story in Genesis 22, known as the Akedah (binding) in Jewish tradition, is invoked in a medieval Jewish chronicle about an episode in 1096 when Jews killed themselves and their children rather than fall into the hands of Christian rioters in Mainz, Germany. The chronicler asks, "Ask now and see, was there ever such a burnt offering as this since the days of Adam? When were there ever a thousand and a hundred sacrifices in one day, each and every one of them like the Akedah of Isaac son of Abraham?" Another poem chanted in the synagogue confronted God with failing to rescue Jews facing contemporary persecution the way God once rescued Isaac.

> O Lord, Mighty one, dwelling on high!
> Once over one Akedah, angels cried out before you.
> But now how many are butchered and burned!
> Why over the blood of children did they not raise a cry?
>
> Before that patriarch could in his haste sacrifice his only one,
> It was heard from heaven: Do not put forth your hand to destroy!
> But now how many sons and daughters of Judah are slain—
> While yet God makes no haste to save those butchered nor those cast on the flames.
>
> On the merit of the Akedah at Moriah once we could lean,
> Safeguarded for the salvation of age after age—
> Now one Akedah follows another, they cannot be counted.[12]

In these ways and others the Genesis story of Abraham's almost-sacrifice of Isaac has mirrored the horrors faced by Jews across thousands of years. These later Jews have felt as if their children were like Isaac in being offered as a sacrifice. Yet Isaac survived in the Genesis Akedah story. Reading it, successive generations of Jews have confronted their God, asking why their children were not rescued too.

Scholars may debate when and how these stories about Abraham were written, but one thing is clear: whenever and however the Abraham story was written, it has spoken to people who suffer. They find themselves in Abraham and his children, and they see a God who, at least in theory, takes care of them. Even in life's worst traumas, even in places where children, the most precious thing that any parent could lose, are lost or threatened. The Genesis Abraham story, particularly the story of Abraham and Isaac, has given Jews and others hope, or at least a basis for protest.

Less clear is how this story gained this power. Of course, one cannot rule out that the historical Abraham, the one who lived, actually underwent challenges like those described in Genesis. Perhaps it is just lucky happenstance that stories about him turned out to comfort later traumatized generations.

Whatever its origins, the Genesis story of Abraham was a story revised in light of trauma for people in trauma. It is an excellent example of how biblical texts came to address universal human experiences of catastrophe.

There is another reason that the Abraham story is particularly important: it introduces the theme of divine promise to the patriarchs that binds the whole Pentateuch, the whole Torah, into a single narrative. Earlier, before the exile, there were separate stories about Jacob and Joseph, Moses and exodus. Originating in the north, these accounts of Israel's ancestors and exodus circulated on separate scrolls and were referred to separately by early prophets like Hosea. And though Judean kings like Josiah invoked exodus-wilderness traditions, there is no clear sign that they yet were joined into a continuous story.[13] The present Pentateuch, however, tells a story in which God's care for Isaac, Jacob, and the generation of Moses is based on God's memory of the promise originally given to Abraham. The exilic theme of Abrahamic promise, in other words, is the thread that now connects the disparate parts of the Pentateuch. Take out the theme of promise in the Isaac, Jacob, and Moses stories, and they largely stand on their own.

Not only that, but this promise thread seems to have been added by exilic authors to earlier, *pre*-exilic writings, such as scriptures about Jacob and Joseph. For example, the story of Isaac in Genesis 26, where he receives the promise once given to Abraham (especially 26:2–5, 24), is an inserted interruption between successive stories about Jacob and Esau's rivalry in Genesis 25 and 27. The story of Jacob's vision of God at Bethel in Genesis 28 features a quotation of the Abrahamic promise (28:13–14) that is only loosely connected to the surrounding story about the holiness of the Bethel sanctuary. One hardly hears about the Abrahamic promise through much of the rest of the Jacob and Joseph stories, with the prominent exception of the reaffirmation of God's promise to Jacob in Genesis 46:2–4. This too seems a later exilic insertion focused on God's promise to Jacob in a broader novella about Joseph, focused on his conflict with his brothers.

The promise to Abraham, then, does not just point to the formation of the Abraham story amidst exilic trauma. The appearance of God's promise to Abraham across the rest of Genesis is like a red marker showing how old Israelite stories about Jacob and Joseph were revised during exile as well. Formed and/or revised amidst exilic trauma, Genesis was poised to speak to later traumas as well.

CHAPTER SIX

The Story of Moses

After Genesis, in the book of Exodus we confront a similar pattern to that seen in the previous chapter: older traditions about distant ancestors reshaped and expanded—sometimes radically—in light of the experience of exile. As I have mentioned, Moses was an ancient historical figure for the Israelite tribes, and he was a focus of some of Israel's earliest writings.

EXODUS AND EXILE

Despite these older origins of the story of Moses, we now have a biblical Moses story because that Israelite story spoke to the experiences of much later, exiled Judeans. This means that the books of Exodus through Deuteronomy worked on two levels. On the one level, there was the story line about Moses and the Israelites leaving Egypt, spending forty years in the wilderness, and receiving the Ten Commandments and other laws at Mount Sinai. This story is set in the distant past and it is based, at least in part, on pre-exilic traditions about figures, like Moses, who are probably historical. Yet on another level, the Moses story connected with the experiences of much later Judeans, that is, Judeans in exile or looking back on exile. These exilic Judeans preserved and reshaped older traditions about Moses into the texts we now have. To be sure, biblical scholars have had trouble achieving consensus on exactly how these texts formed.[1] Nevertheless, the Moses story, as we now have it, revolves around collective trauma, whether in Egypt or in Babylon.

The book of Exodus opens with Jacob's descendants still in Egypt, generations after his family came there in the time of Joseph to find food. They have multiplied into such a huge nation that a frightened Pharaoh, who "did not know Joseph," decides to enslave them. This ancient story of enslavement mirrored the experience of Judean exiles in Babylonia, who had to endure forced labor on the Babylonian building projects. For example, the Babylonian king Nebuchadnezzar boasts in an inscription of having conquered all the lands West of Mesopotamia, and enslaving their peoples to build his temple in Babylon: "The mighty cedars of the mountain of Lebanon were brought to the city of Babylon, the whole of the races, peoples from far places, whom Marduk my Lord delivered to me, I put them to work on the building of Etmenanki, I imposed on them the brick-basket."[2] The story of slavery in

Egypt found in Exodus thus had new resonance for Judean exiles toiling in Babylon.

But the exodus story goes yet farther in its picture of ancient trauma. Not stopping at slavery, this pharaoh develops a genocidal scheme to have midwives murder all newborn Israelite boy babies. When the midwives, Shiphrah and Puah, subversively undermine Pharaoh's order, he orders that all Israelite babies be thrown in the Nile (Exodus 1:15–22). This then is the situation when Moses is born to a couple in the Levitical tribe. Frightened at what might happen to her son, Moses' mother places her baby in a waterproofed basket and sets him adrift on the Nile River. Within the space of a chapter and a half, the book of Exodus has opened with slavery, infant genocide, and an individual mother's decision to let her baby son loose on a river. These first scenes close with Moses' sister standing at a distance "to see what would happen to him" (Exodus 2:1–4).

As the story continues, its Moses figure is developed in a way that his individual life mirrors his people's vulnerability. Not only is he born, like many exiles, in a foreign land. Not only does his mother avoid having him murdered by Egyptians by setting him loose, as a three-month-old baby, in a basket on the mighty Nile. But he then is taken up from the river by an Egyptian princess and grows up in an Egyptian household. The child Moses of this story thus lives like an exile amidst foreigners, even as his mother is hired as his wet nurse (Exodus 2:5–9). The princess gives him an Egyptian name, Moses, but ironically this Egyptian woman explains his name in terms of

Hebrew—as reflecting the fact that she "drew out" (Hebrew *mashah*) Moses from the river water (Exodus 2:10). Here we see the cultural cross-currents that many exiles face while living as a cultural minority. They take on foreign names and/ or customs while maintaining ties to their own cultures. In this exilic version of the story, Moses' mother can parent her son only secretly, and his name is a mix of the slaveowner's culture (Moses) and a Hebrew reinterpretation of it ("I drew him out of the water"). Little does Pharaoh's daughter know, but her link of Moses' name to water deliverance anticipates his later deliverance of his people at the Egyptian Red Sea (Exodus 14).

On one level this story of slavery, genocide, exposure, and secret parenting works powerfully as individual drama, but this story would have resonated in a special way with exiles under forced labor in Babylon. The ancient figure "Moses," after all, could serve as another individual figure who symbolized the destiny of exiled Judeans as a group, much like the figures of Ezekiel, Jeremiah, and the suffering servant. By preserving and revising old narratives about Moses' endangerment as a baby and rescue from the Nile, these exiles could speak, from a safe distance, of their own suffering and hope.

As if to cement this link of Moses with the whole people of Israel, the Bible goes on to tell stories about him that parallel the experiences that his people will soon have. This starts when Moses flees from Pharaoh's wrath into the wilderness, walking the same path out of Egypt on which he later will lead his people (Exodus 2:11–15 here anticipating Exodus

14–17). Moses then sees God in a burning bush at the "mountain of God" (3:1–4:17), a story that looks ahead to when Moses' people will see God on Mount Sinai (19–24). Then, one of the strangest stories in the Bible, found in Exodus 4:24–26, tells of how Yahweh attacks and tries to kill Moses as he returns to Egypt to rescue his people. He is saved only when Zipporah, his wife, circumcises their son and touches Moses' legs with the bloody foreskin. This story anticipates how smears of blood on doorposts will save Moses' people when God sends a divine "destroyer" to kill all of the Egyptian firstborn (12:1–13, 23). Finally, just as Moses was saved in infancy by being pulled out of the Nile (2:5–6), so the Israelite nation is saved when Moses leads them through the Red Sea (14).

The whole story of Moses' life found in chapters 2–4 of Exodus thus anticipates the terror, deliverance, and divine epiphanies experienced by his people in the rest of the book.

Moses	Israel
Baby Moses endangered on Nile and saved	Israel delivered at the Red Sea
Moses grows up in Egyptian family	Israel becomes "nation" in Egypt
Moses flees from Egypt into wilderness	Moses leads Israel from Egypt to wilderness
Moses sees Yahweh at "mountain of God" and receives commission	Israel meets Yahweh at Sinai and receives commandments
Moses almost killed by God and saved by smear of son's blood	Israel threatened by divine destroyer and saved by smear of Passover blood

These parallels helped exiles identify with Moses and the Israelites. Like the exiles (especially children of exiles), Moses grows up amidst the dangers of diaspora life, and his God sometimes seems like a murderous demon. Yet the text's parallels of Moses and his people reinforce the exiled Judean readers' identification with ancient "Israel" as well: they can see themselves in the Israelite people that Moses successfully led out of Egyptian exile.

As emphasized before, we do not know exactly when these stories about Moses and the Israelites were written. Parts of the book of Exodus long predate the Babylonian exile. Yet these stories also evolved over time, as later generations of Israelites and Judeans related them to their own lives. One feature in particular appears to have been added to the exodus story during the exile: the idea that the exodus took a long time. Earlier traditions describe the exodus as a single dramatic event, usually depicting God's liberation of the Israelites from Egypt at the Red Sea, a tradition now reflected in Exodus 14. Many biblical traditions, both old and new, refer to God "bringing Israel up out of Egypt," there are various references to unspecified "signs and wonders" that God did in Egypt, and the pre-exilic northern prophet Hosea knows traditions about Israel in the wilderness.

The plagues in Egypt, however, do not appear in these pre-exilic references to exodus. Deuteronomy knows of plagues in Egypt, but only that Egypt was a place characterized by mass epidemics (Deuteronomy 7:15, 28:60).[3] In Exodus

7–12 this idea of epidemic-plagued Egypt is developed in a new way: God's liberation of Israelites from Egypt comes only after a series of plagues inflicted on the Egyptians. God does not just deliver Israel from Egypt after telling Moses to bring them out. Instead, God hardens Pharaoh's heart while inflicting successive plagues on Egypt. Why? In the narrative, God repeatedly declares that these plagues and hardening of heart will lead to both Israel and Egypt recognizing that "I am Yahweh" (7:5, 8:22, 10:2, 14:4, 18). In other words, the delay of the exodus allows God more room to demonstrate God's power. We saw the theme of God demonstrating power already in Second Isaiah's late-exilic prophecy. The appearance of this theme in the Exodus plague narrative is one of the main indicators that this plague narrative is a specifically exilic creation.

This plague portion of the book of Exodus spoke to the Babylonian exiles' struggle for hope after many disappointments. Toward the beginning of exile some prophets opposed Jeremiah with prophecies that the exile would not happen. If it did, it would be short.[4] Yet the Babylonian exile ended up lasting more than five decades. People died never seeing their homeland again, and many others wondered whether they or their children would get a chance to leave Babylon, their "Egypt," for home. Chastened by decades of waiting, these exiles found a believable story of deliverance in the book of Exodus, with its story of exodus after a long process. Nothing was easy, nothing came immediately, but release from forced exile did eventually come.

CELEBRATING SURVIVAL AT PASSOVER

The Exodus story thus moves beyond trauma to survival of trauma. The Judean exile in Babylonia did not last as long as the Assyrian exile that effectively terminated the nation of Israel. In the year 538 BCE, about fifty years after the destruction of Jerusalem, the Persian king Cyrus defeated the Babylonian Empire and began allowing a trickle of Judean exiles to return home, starting with several groups associated with the priesthood and past Davidic monarchy.[5] Yet this was only the beginning of a process of return, and many Judeans never left Babylon. While the biblical book of Ezra describes several waves of return, Ezra and his group probably did not leave Babylon until more than a century after Cyrus, and even then many Judeans remained abroad. The year 538 BCE marks the end of forced exile, but it is just the beginning of the struggle of Judean exiles (and returnee exiles) to understand and embrace their community's survival, a process they underwent partly through the Moses story.

The story of Exodus should be seen in this context. It is a story not just about slavery but about divine deliverance from slavery. Of course, that deliverance itself is traumatic in many ways. God attacks Moses (Exodus 4:24–26) and later sends a divine "destroyer," averted only by smears of lamb blood on doorposts (12:23). The Israelites complain severely to Moses from beginning to end. "You have put a sword in their [Pharaoh and his officials'] hand to kill us" (5:21). And "was it because there were no graves in Egypt that you took us into the desert to die?" (14:11). In the end, however, the Israelites do leave Egypt. Their doubts are misplaced. They survive.

The instructions about Passover found in Exodus 12 commemorate this survival of trauma. The text looks ahead to new generations who have not experienced the terrors of life in a foreign land and escape from slavery. God commands Moses in the Bible to set up an annual pair of festivals to teach children about Israel's founding trauma. The lessons are reinforced with tactile symbols that engage the senses: unleavened bread to remember the rush to leave Egypt, and blood from a sacrificed animal to recall the divine destroyer who "passed over" Israelite homes in the process of killing Egyptian children. Later Jewish traditions have added yet other sensory reminders, like bitter herbs and a brown mixture symbolizing brick-mortar to remember slavery. Such vivid rituals are ways that cultures ensure the transmission of their most central shared memories: instituting annual ceremonies that teach children about history through sight, smell, and touch. This Passover ritual, which was one of the most important of the ancient Israelite festival year, taught Israelite children to see themselves as the descendants of escaped slaves.

This reproduced ritualized trauma and deliverance is more complex than it first appears. The exilic authors of the Passover text in Exodus 12 did not invent this festival in order to remember experiences of exile. Rather, they reaffirmed and revised more ancient festal regulations, joining an ancient "Passover" festival involving blood smears from a lamb sacrifice to another festival that celebrated the early spring barley harvest and involved unleavened bread.[6] Together these ancient rituals now turned generations of Jewish children into delivered slaves. Those children may or may not have experienced traumas of their own. Nevertheless, the Passover ritual in Exodus 12 made those children into survivors of slavery and genocide. Each year, the text says, you will spread blood on your doorpost in the springtime. Each year your children will ask, "Why are you doing this?" In reply, you will tell them, "It is the Passover sacrifice to Yahweh, for God passed over the houses of the Israelites in Egypt, when God struck down the Egyptians, but spared our houses" (Exodus 12:27).

This affirmation, repeated each year, that "God struck down the Egyptians, but spared our houses" expresses a central quandary of trauma, one discussed in Cathy Caruth's classic 1996 study *Unclaimed Experience: Trauma, Narrative, and History*. Discussing flashbacks, nightmares, and compulsive repetitions, she writes:

> The trauma consists not only in having confronted death but in *having survived, precisely, without knowing it.* What one returns to in the flashback is not the incomprehensibility of one's near death, but the very incomprehensibility of one's own survival. Repetition, in other words, is not simply the attempt to grasp that one has almost died but, more fundamentally and enigmatically, the very attempt *to claim one's own survival.* If history is to be understood as the history of a trauma, it is a history that is experienced as the endless attempt to assume one's survival as one's own.[7]

Survivors of trauma struggle to confront an event that they realize only belatedly almost destroyed them. This confrontation brings the self back, again and again, to survivors' helplessness before the death-dealing power of the event. Indeed, that helplessness is more intense because the person looking back on a death-threatening event can still do nothing at all to somehow protect the self that was vulnerable in the past.

The struggle to confront survival is often accentuated for people who survive amidst situations that kill those around them. They find themselves asking, "Why did I survive, when others did not?" The Passover regulations in Exodus 12 take each generation of Israelites back to a similar survival moment: "God struck down the Egyptians, but spared our houses." In doing so, these laws indirectly echo a more recent survival moment for the Judean authors of these exodus texts: the Judean community's survival of Babylonian exile, when their northern sibling, "Israel," did not. Persian Cyrus defeated the Babylonians fifty years after the Judean deportation and allowed Jews to start returning home. The Judean community asked: Why did our community survive when Israel did not? The history that they told of sins of the Northern Kingdom, found in the biblical books of 1 and 2 Kings, provided a partial explanation, as did prophecies of divine judgment directed at the north (for example, Hosea and Amos). Nevertheless, this was a difficult question, so difficult, in fact, that it could be posed only more abstractly in a story about a far distant time. The story was not about how "God struck down Israel, but spared Judah." Instead, generations to come would tell the story of how "God struck down the Egyptians, but spared our houses."

SURVIVAL AND CHOSENNESS

Much of the rest of the Torah tries to answer the question, "Why did we survive?" Again Caruth's study provides useful pointers, this time to the importance of "chosenness" as a key concept in engaging survival. Her discussion of chosenness is a follow-up to her discussion of the struggle "to claim one's survival" and examines how people deal with the fact of "awakening" belatedly to their survival of a death-threatening catastrophe. This discussion takes her to Freud's argument in *Moses and Monotheism* that Jewish monotheism relates to very ancient Jewish trauma. Building on Freud, Caruth links his theory to her discussion of survival and suggests:

> If monotheism for Freud is an "awakening," it is not simply a return of the past, but of the fact of having survived it, a survival that, in the figure of the new Jewish god, appears not as an act chosen by the Jews, but as the incomprehensible face of *being chosen* for a future that remains, in its promise, yet to be understood. Chosenness is thus not simply a fact of the past but the experience of being shot into a future that is not entirely one's own.[8]

This idea of "being chosen" and "shot into a future that is not entirely one's own" powerfully describes how many trauma victims come to posit a new purpose for their ongoing, fragile existence.

Freud placed the Jewish belief in chosenness in Egypt in the time of Moses (about 1300–1150 BCE), while many scholars believe that this theme probably emerged, at the earliest, in

Israel during the tribal period (c. 1150–1000 BCE). Either way, these texts in Exodus were shaped by Judeans centuries later, probably Judeans who had experienced exile in Babylon and survived. Somehow these traumatized Judeans found healing in stories about ancient Israel and its chosenness. In the wake of the exile, more even than in the time of Josiah, Judah now was "Israel," and Israel's ancient history had become Judah's ancient history.

We should pause to note the resilient power of this post-exilic Judean embrace of Israelite stories and belief in chosenness. Before the exile Judeans had focused on Jerusalem and royal traditions. The Judean exiles that shaped the Torah, however, needed a new focus. Jerusalem/Zion had been destroyed, and the monarchy was gone. The Torah barely mentions either one. Instead, in the wake of their near-destruction, the Judean exiles struggling to engage their suffering embraced an Israelite idea of chosenness not bound to a particular city or political structure. In ancient Israel, chosenness was a way of affirming God's favor for hill country tribes. But for the posttraumatized Judean exiles, chosenness was a durable way to assume Israel's survival and embrace a future not their own. No one could conquer or burn their chosenness like one could burn a city. No one could seize and deport or kill their chosenness like one could a king. Belief in God's particular choice of Israel, out of all the nations of the world, has remained the unmovable foundation of Jewish nationhood across centuries of suffering and life (often) in diaspora.

This theme of chosenness is reflected in different ways in various parts of the Torah. It is the unspoken focal point of the theme of God's promises to Abraham, Isaac, and Jacob. God's special favor for Israel is the subtext of God's deliverance of them from Egypt. When they come to Sinai, the first thing that God tells Moses to tell the people is this:

> If you obey my voice and observe my covenant, you will become for me my personal possession among all the peoples of the earth, for the entire earth is mine. And you shall be a kingdom of priests and a holy nation. (Exodus 19:5–6)

God's speech here adds cultic language to more traditional language about chosenness. The Hebrew word for holiness, *qadash*, means "separate," and that is the concept used here to describe God's choosing of Israel "out of all the peoples of the earth." Israel will not just be a "special possession" but "a kingdom of priests" and "a holy nation." The people as a whole, in other words, are now defined as "separate," as "holy" in terms usually reserved for priests. The nation of Israel is marked off from "the peoples of the earth" by its extra "holiness." And this speech then anticipates regulations in the latter half of Leviticus by which God works through Moses to teach laws of purity primarily relevant for priests—regarding eating, contact with corpses, skin diseases, and so on—to the people as a whole. In Leviticus, God restates the theology standing behind this transfer of priestly regulations to the people: "You shall be holy to me, for I, Yahweh, am holy, and I have separated you from the peoples to belong to me"

(Leviticus 20:26). God's people is now holy, with its daily life regulated by laws of purity.

This focus on the people's "holiness" in the Torah is not by chance. It reflects the particular self-image developed by Judean exiles as they lived in their separate communities in previously depopulated parts of central Babylon: Tel Aviv (a Babylonian Tel Aviv long before the modern Israeli Tel Aviv), a Babylonian town called "city of Judah," and so on. These ideas about the people's purity lifted the separate existence of Judean exiles into a virtue.[9] The result was the radical reshaping of Judean history. In particular, Judah's Torah was refocused on Yahweh's creation of a pure, holy people of Israel whom God had separated from the nations and given a special mission.

TRAUMATIC CHOSENNESS

There is another side to the Bible's story about chosenness, one sometimes missed. In describing Israel as "chosen," the Bible is not asserting that Israel was somehow better than other nations. The Torah does not tell a story of God choosing Israel because of its special virtue. On the contrary, the Bible, if anything, seems to stress the unusually rebellious and obstinate character of Israel. The people it depicts are no model of obedience but are constantly complaining: "Is it because there were no graves in Egypt that you [Moses] took us into the desert to die?" (Exodus 14:11); "Would that we had died at Yahweh's hand in Egypt" (Exodus 16:3); "Why did you bring us out of Egypt to kill us, our children and cattle with thirst?" (Exodus 17:3). This people, God and Moses both emphasize, is "stiff necked and stubborn" (Exodus 32:9, 33:3, 34:9).

Over time, this people's complaining moves God from annoyance to murderous rage. Initially, God gets annoyed at the Israelites when they complain at the Red Sea and then ask for water and food in the desert. Nevertheless, God does deliver them, and also comes through with water and manna (Exodus 15–17). After they make a covenant with God at Sinai, however, the stories take a nastier turn. They make a golden calf at Sinai, and God almost kills all of them (Exodus 32). When they balk at invading Canaan, God promises to kill all of them except for a few people who were willing to go forward (Numbers 13–14). Thus begins a series of stories in the book of Numbers where more and more people die amidst conflicts with God about Moses' leadership, the lack of meat in the desert, water, and relationships with foreigners (Numbers 11–12, 16, 20, 25). In the end, almost no one who escaped from Egypt survives to see Canaan. Even Moses dies just outside the promised land in the last chapter of the Torah, because of either his own sin (Numbers 20:1–13) or his people's sin (Deuteronomy 1:37). As the curtain closes on the Pentateuch, the only Israelites left standing are a couple of characters who proved faithful on the journey (Joshua and Caleb) and the children born to the Israelites during the forty years of wilderness wandering.

One could hardly imagine a starker contrast to the triumphalism more common in national myths. In contrast to celebrations of royal kingship common in ancient Mesopotamia and Egypt, this story of a stiff-necked and stubborn Israel reflects powerfully the type of self-blame all too typical of victims of trauma and seen already in exilic-period books like Lamentations and Ezekiel. In Lamentations Daughter Zion cries out, "I have been such a rebel, what a rebel I have been!" (Lamentations 1:20). Ezekiel reimagined both Samaria and Jerusalem as chronically impure and brazen prostitutes, doomed to destruction for their hypersexuality (Ezekiel 16, 23). Formed in the furnace of exile, this idea of Israel's deep sinfulness is woven through the whole Moses story. As a result, the biblical Moses story now emphasizes at every turn Israel's "stiff necked and stubborn" nature.

Finally, the end of the Pentateuch in Numbers and Deuteronomy mirrors the end of the Babylonian exile. In the Pentateuch, most of those who left Egypt never make it to the Promised Land. The book of Numbers relates that most of them die in the wilderness, and the death of Moses is described at the very end of Deuteronomy. Only the children of the Israelites who left Egypt were able to enter the land of Israel, accompanied by a few faithful members of the people who originally left Egypt. Similarly, most people deported by Babylonians from Judah never had a chance to return home. In a world where most people did not live into their forties, a forced exile lasting fifty-plus years was more than a generation. Only a handful of long-lived Judeans survived to return home. The rest of the Judean "returnees" were actually children born in diaspora to exiled Judean parents.

But the Judean community and its stories about itself were forever shaped by this near-death experience. In an earlier, pre-exilic time, Judeans had lived with the illusion of invulnerability, saying to themselves, "We are safe from Israel's fate, God lives in Zion, God will never abandon the Davidic kings, our life in the land is secure." The destruction of Jerusalem, the end of Davidic monarchy, and decades of exile changed all that. Judeans were forced to engage the precarious, inexplicable fact of their community's survival. The exiled community in Babylon had gone up to the edge of the destruction it had seen Israel undergo . . . and lived.

Though we lack a detailed narrative about how the exiled community underwent this process, we have the biblical Pentateuch. Where we might have had a history of life in Babylon, instead we have a story of what life was like for landless Israelite ancestors like Abraham and Moses. This pentateuchal story is built on older sources. Yet this story—both its old and new parts—echoes exilic themes of self-blame, survival, and emphasis on the chosenness and need for purity of the surviving people.

In particular, the impact of exile is seen in the choice of Judean exiles to see themselves as the Israel that survived. When Judean exiles shaped the Pentateuch into their most central scripture, their Torah, they took on Israel's chosenness as their own. Thus reshaped by exile and its survival, the biblical Moses story and the rest of the Pentateuch helped Babylonian exiles, at least some of them, avoid assimilation and engage their survival into the next chapter of their story.

CHAPTER SEVEN

The Return Home

THE SILENCE SURROUNDING EXILE ends with words from Cyrus, king of the Persian Empire, which defeated the Babylonians. In a proclamation repeated at the end of the books of Chronicles and the beginning of the book of Ezra, Cyrus proclaims that the temple in Jerusalem shall be rebuilt and the exiles may return.

> Yahweh, the God of heaven, gave me all the kingdoms of the earth, and he has commanded me to build him a house [Temple] in Jerusalem, which is in Judah. Anyone of you of all his people, may Yahweh, his God, be with him. Let him go up to Jerusalem in Judah and rebuild the house of Yahweh, the God of Israel, the God who dwells in Jerusalem. (Ezra 1:2–3//2 Chronicles 36:23)

We don't know for sure whether Cyrus actually said this (we have no Persian copy of this decree), but he said something quite similar about the restoration of other temples in a major Persian inscription called the Cyrus Cylinder.[1] Whatever Cyrus said to Judah, this quotation is the way the Bible picks up the narrative thread lost after the destruction of the Temple. This is how Judah begins telling its story again.

Right after Cyrus's decree, the story goes on to tell us that the Babylonian exiles immediately responded by preparing to go back to Jerusalem: "Then the heads of the houses of Judah and Benjamin, along with the priests and Levites, every one whose spirit God had stirred, got ready to return and rebuild the house of Yahweh which is in Jerusalem" (Ezra 1:5). These returnee Judean leaders, priests, and Levites are the protagonists of the rest of the story. Like a drumbeat, the biblical text reminds us of their exilic past. They are the "exiles," "the captive exiles," "sons of the exile," and "the assembly of exiles."[2]

CONFLICTS WITH "FOREIGNERS" UPON RETURNING HOME

The books of Ezra and Nehemiah probably were written long after Cyrus's time, talking of figures who returned to Judah decades after Babylon fell. Yet the main characters in the story remain marked by their experience of exile. They are not just Judeans or Benjaminites but former exiles, the community of those who had once lived in Babylon. Throughout this history they continued to identify with one another, as opposed to others who had not been exiled. Those the Babylonians selected for exile were already separated from their countrypeople by fault lines of class. The Babylonians focused their deportations on the urban inhabitants of Jerusalem and other leading classes that might foment future rebellion. Meanwhile, as mentioned before, the Babylonians left "the poor of the land" alone to remain in Judah (2 Kings 25:12). Thus the Babylonian exiles were already distinguished from those who remained by their comparatively elite status.[3]

As soon as these former elites were exiled to Babylon, they began to vie with those in Judah over who represented the true core of the Judean community. Already we saw how the exilic prophet Ezekiel repudiated the claims of some remaining in the land to be heirs of Abraham and the rightful owners of the land (Ezekiel 33:24–29). Many exiles saw the deported king Jehoiachin as the true ruler of Judah (Psalm 89, 2 Kings 25:27–30), while they rejected the Babylonian-appointed Zedekiah as a pretender. Later, when the Babylonians destroyed the Temple and deported more Judeans to Babylon, the exilic "gathering of the wounded" grew, and it grew yet more when the Babylonians exiled a third group to Babylon. These Babylonian exiles then formed a common "assembly of exile" over the subsequent decades, identifying themselves as the true "Israel" and focusing ever more on ancient Israel's traditions of ancestors, exodus, wilderness, and conquest.

These exiles saw their exit from Babylon as a second exodus and their reentry into the land as a new conquest.

Their communal near-death experience of diaspora living made these exiles yet more distinct from the "poor of the land" who remained in Judah. Before exile they had been marked as special by high positions, by genealogy, and often by literacy. Now these formerly elite exiles were distinguished from those who stayed by an experience of living, for decades, among foreigners in Babylon. Now they had become, as Exodus 19 suggests, "a kingdom of priests, a holy nation" (Exodus 19:6). Now they had taken on priestly purity regulations and emphasized other practices, such as Sabbath observance, which were particularly important in the Temple-less Babylonian context. These exiles felt that their nation's downfall and decades of exile had been caused by the failure of past generations to achieve the kind of purity they had come to value during exile. Return to Jerusalem was a precious second chance to get this right.

When they returned, they did not even recognize those who had remained in Judah as kin. Instead, the former exiles saw those who stayed as virtually Canaanite. On the one side there were the returning "sons of the exile," "Judah and Benjamin," "Israel." On the other side there were the "peoples of the land," "whose abominations are like the Canaanites, Hittites, Perizzites, Jebusites, Ammonites, Moabites, Egyptians and Amorites" (Ezra 9:1).[4] This list of non-Israelite peoples is similar to lists like that in Deuteronomy 7:1 of the peoples whom the nation of Israel needed to dispossess when it conquered the land of Canaan.[5] But now returnee Judeans coming back to the land viewed their former countrymen as virtually equivalent to those

Canaanites and the like, marked by the same sorts of "abominations." The returning exiles thus relived the conquest of Canaan, only now the Judeans who remained, the former "poor of the land," were the new "Canaanites."

What could have possessed returnees from Babylon to see their countrymen as virtual Canaanites? The text is not specific about the "abominations" of these "peoples of the land." On the surface, it seems they were guilty of nothing more than being nonexiles. But this was significant. The Judeans who could remain home did not experience the shifts in perspective of the Judeans who had been deported. The nonexiles did not understand themselves as God's pure, priestly people. The laws of the exilic Pentateuch were unfamiliar and held no authority for them. As a result, those who never left Judah lived the kind of "impure" life that former exiles believed had caused the exile in the first place.[6]

The conflict between returnee and never-left Judeans appears at its most intense in the story of Ezra's return. He is described as a priest and a scribe who had dedicated himself "to study of the Torah of Yahweh, to do it and teach its statutes and commandments in Israel" (Ezra 7:10). Decades after Cyrus's victory over Babylon—scholars disagree on whether it was 80 or 140 years later—a Persian king Artaxerses commissioned this priest-scribe Ezra to return from exile to Judah "to investigate Judah and Jerusalem according to the law of your God" (Ezra 7:14).[7] He came bringing a Torah shaped by more than a century of life in the Babylonian diaspora, and his journey was scripted by that Torah. Ezra delayed his departure to ensure that his group had both Levites and priests at its center, like the Israelites marching in the wilderness (Numbers 1–2), and his group celebrated Passover at the outset of their journey (Ezra 8:15, 31) much as the exodus group had celebrated the first Passover just before leaving Egypt (Exodus 12:1–28). Ezra did not have twelve tribes with him like the original exodus group, but he set aside twelve Levites and priests to symbolize those tribes and entrusted the Temple offering to them (Ezra 8:24–30). This act illustrates that the ten tribes of Israel had not been forgotten, but their legacy was absorbed in this new "Israel" formed of Judean exiles. More than ever before the old Israel has been left behind, and "Israel" in this story refers to the Judeans and Benjaminites coming back from exile.[8] Ezra and other returnees like him now saw themselves as the true successors to the Israel that left Egypt. Their trip from Babylon to Judah mirrored their Israelite ancestors' trip from Egypt to Canaan.

Like many returnee exiles, this deeply Torah-oriented group led by Ezra was profoundly disappointed by the state of the homeland it returned to. Though several waves of exiles had returned earlier and the Temple had been rebuilt, the arriving Ezra group was told:

> The people of Israel and the priests and the Levites have not separated themselves from the peoples of the lands with their abominations, from the Canaanites, the Hittites, the Perizzites, the Jebusites, the Ammonites, the Moabites, the Egyptians, and the Amorites. For they have taken some of their foreign daughters to be wives for themselves and for their sons; so that the holy seed has become contaminated

> with the peoples of the lands. And the princes and officials have led the way in this faithlessness. (Ezra 9:1–2)

Ezra responded to the news as if it were the report of a loved one's death, tearing his clothing and pulling out his hair.

That afternoon, at the time for evening sacrifice, Ezra poured out his heart for his people, offering a prayer of confession. He started by summarizing what he viewed as his people's long history of sinfulness, reflecting the self-blame that we've seen is typical of trauma in general and was felt by the exiles in particular:

> My God I am too ashamed and mortified to lift my face to you. For our grave sins have multiplied upward and our great guilt reaches to heaven. From the days of our fathers we have been buried in immense guilt up to this very day. And because of our grave sins we, our kings, and our priests were handed over to the kings of other lands, [handed over] to the sword, to exile, to plunder, and to shame as is true even today. (Ezra 9:6–7)

As Ezra continues, we see a classic illustration of the trauma victim's struggle to engage and trust the survival of a death-threatening event whose danger was perceived only belatedly. Ezra sees the returnee community perched on the edge of a thin blade. Despite their great sins, God has given the people a precious second chance, allowing a "remnant" to survive exile and making the Persian king look kindly on them. Yet these exiles, as Ezra sees it, have virtually thrown away this second chance by disobeying the command in Deuteronomy not to intermarry. In Deuteronomy 7 that command focused on various Canaanite peoples (Hittites, Girgashites, and others), but Ezra rephrases that command here so that it forbids marriage of exilic "Israel" with the "peoples of the land" who remained in Judah (Ezra 9:10–12). From Ezra's perspective, the exiles' intermarriage with the "peoples of the land" puts their already fragile survival in question. He stands before God in terror that this failure of exiles to be "pure" will cause God to destroy them this time (Ezra 9:13–15). Traumatized once, Ezra now fears the ultimate destruction.

Such fears, particularly of foreignness, are typical of groups that have suffered trauma.[9] In this case, Ezra prompts his people to an act that remains difficult to comprehend. He requires all exiles who had married nonexile women to divorce those women and expel them and their children from the community forever. He lets one of the exiles who intermarried propose it himself. After Ezra's prayer of confession, Shechaniah of Jehiel, a man whose father is later listed among those who divorced their wives (Ezra 10:26), proposes that everyone who has married one of the "peoples of the land" send away his wife and children acting "in accordance with the Torah" (Ezra 10:2–4). Ezra then requires all those present to swear to act accordingly, and a proclamation is issued requiring the "sons of exile" to assemble in Jerusalem within three days or forfeit all of their land and property. On a rainy December day these leaders assemble in the open square in Jerusalem and agree on a process to require all exiles to divorce their "foreign" wives; three months later those wives and children are gone (Ezra 10:9–17). What remains in the Bible is a list of men who divorced their foreign wives (10:8–44). The wives and children whom they abandoned remain nameless. We never hear from any source what happened to them.

This divorce of nonexile wives remains one of the most difficult things to understand in the biblical story. It illustrates all too vividly the negative consequences of beliefs in chosenness and purity that came to the fore during exile. It plays into anti-Jewish caricatures of Judaism as exclusive and legalistic. And this whole event seems a prime example of the powerless—here women and children—being victimized by the powerful—elite, exile leaders like Ezra. "How could Ezra and other exiles have expelled all these wives and children?" my students ask. "Isn't this an example of the dangers of any kind of religious exclusivism?"

In response I feel torn between two impulses. On the one hand, I don't want to minimize the pain of those, like these women and children of Ezra's time, who have suffered because of impulses toward religious purity. We know too little about what ancient Judean marriages and families were like, but these divorces—if historical—probably resulted in significant hardship. On the other hand, I want to guard against the centuries-long tendency of Christians like me to critique and caricature Judaism. Indeed, Christian anti-Judaism has led to countless acts of cruelty—expulsion, ghettoization, genocide—acts that make anything that Ezra did pale in comparison. Given this long history of Christian anti-Judaism, I must be careful even in how I try to put Ezra's acts in context. Though we can recognize how the acts described for Ezra may have led to much suffering, we should also strive to understand how those acts may have been necessary for the survival of the postexilic community.

This was not just a matter of Ezra and the returnee exiles' perceptions of their past sin and God's impending wrath. It was a matter of turning a tiny remnant of Torah-oriented exiles into a community that could survive for centuries. Marriages matter for such survival. Families are not just where children are born, but where they are shaped in the most fundamental ways. For people deeply shaped by exile and the lessons they believed it taught them, a marriage to a foreign woman was not just an individual decision. Such a marriage meant that the next generation, precious to these former exiles, would be raised and taught by a person lacking born attachment to their values and beliefs.

Ezra and the returnee exiles were a minority in the broader Near Eastern world. And they were acutely conscious that they could not take survival for granted. Standing as a tiny "remnant" that had barely survived the exile, Ezra and other exile leaders felt they could not take a chance on having the next generation raised by women who were not part of the "children of exile." So they took steps, awful steps perhaps, to ensure that the crucial female teachers of "Israel's" next generation, their mothers, were part of the returnee exile community.

THE FOUNDING OF TORAH-OBSERVANT "JUDAISM"

We hear of one more act of Ezra, and it is no surprise. The narrative is found in Nehemiah 8, and it concerns another gathering in Jerusalem. It is the first day of the seventh month, Rosh Hashanah (New Year's Day) in the Jewish calendar. The people have asked Ezra to read the Torah, and he has done so all morning long, with priestly Levites circulating among the people to help them understand. We are told that the people wept when they heard the Torah, apparently feeling guilt for the Torah laws they had unwittingly disobeyed. But Ezra and the Levites tell them that such weeping does not keep with the holiness of the day. Instead, they should go to feast with their families and give their tithes to the poor. And that is what they then do, "because they understood the words that had been made known to them" (Nehemiah 8:12).

This is how the Bible talks about the founding of a Torah-focused postexilic community in Jerusalem. And it is in this period that many scholars start to speak of "early Judaism" and "Jews," as opposed to just "Judeans and Benjaminites" or "Israel." As we have seen, this is a community exclusively formed of "sons of the exile." They have come home, but they have brought their exilic identity with them. Led by figures like Ezra, they aim to avoid the mistakes they believe caused the exile in the first place. They are devoted to Torah texts formed in exile. And they see themselves as a "holy seed," separated from the nations by genealogy and priestly purity regulations. Though some initially mixed with those who had not undergone exile, Ezra's leadership changed all that. Moving forward, Judaism would be a religion based on Torah above all, a Torah that told the story of an "Israel" called to be God's "nation of priests, a holy nation."

This leaves aside, of course, the important factor of the postexilic Jerusalem Temple, which served as a focal point for the postexilic Jewish community. To be sure, this second Temple was nothing like the one built by Solomon, and the few old exiles who could remember that first Temple wept when they compared the second, rebuilt temple with the one they'd known (Ezra 3:12). Nevertheless, especially with the Davidic monarchy never restored, the postexilic Jerusalem temple and its priesthood stood at the center of this holy, priestly Jewish people. For centuries to come this second Temple, alongside the Torah, united an otherwise diverse Second Temple Judaism.

In the longer run, however, that Temple too would be destroyed, while the Torah remained. Ezra and others' founding of a Torah-centered, exile-shaped Judaism was to have the most lasting effect. Where the second Temple lasted for five hundred years, postexilic Judaism has lasted more than two millennia. Ezra and other former exiles succeeded in shaping an unusually resilient communal structure. Though Judaism was profoundly oriented to the Promised Land, it was a religion of exiles that could be practiced by those living outside that land. Unlike most ancient forms of peoplehood, this Israel of former exiles needed no monarchy or even tribal political structure to survive. No empire could deport or execute their divine king. And even if this holy people experienced persecutions and setbacks, their Torah helped them understand such suffering as mere bumps in the road compared with God's repeated near-destruction of them in the wilderness.

Ezra and his companions could not know it, but they helped create one of the first "religions" of the ancient world that was not inextricably linked to life in a particular place under a particular political structure. Before Judaism, concepts of God were woven into a broader ethnic-national life supported by some form of self-rule over a particular plot of land. There was no religion separate from land-based culture. When the exiles brought the exile home to Judah, they did not just rebuild a Temple, force some to divorce their wives, or focus on the Mosaic Torah. They formed a diaspora-shaped community in Judah that did not require a monarchy or land to survive. They did so as exiles who had seen everything they trusted in—life in the land, monarchy, city, Temple—stripped away. As former exiles they then built a communal way of life that could survive such stripping. As we have seen, Ezra was profoundly worried that the tiny "remnant" of former exiles would not survive into the next generation (Ezra 9:10–14). But the Judaism he helped create, shaped as it was by trauma's lessons, proved unusually resilient. Future generations of Jews would suffer greatly, but Judaism has persisted while disruptions destroyed the other culture-based religions of the Near East. It was shaped to outlast them.

CHAPTER EIGHT

Traumatic Crystallization of Scripture

We jump forward now to a time two hundred years after Ezra, approximately 175 BCE. Things had been going well, comparatively, for the Jews over the preceding centuries. Though there have been minor wars now and then and occasional struggles with famine, the Jewish people have experienced centuries of life without a catastrophe like they faced under Assyria and then Babylonia. Even when the Greek king Alexander the Great conquered the Persian Empire, Judah's new Hellenistic rulers recognized the rights of Jews to live "according to the laws of the fathers," which included the laws of Torah and provision for regular Temple sacrifices.

There came a time, however, when a Hellenistic ruler decided to end this practice of toleration, forcing Jews into a life-or-death choice about standing by their ancient Hebrew traditions. The result was a crisis that was to permanently shape the future identity of Judaism. More specifically, this crisis prompted the transformation of Jews' loose collection of Torah and prophets into a fixed collection of scriptures resistant to revision for thousands of years.

THE HELLENISTIC CRISIS

This crisis was prompted by at least two developments in the early second century BCE. First, in 175 a new ruler, Antiochus IV, rose to the kingship of the Hellenistic Empire ruling Judah, the Seleucid kingdom based in ancient Antioch (in contemporary Turkey). Antiochus had grown up as a hostage in Rome, held captive as a consequence of his father's failed attempt to wrest parts of the eastern Mediterranean from Roman control. He inherited a kingdom impoverished by Roman tribute requirements, and many of his later actions can be explained as attempts to secure tribute money in any way he could.

A second development was the initiative by leading Jerusalemites to turn Jerusalem into a Greek city (*polis*). Making Jerusalem a Greek polis would allow Jerusalemites and their city to enjoy some of the tax and cultural benefits enjoyed by other nearby Greek cities. This was accomplished when a Jewish priest bearing the Greek name of Jason succeeded in buying for himself the office of high priest of the Jerusalem Temple. He did so by offering the new king,

Antiochus, a huge sum of money from the Temple treasury, with the promise of yet more tribute in years to come. Desperately in need of money, Antiochus accepted. Jason and other Hellenists then built a Greek gymnasium—a site for athletic contests and Greek scholarship—within view of the Jerusalem Temple, and Jerusalem enjoyed the status of a Greek city for about seven years.

Many Jewish traditionalists were unhappy with these changes. They saw the Jerusalem priesthood as increasingly preoccupied with Greek games and prestige rather than with maintaining the Temple sacrifices. Nevertheless, that sacrifice still continued in the Greek polis that was now Jerusalem, and Judaism did not yet face a life-and-death crisis. That changed in 171 BCE, when Jason made the mistake of sending another member of the Hellenizing party, Menelaus, to Antiochus to deliver the annual tribute to him. Menelaus used the opportunity of meeting Antiochus to offer to double the tribute if Antiochus would make him, Menelaus, high priest instead of Jason. The Seleucids installed Menelaus, a nonpriest, as high priest of the Jerusalem Temple, and Jason was driven into exile across the Jordan. Menelaus soon went about plundering the Temple treasury and arranged to have Onias (the rightful high priest before Jason) assassinated. Jason's attempt to retake Jerusalem by force was put down by the army of Antiochus IV, who was returning frustrated from an unsuccessful attempt to take Egypt from the Romans. Having been saved from Jason's attack, Menelaus is said to have guided Antiochus himself into the holy of holies in the Jerusalem Temple, where he seized the equivalent of six years of tribute from the Temple treasures.

Around this time something fundamental shifted, and no one is sure why. Whether through some encouragement of Menelaus or out of his own anger or other motives, Antiochus IV resolved to destroy Judaism. He had shown no particular inclination previously to impose a Greek cultural-religious program in his empire, and before this he had not tried to impede Jewish religious observance. But something apparently snapped at this point, and Antiochus IV took measures that would pollute the Jerusalem Temple and prohibit Jewish observance. In 167 BCE a foreign cult was established in the Jerusalem Temple, perhaps to serve the needs of the new troops Antiochus had garrisoned in Jerusalem. He also issued a decree forbidding observance of Jewish laws in Jerusalem and surrounding towns. Jews were forced to offer sacrifice to foreign gods, Torah scrolls were burned, mothers who had allowed their babies to be circumcised were killed with their children. Anyone with a copy of a Torah scroll was executed, and leading citizens were required, on pain of death, to eat pork in public, thus openly disobeying the Torah's commands. What had started as a mild attempt by Jason and other Jerusalemites to gain Greek privileges for Jerusalem and its citizens had turned into a life-and-death struggle for the continuance of Jewish Torah observance.

It is difficult to identify precisely which parts of the accounts in 1 and 2 Maccabees are historical, but most scholars agree that Judaism had never faced such a profound threat to its religious practice. The Assyrians had destroyed towns, the Babylonians had taken Jerusalem and exiled its inhabitants, but no one before Antiochus IV had tried so hard to eradicate Jewish Torah observance and monotheism.

Faced with the choice of "eat pig or die," Jews reacted differently. Some went ahead and ate some pork or offered the required sacrifices to foreign gods. Others are said to have fled to the barren wilderness to avoid the persecution. Still others openly defied the law and were killed outright. For example, 2 Maccabees 6–7 tells of the killing of an elderly scribe, Eleazar, and also of seven brothers with their mother. 2 Maccabees celebrates these victims as heroic martyrs, a new concept in Judaism that will become important in a later chapter of this book.

Yet others, however, chose to fight. In particular, a provincial priestly family, the Hasmoneans, began a guerrilla operation against the armies of Antiochus. They scored repeated successes against a Seleucid army weakened by problems in other parts of the empire. Within three years, in 164 BCE, the Hasmoneans had fought the Seleucids to a draw. Antiochus IV issued a decree rescinding his prohibition of Judaism:

> King Antiochus to the senate of the Jews and to the other Jews, greeting. If you are well, it is as we desire. We also are in good health. Menelaus has informed us that you wish to return home and look after your own affairs. Therefore those who go home by the thirtieth day of Xanthicus will have our pledge of friendship and full permission for the Jews to enjoy their own food and laws, just as formerly, and none of them shall be molested in any way for what he may have done in ignorance. (2 Maccabees 11:27–31)

Later that year, in December 164, the leader of the Hasmoneans at the time, Judas Maccabeus, retook Jerusalem, trapped the Seleucid forces in the fortress there, and purified the Temple of the non-Yahwistic cult. The holiday of Hanukkah celebrates this event.

Though there was much back and forth, the Seleucids gradually lost control of Jerusalem and the rest of the land. Eventually, around 153 BCE, Judas's brother Jonathan became high priest of the Jerusalem temple and official head of the Jewish people. About a decade later (142 BCE), his brother Simon succeeded Jonathan and managed to achieve complete independence from the Seleucids. Simon's successor John Hyrcanus (135–104 BCE) expanded Judean control into Edom/Idumea to the south and Samaria to the north, and later Hasmonean rulers assumed the title of "king" and expanded yet farther into the Phoenician coastland, Transjordan and Galilee. Over the span of just a few decades, the Hasmonean priest-kings built a virtual mini-empire covering the areas of Judah, Samaria, and surrounding regions.

Their monarchy was a complex cultural mix. On the one hand, they promoted themselves as champions of Hebrew culture. Their monarchy issued coins with ancient Hebrew writing and their scribes produced books, such as 1 and 2 Maccabees, which depicted them as defenders of Torah and liberators of the people from the evil Greek king Antiochus. On the other hand, their monarchy was, in many ways, very Greek itself. They held Greek games; they saw Greek Sparta as a sister kingdom; and one of their main writings, 2 Maccabees, is a Greek-style history written in Greek that celebrates Jewish martyrs with Greek tropes of heroic sacrifice. This complex mix might be described as an anti-Hellenistic Hellenistic monarchy. The Hasmonean kings presented themselves as defenders against the Greeks, yet their monarchy was deeply influenced by Hellenistic culture. Their brand was anti-Greek, but they promoted that brand using Greek means.

THE HASMONEAN DEFINING OF HEBREW SCRIPTURE

This Hasmonean monarchy was where Hebrew scriptures started to be standardized. Previously Jews had worked with a more fluid idea of scripture. Though most postexilic Jews agreed on the holiness of the Pentateuch (the "Torah"), they were much less clear on whether other books contained "prophetic" inspiration, and if so, which ones. Some recognized the Torah alone as scripture. Most recognized the scriptural status of other Hebrew scriptures, like Isaiah or Psalms. Still others, such as the Qumran community of the Dead Sea Scrolls, saw books like Enoch and Jubilees as holy scripture as well. Just as Judaism of this time was highly varied—consisting of diverse groups (Pharisees, Sadducees, and others)—so also the texts recognized by these groups was varied.[1]

The Hasmonean monarchs were hardly in a position to suddenly end this variety, but several bits of data suggest that they began a process of scriptural standardization that would be completed long after them in the Roman period. To start, the Hasmonean monarchy—though it existed for only a few decades—was the only Jewish institution of the time with the power to enforce the selection of certain biblical books as authoritative and the standardization of the manuscripts of those books. There was no comparably powerful Jewish institution either before or after it.

In addition, it is during the period of the Hasmonean monarchy that we first see standardized manuscripts of the books in the Hebrew Bible. Before, Jewish groups produced highly varied copies of the Hebrew manuscripts of the Bible, none of which closely corresponds to the text of the Hebrew Bible we now have. But during the Hasmonean period we see the emergence of Hebrew manuscripts whose texts are almost identical with the traditional Hebrew text of today's Bible. In addition, Jews started to produce Greek translations of Hebrew scriptures matching this emerging standardized Hebrew text. The Hasmonean monarchy provides the most plausible context for this textual standardization, producing both an authorized Hebrew text and Greek translations focused on that newly authorized text.

Finally, the Hasmoneans had a motive to support such scriptural standardization: their wish, first, to promote themselves as defenders of Hebrew culture and, second, to use a standardized Hebrew curriculum of texts to consolidate cultural control over formerly non-Jewish areas that they conquered (for example, Idumea, Galilee, and the Transjordan).[2]

To be sure, our histories of the period speak only generally about the Hasmonean kings as defenders of Judaism and its texts. They do not say that the Hasmoneans decided what books were holy and standardized the Hebrew manuscripts of those books. Yet the very concept of Holy Bible demands that no record be kept of its own genesis.[3] To chronicle that this or that king, priest, or council had decreed that certain books were biblical would undermine the very idea that such books were revealed by God. That said, the Hasmoneans' own books (1 and 2 Maccabees) do not shy away from depictions of them as defenders of the Torah and of the holy Hebrew language. The book of 2 Maccabees even describes Judas the Hasmonean as someone who "collected all the scrolls that had been lost on account of the war that had come upon us" (2 Maccabees 2:14). This verse does not describe the creation of the Bible we now know, but it does depict Judas as a preserver and collector of ancient scrolls.

In addition, the book of 1 Maccabees, a Hasmonean document, contains the first possible reference to the idea that prophecy had ended by the Hellenistic period: "There arose a great distress in Israel, such as had not been since the time that prophets ceased to appear among them" (1 Maccabees 9:27).[4] This is important, since most Jews at the time recognized two major categories of authoritative, scriptural books: "Torah" and "Prophets." Moreover, the category Prophets included the full range of inspired books, not just Isaiah or Hosea, but also Psalms and Proverbs. To imply that the time of such prophetic books had ended with Hellenism is to put an implicit limit to scripture. It suggests that "prophetic" books (including books like Psalms or Proverbs) written up through the Persian period could be inspired, while those written afterward were not. Scripture becomes limited to the Torah and pre-Hellenistic Hebrew "prophets" scrolls.

This idea of an "end to prophecy" would have been the Hasmonean counterpart to the Hellenistic "canon" of pre-Hellenistic classic Greek works. The Greeks had their Homer and a defined list of authoritative Greek authors taught in schools. Now, the Hasmoneans had their own Hebrew corpus of Mosaic Torah and pre-Hellenistic prophetic books. Standing as defenders of Hebrew culture against the Greeks, they standardized an older corpus of Hebrew works and juxtaposed it to the Greek curriculum. Put another way, the Hasmoneans took the Hellenistic idea of a defined corpus of texts and Hebraized it. And in the same way that some Hellenistic-period Greek authors attributed their new works to ancient figures like Homer or Plato, so the Hasmonean period saw an increase in the number of contemporary Jewish works attributed to pre-Hellenistic figures such as Enoch, the patriarchs of Genesis, Moses, and Ezra. Canon, whether Greek or Hebrew, breeds pseudonymity.[5]

Indeed, some seem to have disagreed with the Hasmoneans' limitation and standardization of Hebrew scriptures. One potential indication of such disagreement comes in a Greek work, Sirach, that is included in the Old Testament of many churches. This book is a wisdom instruction by a pre-Hasmonean sage, Ben Sira, that was translated from Hebrew into Greek by Ben Sira's grandson during the Hasmonean period. In the prologue of this work, this grandson seems to protest against an exclusive focus on pre-Hellenistic "Torah and Prophets." In introducing the work, he repeatedly insists on the importance not just of "the law and the prophets" but also of "other writers succeeding them [the prophets]," "other books of the fathers," and "other books." The reference to post-prophetic works is telling, indicating that the grandson did not just value books like Psalms or Proverbs attributed to "prophetic" figures (David and Solomon) but also wanted to promote the worth of books like his grandfather's instruction, which is clearly written in the Hellenistic period. In this way Ben Sira's grandson, writing his prologue during the time of the Hasmonean monarchy, defends the importance of his grandfather's work against any who might dismiss that work as Hellenistic and thus nonprophetic and noninspired. Against such ideas, he argues that Ben Sira's instruction, now translated into Greek, is another important "book of the fathers."

Ironically, Ben Sira's grandson protests here against a form of Hellenization of Hebrew scripture as culturally complex as Hosea's adaptation of Assyrian treaty traditions in advocating monotheism. For it was the Greeks who developed the idea of a limited corpus of pre-Hellenistic works, in their case works by pre-Hellenistic authors like Homer and Plato. Furthermore, it was Greek scholars in Alexandria who were most famed for standardizing and solidifying Greek manuscripts of those Greek works, attempting to purify the manuscript tradition of later copyists' corruptions.

TRAUMA AND SCRIPTURALIZATION

My initial impulse in thinking about impact of communal trauma on scripture was to see standardization of scripture as analogous to the rigidity of traumatic memory. After all, many studies have emphasized that traumatic memory is distinguished from normal memory by how frozen it is. Normal memories shift and are adapted as they are fit into different schemes and stories. Traumatic memories, in contrast, often remain stubbornly fixed as they intrude on life in the form of flashbacks, traumatic memories, and compulsive repetitions. So also scripture is distinguished from other forms of ancient textuality in its fixity, the unchanging focus on certain books, and the effort to make sure the manuscripts of those books do not change.

Yet this analogy does not really fit the Bible. First, the Bible, despite its low points, is not equivalent to a flashback or traumatic nightmare. It tells a more differentiated story of crisis *and* survival, oppression *and* deliverance. Second, the frozenness of traumatic memory is particularly characteristic of individual trauma, while the Hasmonean standardization of Hebrew scripture was a profoundly communal process. Indeed, the Hasmoneans only began a communal process that influenced other parts of the community at a much later time.

Judaism at the time of the Hasmoneans confronted some of the most profound challenges it had ever faced. The obvious challenge, of course, was the ferocious attempt by Antiochus IV to eradicate Torah-observant Judaism. That experience was traumatic enough that "Hellenization" would be posed for centuries to come as an ultimate opponent of "Judaism." More subtle, however, was the inexorable influx of Hellenistic culture into all Jewish practices, whether of the Hellenizers or of their Torah-observant opponents. Like it or not, there was no way to stand completely free of the allure and power of Greek culture. Even the Hasmoneans, as we have seen, were deeply influenced by Greek culture at the same time they promoted themselves (in books like 1 Maccabees) as defenders against its threats.

It is precisely amidst such rapid change that societies are most prone to focus on their ancient traditions—orienting themselves around newly dear "mother tongues," sacred sites of pilgrimage, commemorative festivals, and the like. In each case, older traditions are appropriated to new ends by later societies in transition. A particular older dialect is selected to be the holy "mother tongue." A given site with older associations is given a specific meaning in national mythology. A festival previously of marginal significance is transformed into a major holiday.[6] Such festivals, sites, and languages then provide secure, ancient anchor points for societies undergoing rapid and disorienting transformations.

The Hellenistic crisis—both short and long term—was an analogous time of change for Judaism. Antiochus's attack on Judaism ended up being a mere symbol of a broader Hellenistic threat to Judaism. This threat was real. If things had gone just a bit differently, there is a good chance that Jerusalem would have remained a Greek polis and Hebrew learning would have gradually faded away. We see this happen elsewhere in the Near East during the Hellenistic and Roman periods. Across this time Egyptian and Mesopotamian education was confined to temples and limited to a dwindling number of priests. The same thing could have happened to Hebrew learning if the Hasmoneans had lost.

Instead, the trauma of Antiochus's attack on Judaism spurred a new level of devotion to Torah and a new selection and standardization of "prophets" manuscripts (again including books like Psalms, Proverbs, and Chronicles). It is not as if such books did not exist before. Decades before the Hasmoneans, the above-mentioned sage Ben Sira surveys almost all of the Hebrew Bible in his great "hymn in praise of the fathers" toward the end of his wisdom instruction (Sirach 44–49). And the Hasmoneans do not seem to have had much power to change the contents of the collection they standardized. For example, they could not include Hellenistic-period books celebrating their own monarchy, such as 1 Maccabees, in it. At most they could introduce a few minor changes in their standardized manuscripts of Torah and Prophets that agreed with their political program, changes now seen in the Masoretic text of the Hebrew Bible used today in Judaism and (in translation) in Christianity.

Yet I suggest the Hasmoneans did do something more important to shape what we now know as the Old Testament or Jewish Tanach. In the face of Hellenism's challenge, they introduced the idea that the truly inspired Hebrew scriptures were a fixed collection of Torah and pre-Hellenistic prophetic works. This is a collection of scrolls (not a single "book") and still a long way from the Bible we now know. Nevertheless, this was an important step toward solidifying and preserving biblical tradition. Without ever speaking of it directly, these Jewish kings effected a change as revolutionary in its own way as the earlier creation of Jewish monotheism. Their preliminary development of standardized Hebrew scriptures was a precursor to the Jewish Tanach, the Christian Bible, and even the Muslim Koran.

CHAPTER NINE

Christianity's Founding Trauma

IT WAS A SPECTACULAR late summer morning in New York City. I was at a Sunday worship service at Broadway Presbyterian Church, September 16, 2001, five days after the September 11 attack. The whole country was in shock, but in New York we did not just see images of the catastrophe, we could smell it. The ruins of the World Trade Center continued to smolder for days. Flowers were laid at every firehouse, and posters were posted on lampposts asking after missing loved ones. The pastor, Walter Tennyson, pointed to a saying across the back of the sanctuary that read, "We preach Christ and him crucified." "The Romans used crucifixion as a way to terrorize those they ruled," he said. "They tried to do that with Jesus, but he was resurrected. The cross, Christ crucified, is our faith's symbol of facing and living beyond terror."

I had seen crosses for years: on churches, necklaces, stationary, highways, but I gained a new understanding of the cross that week of September 11 in New York City. For many the cross is a symbol of Christian faith, of piety or religion in general. For me it became a sign of trauma, but not just that: of trauma faced by God alongside us. The cross, a symbol formed in the midst of early Christian trauma, was used effectively by Walter Tennyson to minister to a traumatized Presbyterian community in New York in the wake of 9/11. His sermon invited his church to see Jesus Christ, crucified by the Romans, as the symbol of a traumatized God, a god who was right there with them as they faced and lived beyond their own trauma.

It is important to get clear on what ancient crucifixion was. The word "crucifixion" comes from the Latin word *cruciare*—"torture." The Roman Cicero describes it as "*suma supplicum*, "the most extreme form of punishment," and goes on to say: "To bind a Roman citizen is a crime, to flog him an abomination, to slay him is almost an act of murder, to crucify him is—what? There is not a fitting word that can possibly describe so horrible a deed."[1] The Jewish historian Josephus describes it as "the most pitiable of deaths."[2] The victim was first brutally whipped or otherwise tortured. Then his arms were attached to a crosspiece of wood, usually by nails, sometimes by rope. Finally, the victim was hoisted by way of the crosspiece (*crux* in Latin) onto a pole, and the crosspiece was attached to the pole so that his feet did not touch the ground. There the victim was left on public display until he died. Sometimes death came quickly through suffocation or thirst, but sometimes death was postponed by giving the victim drink. After the victim was dead, the Romans often left the body on the cross as a public display, rotting and eaten by birds.[3] The point was not just to hurt and kill a person but to utterly humiliate a rebel or upstart slave, while terrorizing anyone who looked up to them. Crucifixion was empire-imposed trauma intended to shatter anyone and any movement that opposed Rome.

THE EARLIEST PRESERVED STORY OF JESUS' CRUCIFIXION

The impact of the crucifixion can be felt palpably in the earliest narrative about the crucifixion of Jesus found in the New Testament. This narrative is preserved particularly in chapters 14 through 16 of the book of Mark, the earliest gospel in the New Testament.[4]

The exact contents of this early crucifixion narrative are unknown, but it seems that a form of the story of Jesus' death was known by the authors of the gospels of Mark and John. These two gospels overlap in how they tell of Jesus' death and rarely elsewhere.[5] In addition, these final chapters in Mark stand out from the rest of the gospel in their style and depiction of Jesus.[6] As a result, most scholars agree that parts of Mark 14–16 are an early crucifixion narrative used by Mark's author, though they disagree on whether one can determine its exact contents.[7]

These final chapters of Mark present a bleak picture of Jesus' final days.[8] The story opens in Mark 14 with the decision by "the chief priests and the scribes" to secretly arrest Jesus and kill him before the Passover for fear of starting a riot among the people. Soon thereafter Jesus has a final meal with his disciples at which he predicts that he will be betrayed by one of them, that all of them will desert him, and that Peter, the head disciple, will repeatedly deny to others any association with Jesus. Jesus goes to the garden of Gethsemane to pray to be allowed to avoid death, and his chief disciples fall asleep while waiting for him. Judas then arrives with an armed contingent to arrest Jesus, and Jesus is taken away to be interrogated by the priests of the Jerusalem Temple. While they are interrogating Jesus inside the Temple, his apostle Peter outside denies association with him three times, just as Jesus had predicted. At the outset of Mark 15 the Jewish authorities turn Jesus over to the Roman governor, Pilate, for interrogation and execution. Pilate asks Jesus, "Are you the king of the Jews?" To which Jesus replies, "So you say." Otherwise, Jesus refuses to respond to any of Pilate's questions, just as he had been silent before the Temple priests. Pilate speaks to the Jewish crowds and offers to free Jesus, since (the narrative says) it was the custom for the Roman governor to free a Jewish prisoner at Passover. But the crowd loudly proclaims their preference that Barrabas, an anti-Roman insurgent, be freed instead.

From here the crucifixion narrative describes step by step the torture, mocking, and execution of Jesus. Jesus is flogged.

Then Roman soldiers dress him up as "the king of the Jews," strip him, taunt him, and divide his clothes. Finally, they take Jesus to Golgotha, "the place of the skull," and crucify him between two criminals, who mock him too. Around noon the soldiers offer the dying Jesus sour wine to drink, and he soon dies, crying out in his native Aramaic tongue, "My God, my God, why have you forsaken me?" Hung on the cross, Jesus has been abandoned by all who know him except for three women watching from a distance, among them Mary of Magdala and another Mary identified here in Mark as the mother of "the younger James and Joses." Jesus is hurriedly buried just before the Sabbath. Then, in a section that may or may not have been part of the early crucifixion narrative, three women come after the Sabbath to anoint his body, but they find the tomb empty, and a young man instructs them to tell the disciples that Jesus has risen from the dead. The narrative (and the Gospel of Mark) closes with the women running away "in terror, telling no one anything because of their fear" (Mark 16:8).

This crucifixion narrative reveals the rawness of early responses to Jesus' death. The Jesus remembered here is no hero offering eloquent speeches and welcoming torture and death. Instead, he prays to God to avoid death and is silent or evasive when questioned.[9] This narrative blames the Jewish leadership first and foremost for Jesus' death, while the Roman governor, Pilate, comes off as an indecisive and unwilling participant in the process. Yet Jesus' closest disciples also come off poorly, betraying, denying, and abandoning Jesus in his death. Even the female followers of Jesus who watch his final passing do so from a distance. Formed by the first generation(s) of Jesus' followers, perhaps this crucifixion story of Jesus' abandonment preserves tinges of self-blame. These followers, so the story goes, survived by deserting and denying Jesus, while he suffered a humiliating and solitary death. Be that as it may, the story enjoyed a circulation far beyond Jesus' first disciples, becoming the basis for all four of the New Testament gospel accounts of Jesus' death.

We do not know when this crucifixion narrative was written, but it is about as close as we can come, I believe, to seeing the early impact that Jesus' death had on his followers. It was not just that Jesus did not match up to some messianic expectations laid on him. In crucifying Jesus the Romans used a time-tested strategy to obliterate movements they deemed dangerous, devastating his followers.

Now, thousands of years later, with Christianity a worldwide movement, it is easy to overlook the fact that this Roman attempt to obliterate the Jesus movement was almost successful. One of Paul's early letters, the first one to the Corinthians, acknowledges decades after the fact that "the message about the cross is foolishness to those who are perishing" (1 Corinthians 1:18) and "a stumbling block to Jews, folly to gentiles" (1:23). Even a couple of centuries later we find a prominent critic of the church, Celsus, mocking Christians for following a figure, Jesus, who was "punished to his utter disgrace."[10] For many in the Greco-Roman world, there was not much more to say about a movement that had its leader, a demonstrable failure, crucified. End of story.

RESISTANCE TO ROMAN IMPERIAL TERRORISM AMONG EARLY JESUS FOLLOWERS

But it was not the end of the story. The Messianist community centered on Jesus reinterpreted the crucifixion in ways unanticipated by the Romans. Jesus' crucifixion became the founding event of the movement and not its end. The move was so radical that many Christians now wear symbols of the cross as a mark of their membership in the movement. The cross is no sign of humiliating defeat for Christians. Instead, it is a proud symbol of movement membership. Jesus' followers did not end up fleeing from the reality of his crucifixion, but "took up the cross" themselves. Such a thing would have been incomprehensible to Romans. It is an excellent example of the adaptability of symbols, especially in cases like imperial domination, where a dominated group confronts symbolic actions imposed on it by its oppressor.[11] The Roman symbol of ultimate defeat became the Christian symbol of ultimate victory.

How did the first generation of Jesus' followers accomplish this reinterpretation of crucifixion?

Answering this question is no easy task, since even the above-discussed "crucifixion narrative" probably was written years after Jesus' death. Yet we have another resource available for uncovering early responses to Jesus' crucifixion: the traditions of Jesus' followers preserved in the letters of the New Testament. These letters sometimes date from earlier periods, especially the letters most clearly written by Paul (Romans,

1 and 2 Corinthians, Galatians, Philippians, 1 Thessalonians, and Philemon).[12] Through uncovering early traditions known by Paul and other early Jesus followers, we may gain clues to how the early church first responded to Jesus' death and reinterpreted it. These traditions about the crucifixion may date only years or even mere months after Jesus' death.

JESUS AS THE SUFFERING SERVANT OF THE HEBREW BIBLE

I start with a quotation of early tradition about Jesus found in Paul's first letter to the church at Corinth, which he had founded. Writing about 53 or 54 CE, about twenty years after Jesus' death, Paul says in chapter 15 of that letter:

> For I handed on to you as of first importance what I in turn had received: that Christ died for our sins in accordance with the scriptures, and that he was buried, and that he was raised on the third day in accordance with the scriptures. (1 Corinthians 15:3–4)

Paul's reference to "what I in turn received" indicates that he is reciting here an earlier teaching, one Paul himself was told in the founding years of the church. And this brief teaching tells us at least two important things up front. Both assertions, that "Christ died for our sins" and that "he was buried and then raised on the third day" are according to the (Hebrew) scriptures.

This indicates the importance for early followers of Jesus of interpreting Jesus' death and resurrection through the lens of scripture. These early followers of Jesus, like Jesus himself, were Jewish. Being Jewish, they drew on the Hebrew Bible to make sense of their lives. They readily identified themselves and figures like Jesus with the major actors of the Bible, and they could invoke a given text from the Torah and Prophets through mentioning just some key phrases or a mere rare word found in the given text.

In addition, the first-generation Jesus community did not choose just any Hebrew scripture to understand Jesus' crucifixion. Rather, in the wake of Jesus' crucifixion, early Jesus followers found themselves focusing on Hebrew scriptures formed in the midst of earlier Jewish traumas. The scripture best corresponding to the assertion that "Christ was raised on the third day according to the scriptures" comes from the book of Hosea, formed amidst Assyrian trauma. In it, his people look forward to being resurrected as a community—"In two days God will make us whole again, on the third day God will raise us up" (Hosea 6:2). Apparently Jesus' followers found comfort in this text, finding in it a promise of their community's revival in the wake of his death. This idea of communal survival after Jesus' death will be important shortly.

But let us turn to Paul's other statement that "Christ died for our sins in accordance with the scriptures." This quote is reminiscent of the suffering servant song in Isaiah 53 formed amidst Babylonian trauma. Recall its repeated focus on the servant's bearing of the community's sin—"ours were the sins that he bore; our pains he endured" (verse 4); "he was wounded for our crimes, crushed because of our bloodguilt"

(5); "Yahweh allowed the bloodguilt belonging to all of us to harm him" (6). The tradition quoted by Paul looks back on this song, asserting that Jesus' death on the cross for "our sins" was analogous to the exilic servant's suffering for the sins of his community. In this sense, Jesus "died for our sins in accordance with the scriptures" and was a "suffering servant."[13]

Some other early Christian sayings are yet more explicit in seeing Jesus as a suffering servant. For example, the author of the late-first-century letter of 1 Peter says that "Christ suffered for you" and then quotes an early hymn that describes Jesus' death in terms that repeatedly echo the suffering servant song in Isaiah:

1 Peter 2:22–24	Parallel parts of Isaiah 53
(22) He [Jesus] committed no sin,	No lie was in his mouth (53:9)
and no deceit was found in his mouth.	He was struck, but he submitted he did not open his mouth (53:7)
(23) When he was abused, he did not return abuse;	Like a sheep led to slaughter . . .
when he suffered, he did not threaten;	he did not open his mouth (53:8)
but he entrusted himself to the one who judges justly.	Ours were the sicknesses he bore (53:4)
(24) He himself bore our sins in his body on the cross,	He bore the sin of many (53:12)
so that, free from sins, we might live for righteousness;	my . . . servant shall make many righteous (53:11)
by his wounds you have been healed.	with his wounds we have been healed (53:5)

Many Christians assume from texts like this that the suffering servant song in Isaiah 53 accurately prophesied Jesus' death. Yet it is far more likely that ancient hymns like the one in 1 Peter represent an attempt by Jesus' followers to retell his story so that it matched and could be interpreted in terms of Isaiah 53. In and of itself, Jesus' execution at the hands of Romans featured few parallels to the suffering servant seen in Isaiah 53. He died unjustly. But early traditions like the hymn in 1 Peter discussed here connected Jesus' brutal and apparently senseless death to the poem in Isaiah 53, arguing that Jesus' death—like the suffering servant's—made a positive difference for the community that survived him. Jesus died on his people's account, so that they could, as 1 Peter says, "be healed" and "live for righteousness."

Through singing this hymn, early Jesus Jews make themselves the "we" seen in Isaiah 53, the "us" whose sins were borne by Jesus, and the "many" made righteous by his pain. Thanks to this redescription and reinterpretation of his death, they behold not just the Roman humiliation but the suffering and vindication of Jesus. They see how his suffering on the cross benefited them.

This link of the suffering servant song to the death of a contemporary figure Jesus was unprecedented. Earlier Jewish texts do not depict Jewish heroes, like those who died resisting Antiochus IV in the Hellenistic crisis, as suffering servants. And Jews before Jesus did not read Isaiah 53 as a prediction of a suffering Messiah.[14] Instead, the closest contemporary analogy to the idea that "Christ died for our sins" was the widespread idea in Greco-Roman culture of heroic figures dying "for" others—their family, friends, or their community. These Greco-Roman ideas probably helped Jesus' followers understand the significance of his death as well.[15]

Nevertheless, both the brief pre-Pauline teaching that "Christ died for our sins according to the scriptures" and the longer hymn in 1 Peter add an element of communal guilt to the story of Jesus' noble death. If we look for a precursor to that element, we find it repeatedly in Isaiah 53 ("our sins," "our pains," "our crimes," "our bloodguilt") but not in the Greco-Roman parallels. To be sure, the early followers of Jesus probably saw him as another hero who had "died for" others. But they seem to have seen Jesus as a particular type of such a hero, one modeled on the suffering servant of Isaiah 53.

JESUS' DEATH FOR HIS PEOPLE COMPARED WITH MOSES'

I have not yet explained, however, how Jesus' early followers believed Jesus had "died for our sins." Later Christians have believed that Jesus died as a sacrificial offering for the sins of others. God needed a victim to atone for the sins of the world, and Jesus—being innocent of sin—served as a substitute sacrifice instead of guilty humanity.

Recent research by Ellen Aitken, however, has uncovered a different way that early Jesus followers understood his death.

According to this alternative understanding, Jesus did not die for others as a sacrificial offering to an angry God. Instead, Jesus, like Moses, died on the threshold of salvation so that his followers could move forward.

After all, Moses is the most important figure in the Old Testament, and he dies just before his people enter the Promised Land.[16] There are various biblical explanations for this, but one prominent one is that Moses died when he did because of his people's sin. In Deuteronomy, Moses pronounces to his people, "Yahweh was angry with me on your account, saying 'you shall not enter [the land]' " (Deuteronomy 1:37). The book of Psalms mentions Meribah, where God declared that Moses would not enter the land, and says, "[Our fathers] provoked God's anger at Meribah, and Moses suffered on their account" (Psalm 106:32). This biblical picture of Moses suffering and dying outside the land on account of his people has even led some to propose that the song about the suffering servant in Isaiah 53 was originally written with Moses in mind.[17]

Aitken's proposal, however, depends not on ideas of what Isaiah 53 originally meant but on how that song was interpreted in relation to Jesus by his first followers. She notes that the review of Jesus' death in the hymn in 1 Peter uses an unusual and rare Greek word at the point that it says, "When he [Jesus] was abused [Greek: *loidoreo*], he did not return abuse."[18] This same rare word *loidoreo* is used in the ancient Greek translation of the Old Testament, multiple times, to describe the "abuse" that Moses suffered at Meribah (Numbers

20:3, 13). The occurrence of this rare word in the 1 Peter hymn may mean that its author saw Moses as the suffering servant who prefigured Jesus. Just as Moses was "abused" (*eloidoreito*) by his own people and prevented from entering the land on their account, so also Jesus suffered similar "abuse" (*loidoroumenos*). Those singing the 1 Peter hymn believed that Jesus was a suffering servant akin to Moses.

In this way the first followers of Jesus used Old Testament texts formed amidst exilic trauma (Isaiah 53 and the Moses story) to deal with the Roman-imposed trauma of Jesus' crucifixion. Their rereading of texts about Moses and the suffering servant allowed them to see Jesus' death as empowering them. Like Moses, like the exilic suffering servant, Jesus bore their sins and died, so that they could live.

Aitken makes an additional point that can give us a new perspective on how some early Jesus followers interpreted Jesus' death. She notes an important gap in the 1 Peter hymn: any word about Jesus' resurrection. In this respect the gap in the hymn parallels a gap found at the end of the Gospel of Mark. Where other gospels end with disciples seeing and talking with the resurrected Jesus, Mark's crucifixion narrative ends with an empty tomb, Jesus' missing body.

The first followers of Jesus may have been challenged by the fact that they lacked an identifiable tomb for their hero, Jesus. Many savior figures at the time were honored at their burial places. Their graves were focal points for their followers. Jesus had nothing.

Yet here the Moses traditions came to the rescue. Jesus' empty tomb linked him to Moses, whose burial place was likewise unknown.[19] The Pentateuch ends with uncertainty about where Moses was buried, saying, "Moses, the servant of the LORD, died in the land of Moab . . . and they buried him in Gai in the land of Moab opposite Baal Peor, and no one knows his tomb to this day" (Deuteronomy 34:5–6). The Jesus seen in Mark's early crucifixion narrative likewise lacks an identifiable burial place. And the announcement of his resurrection dies on the lips of the terrified women fleeing in fear.

Yet, one might ask, "Where is the vindication? Where is some kind of happy ending?"

Here again, the Moses story provided a guide for the Jesus community. The vindication of Moses, God's "servant," came not in his own resurrection. His life and death were vindicated by the ongoing life of his community, which entered Canaan and lived on as Israel. So also the hymn in 1 Peter and the Gospel of Mark do not emphasize Jesus' resurrection. The suffering Jesus they depict is vindicated in the redeemed community that survives him. The church's survival, its ongoing life and flourishing, becomes a testimony to the healing and making-righteous that Jesus' death accomplished. Not only Jesus but the whole community, the whole Jesus movement, stands as proof of the failure of Roman imperial terrorism.

The flourishing of the Jesus community thus became a transformative response to the Roman crucifixion of Jesus. According to this understanding of the cross, the Jesus community survived because of Jesus' death, not in spite of it. What the Romans intended as shameful, community-disintegrating, traumatic memory of crucifixion became the community-founding memory of the Christian community.

Members of the Jesus movement could say, "You thought you could end us by killing our founder, our savior, our Jesus. Here we still are, and our life as a community proves his death was not in vain. Jesus' death freed us—from sin, and from fear of death. Like God's servant Moses, our Jesus bore our sins so that we could live. His death did not hold us back but allowed us to go forward like the wilderness Israelites into new life in the promised land."

THE CRUCIFIED JESUS AND FUTURE UNSPEAKABLE SUFFERING

It would be a severe mistake, however, to see this as a story that moves in a simple way from suffering to redemption, wilderness to Promised Land. Instead, Jesus' followers faced far more suffering to come, both in the near term at the hands of fellow Jews and Roman authorities, and in the longer term dealing with other burdens and crises. When that suffering became overwhelming, even traumatic, the figure of the crucified Jesus—now seen through the lens of suffering servant traditions—served as a focal point for sufferers. Back in exile, the suffering servant and other figures (Daughter Zion, prophets) helped symbolize to Judeans a pain they did not verbalize directly. Similarly, the figure of Jesus, the crucified savior, became a picture of divine solidarity that comforted Jesus' followers facing other kinds of unspeakable pain.

We see this already in an early hymn quoted by Paul in Philippians, that describes God's becoming human in Jesus Christ:

> who, though in the form of God,
> did not regard equality with God
> as something to be exploited,
> but emptied himself,
> taking the form of a slave,
> being born in human likeness.
> And being found in human form,
> he humbled himself
> and became obedient to the point of death—
> even death on a cross. (Philippians 2:6–8)

Centuries later African slaves in the American South took comfort in this Jesus, who was crucified for them. In the words of one spiritual,

> Nobody knows the trouble I've seen
> Nobody knows but Jesus
> Nobody knows the trouble I've seen
> Glory hallelujah!

The slaves who sang this song and their descendants found hope in a savior who profoundly suffered like them and yet somehow survived. As my Union Seminary colleague James Cone notes in his book *The Cross and the Lynching Tree*, African Americans in the segregated South would "keep hope alive" by focusing on the crucified Jesus. Impoverished, landless, and facing the terror of lynchings, they "found in the cross the spiritual power to resist the violence they so often suffered. They came to know, as the black historian Lerone Bennett wrote, 'at the deepest level . . . what it was like to be crucified.' "[20] Some church traditions might focus on Christ's teachings or his resurrection, but for African slaves and their descendants, the crucified Jesus was first a brother who showed that God knew their suffering in a way that no one else did.

This is a particularly powerful example of how the image of Jesus has come to function for others, too. For millions of Christians the crucified Jesus has become what the suffering servant and other exilic figures were for exiles—a symbol of often unspeakable suffering. The cross that Romans intended to bring despair instead became a beacon of hope.

CHAPTER TEN

The Traumatized Apostle

THE APOSTLE PAUL STANDS at the crossroads of Christianity. Though not a disciple during Jesus' lifetime, Paul became one of the most influential apostles after his death, perhaps *the* most important apostle. Paul was a card-carrying member of the Pharisees, the Jesus movement's greatest competitor in Judaism. He personally was one of the Jesus movement's earliest opponents. Yet he soon became one of that movement's greatest evangelists. Most important, he provided the rationale for Christianity's global mission beyond Judaism to gentiles (non-Jews).

Despite his importance, Paul's basic message has proven notoriously difficult to nail down. Theologians like Augustine and Luther rightly saw Paul as the founder of Christian theology. Recent scholarship has found good grounds to conclude that Paul remained Jewish. And scholarship over the centuries has been particularly divided on how Paul viewed the ongoing significance of Jewish law. In sum, no treatment can do full justice to the complexity of Paul's thought. And this is not just because our only direct record of Paul's theology is found in diverse New Testament letters written by him. Instead, Paul remains so fascinating and yet irreducibly complicated in part because of the ways in which his message was influenced by multiple crises.

Paul wrote amidst traumatic force fields of past Jewish zeal and present gentile mission without fully resolving them. He loved the law. He hated excessive focus on it, particularly by gentiles. He steadfastly remained a Jew and believed in God's ongoing covenant with Israel. At the same time, he decisively affirmed the membership of gentiles in the church as gentiles. And this only begins to touch on the ways Paul's theology grew out of fractures in his being. As a result of these and other struggles, debates about him reflect irresolvable disjunctions in his identity. Given his traumatic past, there is no way to pin him down.

Yet Paul's traumas are not important only because they provide background to his complex theology. Paul is important because of how his traumas influenced Christianity as a whole. Paul did not just suffer personally. His writings, deeply shaped by his complicated past and later afflictions, bequeathed a model of Christian suffering to millennia of Christians who have followed him.

PAUL'S MOVE FROM PERSECUTOR OF CHRISTIANITY TO EVANGELIST

To start, Paul was a deeply religious Jew. Describing himself to a church community at Philippi, Paul emphasizes his Judaism: "circumcised on the eighth day, a member of the people of Israel, of the tribe of Benjamin, a Hebrew born of Hebrews; as to the law, a Pharisee . . . as to righteousness under the law, blameless" (Philippians 3:5–6). In his letter to the churches in Galatia (located in modern Turkey), he responds to reports they have heard of his earlier life "in Judaism" and affirms: "I advanced in Judaism beyond many among my people of the same age, for I was far more zealous for the traditions of my ancestors" (Galatians 1:14). Paul never retreats from the fact that he had been, and still was, Jewish, indeed a more observant Jew than most. And Paul's letters betray his profound bond with his Jewish heritage, constantly citing Old Testament texts and interpreting them through the lens of contemporary Jewish interpretations.

Yet Paul was also haunted by his past, not by his Judaism but by the way he had persecuted Jesus' followers, and in so doing, implicitly persecuted Jesus himself. In the earlier quoted statement to the Philippians, he admits to being a "persecutor of the church," and to the Galatians he confesses, "I was violently persecuting the church of God and was trying to destroy it" (Galatians 1:13). The biblical book of Acts also tells stories of Paul's persecution of Jesus' followers. It says that he kept the coats of the people who stoned Stephen to death and approved of their killing of him. In the persecution that followed, he entered house after house of Jesus' followers, taking them to prison.

That was Paul before. Then a transformative experience of unknown character happened. Paul reports it as a vision of the resurrected Jesus. Nevertheless, this experience, however positive and real it was for him, also has analogies to trauma.

The book of Acts describes Paul's vision as involving collapse, extended blindness, and an inability to eat or drink for three days. Only when he is visited by a member of the Jesus movement (Ananias), does he regain his ability to eat and drink and eventually start promoting Jesus as "the Son of God" in the Jewish synagogues (Acts 9:3–22).

Paul's own letters offer fewer details on the experience. In his first letter to the Corinthian church, he concludes a list of Jesus' resurrection appearances by saying, "Last of all, as to a fetus born prematurely, he appeared also to me. For I am the least of the apostles, unfit to be called an apostle, because I persecuted the church of God" (1 Corinthians 15:8–9). Early in Galatians, he follows a description of his persecution of Jesus' followers by insisting that his change came not through any human evangelism but through a direct appearance of Jesus Christ to him: "God, who had set me apart before I was born and called me through his grace, was pleased to reveal his Son to me, so that I might proclaim him among the Gentiles" (Galatians 1:15–16).

Finally, in his second letter to the Corinthian church, he speaks enigmatically of having experienced a heavenly ascent that may have culminated in the vision of Christ spoken of in 1 Corinthians and Galatians:

> I know a person in Christ who fourteen years ago was caught up to the third heaven—whether in the body or out of the body I do not know; God knows. And I know that such a person—whether in the body or out of the body I do not know; God knows—was caught up into Paradise and heard things that must not be told, that no mortal is permitted to repeat. (2 Corinthians 12:2–4)

Several features of this report by Paul resemble how victims of trauma speak of their experience—Paul's initial presentation of it as if it happened to another person ("a person in Christ"), his repeated emphasis on the idea that the experience might have been out of his body ("whether in the body or out of the body I do not know"), and his statement that he cannot speak in detail of the contents of his vision ("heard things that must not be told, that no mortal is permitted to repeat"). Many scholars reject an association of this vision with Paul's call because his dating of the vision ("fourteen years ago") does not agree with their dating schemes for his career, but those schemes are based on the biblical book of Acts, hardly a reliable source for details of historical dating.[1] Moreover, even if this vision in 2 Corinthians is separate from his call experience, it is evidence for Paul's possibly having lived through traumalike experiences that he later reported as mystical visions.[2]

In suggesting all this, I must emphasize that we will never know for sure what happened to Paul. The history of Pauline studies features multiple examples of attempts to psychologize him, but few today would venture guesses about Paul's internal thinking processes.[3] After all, our only evidence for Paul's state of mind consists of his own stylized letters and later legends about him in Acts. This is more than we have for uncovering the inner dynamics of any other biblical character, but it is limited nevertheless.

With these qualifications in mind, my first point about Paul is this: that the pivotal experience that turned him into a Jesus follower had analogies to trauma. It exploded Paul's prior worldview and divided his life in half, much like a traumatic event would. Like many survivors of trauma, Paul subsequently told his life story in two parts—his past leading up to the Damascus road event and his present in the wake of that event.[4] We must be careful, of course, not to then envelop all life-changing experience under the ever-expanding umbrella of "trauma." Nevertheless, this case of Paul's encounter with the resurrected Christ can help us recognize how even positive life-altering events can have more analogies to traumatic occurrences than one might first presuppose.

PAUL'S CONVERSION FROM HIS PHARISAIC PAST

Whatever happened to Paul in this experience, it complicated his relationship with the law so central to his pre-call life. As a Pharisee, Paul had thought that Jewish Torah observance was the main way to live a life that pleased God, rejecting the claims of Jesus' followers that Jesus was God's Messiah. Then he himself met Jesus as the resurrected Messiah and both assumptions fell away: Jesus was God's divine son, and Jesus' care for Paul was not based on Paul's past behavior. After all, Paul, the persecutor, was the last person one would think Jesus would have deigned to appear to. Yet according to Paul's understanding of his experience, Jesus had appeared to him nevertheless, and called him, of all people, to be an apostle to the gentiles. This experience of unconditional call taught Paul that faith in God, not Torah obedience, was what most mattered. Everything centered on "faith," a total trust in God exemplified by the crucified Jesus. Through obeying God even to the cross, Jesus exemplified an absolute and total faith, a "faith of Christ," that Paul now believed to be the key to a relationship with God.[5] This faith was the gift Paul himself received through Christ, the one he'd once persecuted, and it was the center of the gospel that Paul then preached to gentiles.

This also gave Paul a new understanding of his own Jewish identity. Later he described his Jewish self-understanding to the Galatians in this way:

> We ourselves are Jews by birth and not Gentile sinners, yet we know that a person is determined [by God] to be righteous not by the works of the law, but through the faith of Jesus Christ. And we have come to believe in Christ Jesus, so that we might be marked as righteous by having the faith of Christ, and not by doing the works of the law, for no one will be reckoned as righteous by works of the law. (Galatians 2:15–16)

This quotation reminds us again that Paul was Jewish. But his encounter with Jesus, whatever it entailed, was so

'ORD OF THE WEEK

ıe Subject: God ordains certain men to hell on purpose

Isaiah 64:8 - 0 Lord, thou art our Father; we are the clay; and thou our potter; and we all are the work of thy hand.

work - Hebrew: Maaseh · an action (good or bad); product; transaction; business

Romans 9:20-23 - Who art thou that repliest against God? Shall the thing formed say to him that formed it, why hast thou made me thus? Hath not the potter the power over the clay of the same lump, to make one vessel unto honour and another unto dishonour - What if God willing to show his wrath, and to make his power known, endured with much long suffering the vessels of wrath fitted to destruction: And that he might make known the riches of his glory on the vessels of mercy, which he hath afore prepared unto glory.

fitted - Greek: katartizo · to complete thoroughly; fit; frame; arrange; prepare. Thayer says this word speaks of men whose souls God has so constituted that they cannot escape destruction; their mind is fixed that they frame themselves.

Ien get angry to think that we serve a God that can do as it pleases him. They ctually think that an almighty God thinks the way they think and that he could ot possibly form-fit a vessel to hell merely to show his wrath and power. Paul said e does. Men have difficulty perceiving a God that predestinates men (Rom. 8:29) n whom he desires to show his grace (unmerited favor) and mercy, that he may hower them throughout eternity with the riches of his glory. We like to believe ıat we must give him permission if he is to operate in our hearts and minds. The ,ord said, "My thoughts are not your thoughts, neither are your ways my ways. As ıe heavens are higher than the earth, so are my ways higher than your ways and my ıoughts than your thoughts (Isaiah 55:8,9)". Our God is in the heavens: he hath 'one whatsoever he hath pleased (Psalms 115:3). He doeth whatsoever pleaseth him Eccl 8:3). Thou, 0 Lord, hast done as it pleased thee (Jonah 1:14). Whatsoever the ,ord pleased, that did he in heaven, and earth, and in the seas, and in all deep laces (Psalms 135:6). He does all his pleasure (Isa. 46:10; Isa. 44:24-28; Eph. :5,9; Philippians 2:13). It is Jesus that holds the keys to death and hell (Rev. 1:18), ot Satan. God will intentionally cast these evil vessels of wrath into hell and lock ıem up for eternity because it is not his pleasure to draw them to him (John 6:44). 'his doctrine angers men, though it is taught throughout the pages of God's Holy ook. Men do not have a Biblical view of the living God when they think he is not n control of all things including the minds and hearts of all men. God is not only ove to the vessels of mercy, but he is a consuming fire (Deut. 4:24) upon the vessels f wrath fitted to destruction. We do not serve a God who is Superman that can nly shake mountains, implode blackholes, and explode quasars. The God of the niverse can harden and soften the hearts of men at will (Rom. 9:18; Ezek. 36:26). Ie giveth not account of any of his matters (Job 33:13).

GRACE AND TRUTH MINISTRIES
P.O. Box 1109, Hendersonville, TN 37077
Jim Brown - Bible Teacher · Local: (615) 824-8502 | Toll Free: (800) 625-5409
https://www.graceandtruth.net/

determinative for him that he came to believe that this kind of Christ-enabled, faith-based relationship was now everything. As he put it a bit later in his letter to the Galatians:

> The law was our guardian until Christ came, so that we might be determined as righteous by faith. But now that faith has come, we are no longer subject to a guardian, for in Christ Jesus you are all children of God through faith. . . . There is no longer Jew or Greek, there is no longer slave or free, there is no longer male and female; for all of you are one in Christ Jesus. (Galatians 3:24–26, 28)

Thus, with the coming of Jesus, any way of life—whether Jewish or gentile—was mere window-dressing on this more fundamental relationship of faith in God made possible by Jesus. Jews could discover this amazing faith-based relationship, even as they remained Jews and obeyed the law. But gentiles could discover this amazing faith-based relationship too, and such non-Jews did not need to take on Jewish laws to get this relationship with the God of Israel. They just needed faith.

Indeed—and this would confuse later readers of Paul—he saw danger for some, especially gentiles and especially gentiles in certain communities (Galatia, for example), that becoming circumcised or observing other Jewish laws might confuse them about the deeper importance of this all-important faith relationship with God. By the end of his letter to the Galatians he presented that church with two sharply opposing paths—seek either circumcision or Christ:

> If you let yourselves be circumcised, Christ will be of no benefit to you. . . . You who want to be determined as

> righteous by the law have cut yourselves off from Christ; you have fallen away from grace. For through the Spirit, by faith, we eagerly wait for the hope of righteousness. For in Christ Jesus neither circumcision nor uncircumcision counts for anything; the only thing that counts is faith made real through love. (Galatians 5:2, 4–6)

In this way, Paul hammered away at those in Galatia who promoted what he viewed as outmoded ideas about the need for circumcision. In doing so, he hammered away at his past.

The opponents that Paul criticized had views close to those he had abandoned. They, like Paul in former days, were focused on the importance of Jewish legal observance. Since the Jesus movement was Jewish, they believed that gentiles who joined it had to be circumcised and observe Jewish law. That reminded Paul of his past zeal for the law, a zeal he now thought to be inappropriate in the messianic age brought about by Jesus. He believed that Jesus' death and resurrection was a sign of the beginning of the end of the world. As the world clock came closer to striking midnight, God was offering gentiles—through Jesus Christ—a precious opportunity to be saved. They did not need to be circumcised, or engage in any specifically "Jewish" practices. In the supercharged atmosphere of the final apocalypse, Paul believed the imposition of Torah requirements on gentiles to be a misleading distraction from the "faith" in God that Gentiles needed to be saved.[6]

This often led Paul to stress the distance between a faith-based relationship with Christ on the one hand and "works of the law" (like circumcision) on the other. It is as if Paul could not get far enough away from his past.[7] Like others haunted by what they have done to others, Paul lived with unresolved issues about his past persecution of the Jesus movement.[8] Neither he, nor those around him, could forget this history. On one level, he seems to have found a way to talk about his past. In fact, he could not stop talking about it, and he kept talking of his past persecution before telling of his conversion. Yet on another level, this past still seemed to possess him. And not just in the sense that he prefaced his conversion story with an account of his violent past. But also that he could not stop living the story that he talked about. Paul was a man possessed by a history of "pursuit" that would not let him go.

PAUL'S FOUNDING OF MISSIONARY MONOTHEISM

We see Paul's postconversion zeal in the angry way he attacked those in the Jesus movement who advocated an obedience to the law similar to the one he once advocated. He developed a theology that stressed the importance of faith over law as the key to creating a right relationship with God. In the process he achieved something unprecedented in Judaism: the formation of a monotheistic faith unusually open to non-Jews. This responded to a problem implicit in Jewish monotheism ever since the exile: if the God of Israel is the only God in the whole world, how might non-Jewish foreigners gain a relationship with that God?

For Judaism up to Paul's time had been only minimally open to new converts. Aside from the forced mass conversion of conquered populations by Jewish-Hasmonean leaders in the Hellenistic period, early Jewish communities did not seek converts on any kind of wide scale. Moreover, conversion to Judaism involved overcoming some serious obstacles, such as the painful and socially stigmatizing process of adult male circumcision. As a result, though many gentiles in the Greco-Roman world were attracted to the antiquity of Judaism and its practices, few made the ultimate decision to become members of the Jewish people.

The early Jesus movement, being Jewish, thus faced major questions about the terms on which it would welcome non-Jewish members. It was in this context that Paul, reacting to his Pharisaic, church-persecuting past, offered a new way. He argued that non-Jews could fully embrace the God of Israel without focusing on the law that Paul once viewed as essential to righteousness. They could, he suggested, be "counted by God as righteous" because of their faith, before ever embracing circumcision or other aspects of Jewish legal observance. In this respect these Gentiles could model their conversion to Judaism on the first Jew, Abraham, who "had faith and was counted by God as righteous" well before he was circumcised (Romans 4:1–12).[9]

Out of this perspective, Paul energetically criticized what he believed to be wrongly directed legal observance by gentiles. Indeed, with some communities, like the churches in Galatia, all too prone to overemphasize the value of circumcision, Paul could not conceive any productive way that circumcision could be used that did not confuse the more fundamental faith relationship. He criticized circumcision as a way to "end with the flesh" when they had started "with the spirit" (Galatians 3:3). Elsewhere, in his first letter to the Corinthians, he urges gentile believers to just "remain in the condition in which you were called," for "circumcision is nothing, and uncircumcision is nothing, but obeying the commandments of God is everything" (1 Corinthians 7:19–20).

Initially, these ideas about circumcision were controversial, not only with other Jews but in the Jesus movement itself. Acts tells of how Paul, while working in the church in Antioch, was confronted by other Christians "from Judah" who insisted that "unless you are circumcised according to the custom of Moses, you cannot be saved" (Acts 15:1). The church in Antioch appointed Paul and his coworker Barnabas to go back to Judah and to the church in Jerusalem to get a judgment from leaders there about what should be required of gentile converts to the Jesus movement. Once they arrived, the church leaders there met in an apostolic council and affirmed Paul's mission to the gentiles. Acts 15:19–20 reports that James, the leader of the Jerusalem church, affirmed that noncircumcised Gentiles could join the Jesus movement, but had to abstain from eating any food "polluted by idols"—that is, they had to stop participating in Greco-Roman banquets devoted to other gods. Paul's own account of this meeting in Galatians 2 says nothing about this provision, but he goes on later in that same letter to denounce idolatry as a "work of the flesh" avoided by all believers (Galatians 5:20), and his first letter to the Corinthians goes on at length about the problem of eating "food dedicated to idols" (1 Corinthians 8–10).

Thus Paul, perhaps partly at the prompting of leaders in Jerusalem, seems to have developed something unprecedented in the ancient world: a virulently missionary monotheism that did away with the requirement of circumcision. It was a form of Jesus-Judaism boiled down to its monotheistic essentials: faith in the God of Israel and rejection of other gods ("idols") and practices associated with them.

This stripped-down form of messianic Judaism proved incredibly popular and effective among the gentiles who were Paul's target audience. Paul's radical ideas spread rapidly through his own missionary travels and the circulation of his writings among churches. Especially outside Judah, the Jesus movement became dominated by communities that consisted largely of gentile believers who did not observe the Torah. Males were not circumcised. Believers did not observe Sabbath or basic dietary laws. Even in the diverse world of first-century Judaism, such gentiles would not have appeared "Jewish" to other Jews. To be sure, Paul himself believed such gentiles to be joined somehow to historic Israel, but even he saw a difference between these gentile followers of Jesus and ethnic Jews. For Paul, gentiles could be "grafted" onto the people of Israel like a "wild olive shoot" might be grafted onto a cultivated olive tree (Romans 11:17–24). They were part of the plant, but still a "wild" shoot. In this way Paul sowed the seeds, so to speak, for a Jesus movement that would become a religion separate from the Judaism out of which it emerged.

Paul's basic ideas about gentile Jesus-Judaism proved more successful than he could have imagined. The vast majority of the millions who practice Christianity today have no interest whatsoever in observing Jewish law. Where Paul was conflicted on the role of law in the ongoing life of Jesus' followers, the later church came to see this as a nonissue. Where Paul as a Jew continued to affirm Israel's prior claim to relationship with God, later Christian theologians portrayed Judaism as a "has-been" religion, superseded by the Christian church, which was the new Israel. In this sense, the later gentile church forgot Paul's complex ideas about gentiles, Jewish practices, and the status of "Israel."

Even as it left behind Paul's complex bond with Judaism, the church developed its own later version of Paul's tortured relationship to his Pharisaic past. Where Paul himself was never fully at peace with his past life as persecutor of the church, the gentile Christian movement he helped found has continued to struggle with its Jewish past, "pursuing" Judaism in age after age, persecuting it. It is as if Christianity, the gentile heir of Paul's theological legacy, remains insecure about its non-Jewish status. Large sectors of Christianity have remained challenged by the church's tenuous relationship with its Israelite heritage and threatened by Judaism's more obvious claims to be the continuation of historic Israel. These factors have contributed to the tendency of the

Christian church, over centuries, to persecute the Jewish people.

In addition, there is a more subtle way that Christianity is haunted by Paul's struggles. Much of Christianity, especially Protestant Christianity, has been preoccupied with contrasts between "grace" and "law," "faith" and "works," Christian love and Jewish "legalism." Paul's letters have contributed to these contrasts, especially since he himself was ambivalent about his past and the significance of Jewish law. But what started as Paul's struggles with himself became—especially with influential interpretations of Paul like those of Martin Luther—a Christian belief in the absolute contrast between a grace-focused Christianity and a supposedly legalistic Judaism focused only on "works." Yet Judaism is not haunted by such a contrast between grace and works.[10] Instead, classical Judaism has stressed how Jewish obedience to Torah happens in the context of God's forgiving, saving, and sustaining love. Obedience and faith in God's grace are inherently compatible for Jews. In sum, Judaism is not afflicted with Paul's deep contradictions surrounding righteousness, works, and the law.

But Christianity, founded on Paul's conversion from his past self, is more complicated. Christianity, particularly Protestantism, has been shaped by Paul's vision of a faith-based relationship with God not founded on obedience to Torah. It remains haunted—by way of its Pauline scriptures—with Paul's struggle to repudiate the sort of zeal for the law that he once embraced.

PAUL'S SUFFERING AND THE DRIVE FOR MARTYRDOM

Paul did not just struggle with a traumatic past. He also faced challenges in his postconversion present. Shortly after the description by Paul of his disembodied heavenly ascent, he describes suffering from an enigmatic "thorn of the flesh" that led him to conclude that "power is made perfect in weakness" (2 Corinthians 12:7–10). Then there is the passage in Galatians where he sets his whole mission to Galatia in the context of suffering: "you know that it was because of a physical infirmity that I first announced the Gospel to you" (Galatians 4:13). These passages do not provide enough data to be more specific about Paul's specific ailment(s). Nevertheless, they indicate that he suffered some kind of illness(es) perceived as debilitating "weakness" by others in the church who opposed him.

In addition, as Paul worked energetically to spread the gospel, he repeatedly experienced suffering at the hands of synagogue authorities and pagan opponents of his message. The book of Acts describes Jewish leaders and pagan opponents of Paul driving him and his colleagues away (Acts 14:2; 17:5–10, 13–14), stoning him (14:19), stripping him and beating him with rods and whips, imprisoning him, and vowing to kill him (16:22–23, 21:31–32, 22:24–29, 23:2). But we need not rely only on the sometimes unreliable stories in Acts. Paul himself lists similar sufferings in his second letter to the Corinthians:

> Five times I have received from the Jews the forty lashes minus one. Three times I was beaten with rods. Once I received a stoning. Three times I was shipwrecked; for a night and a day I was adrift at sea; on frequent journeys, in danger from rivers, danger from bandits, danger from my own people, danger from Gentiles, danger in the city, danger in the wilderness, danger at sea, danger from false brothers and sisters; in toil and hardship, through many a sleepless night, hungry and thirsty, often without food, cold and naked. And, besides other things, I am under daily pressure because of my anxiety for all the churches. Who is weak, and I am not weak? Who is made to stumble, and I am not indignant? (2 Corinthians 11:23–29)

Imprisoned, whipped, beaten, stoned, shipwrecked, in constant danger and anxiety, Paul presents himself in this passage as a model of a suffering individual.

Many in Paul's Roman context, even some in his churches, were inclined to see Paul's health struggles and beatings as weaknesses that disqualified him from leadership, but Paul developed a theology focused on Christ's cross that turned these weaknesses into a strength. Repeatedly, Paul takes Christ's crucifixion as a model for his own suffering. As he puts it in Philippians, "I want to know Christ and the power of his resurrection and the sharing of his sufferings by becoming like him in his death" (3:10). In his second letter to the Corinthians, Paul is even more explicit:

> We are afflicted in every way, but not crushed; perplexed, but not driven to despair; persecuted, but not forsaken; struck down, but not destroyed; always carrying in the body the death of Jesus, so that the life of Jesus may be made

> visible in our bodies. For while we live, we are always being given up to death for Jesus' sake, so that the life of Jesus may be made visible in our mortal flesh. (2 Corinthians 4:8–11)

Some of Paul's contemporaries might have looked down on him because of his afflictions, but he maintained that his suffering body was a symbol of Christ crucified. Those who criticized him for weakness were criticizing Christ himself.

Thus Paul, interpreting his own experiences of suffering, came to see the essence of Jesus Christ in one main thing: Jesus' miraculous transformation of humiliation on the cross into ultimate glory. Early in his letter to the Philippians, Paul quotes the older Christian hymn quoted in the previous chapter, "[Jesus Christ] emptied himself, taking the form of a slave . . . humbled himself and became obedient to the point of death—even death on the cross" so that God "highly exalted him" (Philippians 2:7–9). Paul read his own life through this basic principle: glory can be achieved through humiliating suffering. Christ was the ultimate model of achieving ultimate power through ultimate weakness.

Yet it would be a mistake to believe that Paul applied this lesson only to himself. For Paul did not see Jesus' crucifixion just as a way to reinterpret his own personal shortcomings. He believed that his adoption of Jesus' suffering was a model for others. The clearest statement of this comes toward the end of Philippians, where he says, "Brothers and sisters, join in imitating me, and observe those who live according to the example you have in us" (Philippians 3:17). But there are multiple statements in 1 Thessalonians as well of the community's need to "become imitators of us [Paul and company] and of the Lord [Jesus]" (1 Thessalonians 1:6).[11]

In this way, the trauma of the cross and Paul's own trauma became a paradigm for Christian living in general. The crucifixion became part of the Christian path. And this then defined, for Paul, who was in and who was out. We see this toward the end of the letter to Philippians. On the one side were those who imitate his and Christ's suffering. On the other side were "enemies of the cross" (Philippians 3:18). The cross, the church's signal trauma, marked the divide, for Paul, between the true community of Christ's followers and everyone else.

PAUL'S CONTRADICTIONS, CHRISTIANITY'S CONTRADICTIONS

The cross-focused Jesus follower movement marked a new stage for a monotheism that, until Paul's day, had been confined to ethnic Judaism. Paul occupies a special place in the broader scope of the development of that monotheism. He is a profoundly Jewish founder of what becomes a profoundly gentile religious movement. Recall that in adopting the identity of "Israel," Judaism had its own complicated origins. The Judaism of Paul's time was built on a tenuous reidentification of itself with an "other." "Jews" were Israelites, and their most precious text, the Torah that Paul also loved, was an

Israelite text. Not only that, but this "Israelite" Judaism, in the wake of Assyrian and then Babylonian traumas, had a fundamental fissure with its non-Israelite, pagan past.

That past was its own. That past, however, had to be identified as fundamentally other, "foreign." The more this fissure was solidified in the postexilic period, the more it got reflected in preoccupation, from the beginning of the Hebrew Bible to its end, with foreigners. This is reflected even in that paradigmatic "expulsion": the divorce of foreign wives that is such a key theme in the postexilic period.

Thus Judaism found itself a religion built on a leap of identification: adopting the displaced identity of the replacement child and denying its own parental origins. Should it be any surprise that the church, Judaism's younger sibling, might not also have identity issues? That the church of Jesus would struggle profoundly with its own "foreignness"? With its own parentage?

The importance of Paul in this respect can be grasped by comparing him with another bridge figure, Hosea. Recall that Hosea is unique in Hebrew Bible as a specifically Israelite prophet, and not only that, but the prophet who introduced the idea of exclusive fidelity to God as the prime metaphor for the divine-human relationship. Looking closer, there are many ways this anticipates Paul. Much as Hosea was an "Israelite" among a people who would adopt Israelite identity along with their Judean one, so Paul is an identifiable Pharisaic Jew among a people who will adopt a semi-Jewish identity on top of their pagan one. Hosea is the father of the problem Paul aims to solve: where Hosea anticipated monotheism in his stress on the importance of (Israel) worshiping only Yahweh, Paul offers a solution to the problem in monotheism about Yahweh's relation with foreigners. The God preached by Paul offers a new relationship to non-Israelites through Jesus Christ.

Both Hosea and Paul end up stressing the all-encompassing importance of divine-human relationship characterized by certain emotions: for Hosea the love of a child to the parent, of a wife to a husband. Paul stresses a divine-human relationship of faith founded on Christ's death and resurrection. Both Hosea and Paul are passionately against something, yet each is a complicated figure to pin down, his exact targets intensely debated. Nevertheless, we can say this about what each opposed: Hosea urged a rejection of non-Yahwistic gods as foreign. Paul fought a focus by Jesus' followers on Torah observance. Post-Hosea Judaism came to see worship of other gods as idolatry. Post-Pauline Christianity came to see Torah observance—and "works of the law" more generally—as "Jewish."

Where Israelite Hosea comes to found a Judaism that fundamentally rejects its foreign heritage, Jewish Paul comes to found a Christianity that sporadically hunts down its Jewish sibling. Each is a religious formation founded partly on rejection of past attachments. As such, both forms of religious devotion are formed around a tear in the religious self. Both require the self and communities to battle and repress internal elements that threaten reattachment to a rejected past.

CHAPTER ELEVEN

The Traumatic Origins of Judaism and Christianity

BEFORE CLOSING THIS BOOK, there is one more communal trauma to be described, one that played a fundamental role in origins of religions we now call Judaism and Christianity. That trauma was the Roman destruction of Jerusalem, its Temple, and any form of Judaism focused on either. Like the earlier Babylonian destruction of Jerusalem and its Temple, this Roman devastation of Second Temple Judaism was explosive and haunting in a way that qualifies it as "traumatic" rather than just intensely painful. Before this, there was an incredible range of different types of Judaism and Jewish groups: Sadducees, Pharisees, Essenes, Gnostics, various forms of revolutionaries, Christ followers like Paul, and others. They disagreed passionately, but were loosely bound together by their varied connections to Jerusalem and its Temple.

Afterward, only two main strands of this religious matrix survived: rabbinic Judaism on the one hand and Christianity on the other. In this chapter I tell the story of how each was shaped by this trauma.

THE ROMAN DESTRUCTION OF SECOND TEMPLE JUDAISM

Like the Babylonian destruction, this Roman obliteration of early Judaism was a longer process that later came to be seen as concentrated in a single event—the destruction of Jerusalem and its Temple in 70 CE.

Ever since the Romans had seized power from the Hasmoneans, Roman rule over what it called Palestine was complicated. The first governor, an Edomite Jew named Herod, was famed for brutally attempting to secure his rule against many feared and often imagined plots. The Romans appointed a series of governors after Herod, basing many such appointments on patronage. The resulting Roman governors of Palestine were remarkable for their mediocrity and even incompetence. Notably, none is reported as holding higher office after leaving his job in Palestine, and most seem to have distinguished themselves by failures to manage relations with the often religiously charged populace.

Trouble started already in the early 40s, when the Roman emperor Caligula ordered that a statue of him be erected in Jerusalem. Later, Jews rioted over reported burning of the Torah by Roman soldiers and indecent exposure at the temple.

Finally, in 64 CE, a Roman governor, Gessius Florus, mismanaged a conflict between Jews and Greeks in the Roman capital of Caesarea. The crisis soon spiraled out of control, Gessius Florus ordered that the Jerusalem Temple treasures be seized, and the country exploded in an insurrection so powerful that Roman forces were initially expelled from the region. Emperor Nero dispatched three Roman legions to quell the rebellion, and they succeeded in retaking much of the country. But then Nero died, and the general in charge, Vespasian, paused the counterinsurgency so that he could return to Rome to seize imperial power for himself. Once Vespasian was made emperor, he commissioned his son, Titus, to return to Palestine in March 70 to finish the job of quelling the rebellion.

Eager to make Jerusalem an example, Titus did not merely lay siege to the city and starve the rebels out. Instead, he set the full power of his Roman legions into a frontal assault on the city, seizing it quickly at the cost of many extra lives of Roman soldiers.[1] Once the walls were breached, the Roman army plundered Jerusalem, burned the Temple, and decimated the city's populace. Many were killed, and thousands of survivors were sold into slavery. The Romans assumed ownership of the entire Palestinian province, seizing much of its best land from Jewish inhabitants and awarding it to Roman soldiers as a reward for their service. The major institutions of Jewish self-rule—the high priesthood of the Jerusalem Temple, the Sanhedrin council of priests and civic leaders—were dissolved and no longer held sway over the populace.[2]

We should be clear that this was not a purely local affair. Already the Jews' initially successful revolt was a threatening challenge to the Roman air of invincibility. This in part explains the direct assault on Jerusalem and subsequent Roman commemoration of the event. Coming at the outset of Vespasian's rule, the destruction of Jerusalem was a founding moment in his whole Flavian dynasty. It signified the awesome military power of Rome and the awful fate that would befall any who would defy the empire. Thus the destruction of Jerusalem was not just a calamitous event, it became a virtually mythic event in Roman ideology: the paradigmatic destruction of all who would oppose Rome.

In the aftermath of taking Jerusalem, the Romans erected an arch in Rome, still standing as "the arch of Titus," to commemorate the suppression of the Jewish revolt; it includes a famous depiction of the Roman removal of treasures from the Temple in flames, including a prominent menorah, shewbread table, and trumpets. And they printed and circulated across the realm coins with pictures of the victorious emperor Vespasian on one side and a weeping Jerusalem under a palm tree to publicize Rome's conquest to those farther abroad. As if to make the point, a Jew stands to the left of the palm tree with his hands bound behind his back. Images on coins speak louder than words in a largely illiterate populace. They were issued for a quarter century after the event, through the reign of Titus and into that of his brother Domitian.

Meanwhile, Jews scattered across the Roman Empire were increasingly seen as prototypical rebels and criminals. They

Figure 2: Judea Capta Coin. Photo from David Hendin, *Guide to Biblical Coins*, 5th ed. (New York: Amphora, 2010). Reprinted with permission.

were blamed just months after the destruction of Jerusalem for having started a fire in Antioch, one of the empire's greatest cities. Antioch's Jewish community and those of other major Roman cities then came under sustained attack by their non-Jewish neighbors. In addition, Jews across the empire were punished through the imposition of a special tax on them, a Jewish poll tax. Before this, Jewish males aged twenty to fifty, both in Israel and abroad, were obliged to pay a one-shekel tax per year to support the operations of the Jerusalem Temple. This tax united Jews near and far in common support of the Temple. Now that the Romans had destroyed that Temple, the Romans replaced the Jewish Temple tax with a two-denarii

Roman tax levied on all Jews, male, female, and children, ages three to sixty. This expanded tax, the *Fiscus Judaicus,* was then used to rebuild the great temple to Jupiter in Rome. This was a double insult to Jews. Not only did they have to pay a significant tax, but the tax funded a pagan temple.[3]

As one would expect, Jewish communities fought back at times against these local and imperial impositions. A revolt in Cypus, North Africa, and Cyrene over the years 115–17 led to the banishment of Jews from Cypus, the loss of Jewish communities across the Eastern Mediterranean, and even the devastation of the once-great Jewish community in Alexandria. Finally, there was one more major Jewish revolt in Palestine around the years 132–35 led by a figure named Bar Kochba, who claimed to be the Messiah. Once again Jewish forces successfully expelled the Roman armies from Jerusalem. But once again, this expulsion was only temporary. Emperor Hadrian sent his legions in, they wiped out Bar Kochba's forces, and a pagan temple was built on the site of the former Jewish Temple in Jerusalem. Jews were forbidden on pain of death even to set foot in Jerusalem. Circumcision, Sabbath, and Torah reading were forbidden for several years. And once again, coins were cast commemorating this further destruction of rebellious Jews.[4]

THE FORMATION OF RABBINIC JUDAISM

It is hard to fully appreciate just how devastating this whole process was to Jews and Judaism. A major part of the Jewish populace, both inside and outside Palestine, died. In addition, Jerusalem and its Temple, which had served as a central nerve center connecting the diverse diaspora communities of Jews, was gone. Jews living outside Judea, once united with one another by a common bond to Jerusalem and the common payment of a tax for the Temple, were now cast adrift. In the post-Temple age they were united only by the Torah, a common ethnic heritage, and their common obligation to pay the oppressive *Fiscus Judaicus.*

Diaspora Jews now also bore the intense hostility of their neighbors for their Judean identity and were seen as symbols of failed rebellion against Rome. They were arsonists. They were atheists, denying the imperial and other gods, and there was an ongoing suspicion that Jews might start converting others to their god-denying, "atheistic" ways. Despite all this, these large Jewish diaspora communities did not immediately fade away. For centuries we still see traces of these communities through Jewish names on epitaphs and other remains, and some grand diaspora synagogues were built well after the end of both Jewish wars with Rome.[5]

Eventually, however, much Judaism in the Jewish diaspora did fade away, whether through assimilation or through local persecution. Already just after the first Jewish rebellion the Romans shut down the centuries-old temple in Egyptian Leontopolis, set up by the Jerusalem high priest Onias when he fled the wrath of Antiochus IV and the Jewish Hellenizers of Jerusalem. The revolts of 115–17 led to the loss of Jewish communities in Cyprus, Cyrene, and possibly Alexandria. This left some diaspora Jewish communities to continue in northern

Syria (especially Antioch), Asia Minor (present-day Turkey), some cities of Greece and Rome, and areas not controlled by the Roman Empire. The Jews in these communities continued basic Jewish practices—circumcision of male infants, Sabbath, ritual immersion, following dietary laws in the Bible (not yet rabbinic kosher requirements), and wearing tefillin—but they were open to religious and cultural influences of the surrounding communities.[6]

Meanwhile, there was a core of Jews in Palestine who began to build a Jewish identity that could survive the catastrophe. Ironically, they appear to have been centered in Jabneh, a town on the coast of Judah, where the Romans had settled Jews who had surrendered to Roman forces during the first major revolt of Judah against Rome.[7] Among those who ended up at Jabneh was a rabbi named Jonathan ben Zakkai, who had defected from the defense of Jerusalem. His background is uncertain, but he seems to have alienated some fellow Jews by his opposition to the war against Rome. The Romans, however, liked Jonathan ben Zakkai enough to allow him to establish a rabbinic academy in Jabneh that started debating and making rulings on various matters of Jewish law.

Over time this rabbinic academy became a successor institution to the Sanhedrin, a council of priests, Pharisees, and other leaders that had existed in predestruction Jerusalem. This multiparty council had long served as the main recognized body by which Jews regulated their own affairs. The rabbinic academy at Jabneh, however, was defined by its rejection of past divisions that had contributed to past Jewish defeats by the Romans. To be sure, the academy was dominated by rabbis who had once been part of the popular Pharisaic movement. In this sense, rabbinic Judaism was a Pharisaic form of postdestruction Judaism. Nevertheless, it also included some Sadducees and leaders from other parts of Judaism. Most important, the members of the Jabneh academy did not emphasize their prior affiliations to various Jewish subgroups, at least not in the writings they later produced. Whatever their prior affiliations, they called themselves "the wise," and these sages began a discussion aimed at achieving group rulings on matters of Jewish law.[8]

This rabbinic academy started at Jabneh represented a new way to seek Jewish unity in a world where anti-Roman war and party divisions in Judaism had proved ruinous. Where once Jews had the Temple and the Sanhedrin as orientation points, now there was this academy of sages deliberating over the central matters of Jewish practice. These rabbis, these "wise," did not exclude any Jew on principle. The only ones they pronounced judgment on were Jewish groups—called "minim" by the rabbis—that refused to participate in the discussion and/or submit to their group opinions on the contours of Jewish law and practice. Thus was founded a tradition of rabbinic learning that started small but embraced much of Judaism in the Holy Land within a couple of centuries, and surviving Jewish communities in the diaspora a few centuries after that.

This emergent rabbinic academy developed a post-Temple form of Judaism that could survive the loss of the Temple and expulsion from Jerusalem. In this, the rabbis continued and expanded upon the religious innovations begun by their ancestors in Babylonian exile. Earlier, the exile of Jews to Babylon had forced Jews to develop a form of communal life that was not state oriented. Instead the exiled Jews in Babylonia came to understand themselves as a holy, pure people, a priesthood among nations, bound by rules of purity once applied only to priests. This nonmonarchal "Israel" of the Pentateuch was the model for the Jews in Babylon, and it proved a model that could survive the exile and subsequent centuries of life under various rulers.

Under Roman persecution this model faced an important test. Building particularly on the teachings of earlier Pharisees, these postdestruction rabbis developed a body of oral law through which post-Temple Jews could live as a pure, holy people of God. As they put it, they "built a fence around the Torah" by elaborating on laws of Sabbath, purification, diet, clothing, and other matters. These rulings ensured that Temple-less Jewish life was structured by Torah devotion. The point, of course, was not to create a huge burden of law, though some Christians persist in viewing Judaism this way. Rather, the aim was to build a life structured by God's gift of Torah.

All this was deeply connected to the Roman obliteration of Second Temple Judaism. Stephen Wilson puts it well when he says:

> Faced with a Temple in ruins, banishment from their holy city, and the disruption of everyday routines, the rabbis appear to have created, by force of will and imagination, a

> fixed point in the turning world. For in their obsessive concern with sanctification, whether in daily life or Temple cult, and in their unflagging urge to demarcate and define, they try to create a fixed, stable, and ideal universe. It is a utopia, a world fully perfected and therefore fully at rest. In a context of unpredictable chaos it is a vision of predictable order.[9]

With this new vision, came a new sense of scripture. First, one way the rabbis established a "fixed point" in the wake of Rome-inflicted chaos was by establishing the defined Hebrew Bible canon that the Hasmoneans had initiated but could never fully enforce. Postwar rabbinic Judaism was united in its focus on a group of scriptural books, variously numbered as twenty-two or twenty-four (depending on how one counts some of them), now known as the Hebrew Bible. To be sure, we see some resistance to the emerging dominance of this defined corpus of Hebrew scriptures. An apocalyptic work written just decades after the first revolt, 4 Ezra (14:38–47), implies that the twenty-four Hebrew scriptural books known to all of Judaism are just part of a broader group of important books that were revealed by God to Ezra, but kept secret by him. In making this argument, 4 Ezra is attempting to secure an ongoing privileged place for apocalyptic works like itself that are not yet seen as scripture by many Jews. This text thus testifies to the ongoing diversity of post-Temple Judaism, even as its resistance to a twenty-four-book canon of scripture bears witness to the new dominance of a clearly defined corpus of Hebrew "Torah and Prophets."[10]

In addition to affirming the prior Hasmonean canon of Hebrew scriptures, the rabbis began to compile a new set of secondary scriptures. These scriptures started not as written texts but as a body of oral legal rulings by the rabbis working at Jabneh. They called this body of legal rulings the Oral Torah, in contrast to the written Torah, Genesis–Deuteronomy, that they had inherited. Then, starting around 200 CE, specific versions of this body of oral law were transformed into stylized, written "reports" of rabbinic discussions, and these rabbinic compositions came to have a semiscriptural character of their own. We now know these post-Temple rabbinic compositions as the Mishnah, Tosefta, and two major Talmuds of classic Judaism, along with many Midrashim (collections of comments on biblical books) and other important texts.

It took centuries for this postdestruction rabbinic Judaism to become the dominant form of Judaism worldwide. In retrospect, its founders look like giants; the tradition they set in motion encompasses libraries of volumes, and their Jewish heirs number in the millions. Yet this impressive tradition has its roots in a handful of scholars and their followers working in Judean Jabneh, then Usha in Galilee, and still later in Babylon and elsewhere. These scholars had little to work with other than their mastery of Jewish biblical and other traditions that had been formed in the crucible of centuries of trauma. Eventually, the rabbinic Judaism that they founded embraced thousands and then millions of people, and it survived millennia of brutal persecution.

Survival, it should be emphasized, was not easy for post-Temple Judaism, including rabbinic Judaism. The Romans and other populations in the empire had mixed feelings about Judaism. They respected its antiquity but were deeply suspicious of Jewish particularism and rejection of other people's gods. The Roman historian Tacitus, for example, derided Jews as "the worst rascals among other peoples, renouncing their ancestral religions" and conceiving "of one god only." He goes on to assert that the earliest lesson that Jewish converts receive is "to despise the gods, to disown their country, and to regard their parents, children, and brothers as of little account."[11] From a non-Jewish perspective, such renunciation of gods constituted "atheism," and Jews in general were thought guilty of "hatred of the human race." Yet Romans like Tacitus also had a certain regard for the antiquity of Jewish religion. This led to a compromise. Jews were permitted to continue their monotheistic religious practices, thus making Judaism a form of "legalized atheism," from a Roman perspective. Jews did not even have to offer the normally required sacrifice to the emperor (which would have been unlawful to them), but were allowed to offer prayers for his welfare instead. The one condition for these privileges was this: Jews were forbidden from attempting missionary efforts that would enforce such "atheism" on others.[12]

Jews continued to be viewed with suspicion, however, especially after the wars against Rome in Palestine and various riots between them.[13] Josephus reports a couple of cases where Jewish diaspora communities were damaged by the actions of anti-Roman radicals who came into their midst. Though the leaders of the Alexandrian Jewish community executed Zealots trying to stir insurrection in their community, the Roman governor still heard of the incident and—"suspicious of the interminable tendency of the Jews to revolution"—decided to close the more than two-centuries-old Jewish temple nearby in Leontopolis.[14] Similarly, the Jews in Cyrene reported to the Romans the actions of a certain Jonathan, who had led a multitude of poor Jews into the desert, promising to show them wonders. The Roman governor there is said to have used the affair as an opportunity to kill innocent Jews and confiscate their property.[15] These stories in Josephus, if historical, illustrate the precarious situation of Jews living in the diaspora, especially in the wake of the Jewish wars. A diaspora Jewish community that found a group of suspect radicals in its midst felt very vulnerable indeed.

Nevertheless, most of the time, as long as the Jews kept to themselves, the Romans allowed them to practice what most Romans viewed as an atheistic, albeit ancient faith. The main exception to this was a three-year Roman prohibition of Jewish practice in Judah from 135 to 138 CE. This episode, however, was restricted to Judah and prompted by the Bar Kochba rebellion. Jews continued to struggle with anti-Jewish hostility and occasional deadly conflicts in the diaspora with their non-Jewish neighbors. Nevertheless, they retained a tenuous hold—despite the rebellions against Rome in 66–72 and 132–35—on Roman imperial recognition of their right to follow their ancient ways and beliefs.

THE FORMATION OF "CHRISTIANITY"

The Jesus movement found itself in a precarious position amidst this Jewish unrest inside and outside Palestine. Most churches rejected association with the emerging Pharisee-influenced, postdestruction rabbinic movement. Meanwhile, their fellow Jews had trouble recognizing Jesus Jews as Jewish, especially as more and more of them were noncircumcised, non–law observant gentiles.

Yet the Romans did not like the Jesus movement either. Indeed, Jesus Judaism represented a particularly toxic form of Judaism from the Roman perspective. Unlike other forms of Judaism, the Jesus movement focused on converting gentiles away from worship of their former gods. Its founder, Jesus, was known to have been executed as an insurrectionist by the Romans. We see these associations come together when the Roman historian Tacitus describes the scapegoating of Christians by Nero in 64 CE:

> Nero substituted as culprits and punished with the utmost refinements of cruelty, a class of men, loathed for their vices, whom the crowd styled Christians. Christus, the founder of the name, had undergone the death penalty in the reign of Tiberius, by sentence of the procurator Pontius Pilatus, and the pernicious superstition was checked for a moment, only to break out once more, not merely in Judaea, the home of the disease, but in the capital itself, where all things horrible or shameful in the world collect and find a vogue.[16]

Tacitus writes from a later time, when the term "Christian" was starting to be used for the community of Jesus followers, and his use of the term for this period is anachronistic. Nevertheless, his comments well illustrate developing Roman attitudes toward this Jesus Judaism as a "pernicious superstition" founded and named after a convicted and executed anti-Roman insurrectionist. Note the emphasis toward the end of the quotation on the dangerous spread of this particularly virulent form of Judaism. Tacitus says it was initially suppressed "only to break out once more, not merely in Judaea, the home of the disease, but in the capital itself." This concept of Christianity as disease might be imagined as "malignant monotheism." For Tacitus and other Romans like him, Christianity appears to be a form of metathesizing atheism threatening to spread rejection of ancient gods from Judah to the city of Rome itself.[17]

Meanwhile, the Jesus movement fit neither into the program of anti-Roman rebels nor into that of Jews seeking an accommodation with Rome. According to at least one tradition, church leaders abandoned Jerusalem when it was attacked by Rome, and Josephus says that hundreds of Christians were sought out and executed by the later followers of Bar Kochba during the war against Rome in 132–35. Several late-first-century writings of the church stress the importance of obeying, not resisting, Roman authorities. We can see this, for example, in the following exhortation found in 1 Peter:

> Always behave honourably among gentiles so that they can see for themselves what moral lives you lead, and when the day of reckoning comes, give thanks to God for the things which now make them denounce you as criminals. For the

> sake of the Lord, accept the authority of every human institution: the emperor, as the supreme authority, and the governors as commissioned by him to punish criminals and praise those who do good. It is God's will that by your good deeds you should silence the ignorant talk of fools. (1 Peter 2:12–15 NJV)

It is in this way—"conduct yourselves honorably," "accept authority," "good deeds"—this early Christian author aims to "silence the ignorance of the foolish."

Yet as we see from the writing of Tacitus a few decades later, the reputation of "Christians" for virulent monotheism and sedition only grew. And this—along with the increasingly gentile cast of much of the Jesus movement—led fellow Jews to either suppress Jesus missionaries like Paul or emphatically distinguish their form of Judaism from the Jesus movement.[18] Already the history of the early church in Acts includes scenes in which Paul and his companions are whipped in synagogues as punishment for their missionary activities. In the previous chapter I reviewed testimony in Paul's own writings and Acts to his suffering, often at the hands of Jewish authorities. The book of Acts also features descriptions of the imprisonment of church leaders (Acts 4:3–21, 5:17–19), execution of Stephen by stoning (6:1–7:60), and more general persecution of Jesus followers (8:1–3, 9:1–2). The stoning of Stephen seems an act of mob violence, but the beatings and other punishments were a way, sanctioned by Rome, that Jewish communities could police themselves and their own members.

In time, however, at different rates in different places, the increasingly gentile church saw itself as separate from contemporary forms of Judaism and vice versa. This probably happened earliest in the largely gentile churches in Greek cities of Asia Minor and Rome, while it occurred later in churches of Palestine and Syria. Yet especially as Judaism fragmented with the destruction of Jerusalem and its Temple, these forces separating missionary, reputedly seditious Christianity from other forms of Judaism continued to work. Christian communities increasingly understood themselves as distinct from "Judaism," while Jewish groups increasingly distanced themselves from this missionary Jewish movement designated as "Christian."[19] Whatever Torah-observant ethnically Jewish church communities survived found themselves increasingly rejected by both rabbinic Judaism and orthodox Christianity.

Oddly enough, at the very time that the Jesus movement was separating from other forms of Judaism, its theologians claimed all the more energetically that the church was the rightful heir of Judaism's famous ancient heritage. After all, the one thing that provided Judaism a small measure of protection and respect under Rome was its claim to be an ancient faith. In response, we see early Christian writers claim that the destruction of Jerusalem was God's punishment and rejection of non-Jesus forms of Judaism. In the wake of that destruction, these writers claimed, the church, not the synagogue, was the rightful claimant of Judaism's privileges in the Greco-Roman world.[20] Indeed, this impulse toward claiming Judaism's inheritance reinforced the gentile church's attachment to Judaism's ancient scriptures, the Christian "Old Testament."

For example, Ignatius, a leader of the church in Antioch in the early second century CE, claims that the prophets of the Old Testament are actually not Jewish but Christian, indeed living out Christian lives of martyrdom. On his way to his own martyrdom in Rome, he writes to one church:

> Do not be led astray by strange doctrines or by old fables, which give no profit. For if we are living until now according to Judaism, we confess that we have not received grace. For the divine prophets lived according to Jesus Christ. Therefore they were persecuted like him, being inspired by his grace, to convince the disobedient that there is one God, who manifested himself through Jesus Christ his son.[21]

This quotation is just one early example of the many ways that Christian theologians like Ignatius presented Jesus and his church as the divinely intended sequel to the story of Old Testament Israel. The church, they claimed, was the true Israel. It was not the newfangled "superstition" that Tacitus and others thought it to be. As such, the church rightfully deserved the protections Rome had historically given the Jewish people.[22]

Despite such arguments, things got worse for Jesus followers before they got better. The fact is that—despite their missionary efforts—they were a small group when compared to the millions of other types of Jews. Not only that, but church membership was increasingly dominated by non-Torah-observing gentiles who did not even consider themselves to be Jews.[23] It was a hard sell to have Jews outside the church consider these gentile communities to be "Jewish."

And existing Jewish communities across the empire had established and recognized leadership structures and connections to gentile authorities that the new Jesus Jewish movement could not compete with. The Jesus Jew movement had little hope of convincing fellow Jews or the Romans that they were the true continuation of ancient Israel.

This is where the emergent, multiparty rabbinic academy established at Jabneh ended up being more successful. Though that academy was as small a minority as the Jesus movement at its outset (perhaps more so), it was formed of known defectors from the Jewish war, probably with some kind of allowance from Rome. Thus the academy at Jabneh stood for the opposite of sedition against Rome. It advocated a vision of Judaism that was inward focused and resolutely nonproselytizing, thus cooperating with the Roman injunction against missionary "atheism." The academy's vision built on and elaborated the older Jewish idea of sanctified peoplehood, rather than replacing that idea—as Christians did—with a gentile-Jewish mix unrecognizable as "Israel" to most Jews. Over time, this rabbinic concept of post-Temple Judaism proved more attractive to fellow Jews and more acceptable to Rome than the Christian alternative. By 200 CE the Romans recognized the leader of the rabbinic academy, Judah the Prince, to be the true representative of Judaism in the land of Israel, and this was only one of the ways that rabbinic Judaism grew to be recognized as the authoritative center of post-Temple Jewish life.[24]

There was one more factor, however, that proved decisive in helping define Judaism and Christianity as separate religious movements: the poll tax levied by the Romans on Jews in the wake of the first Jewish war. This tax represented a recognition of the legality of certain kinds of Judaism (for example, rabbinic Judaism) and the potential rejection of others (increasingly, the Jesus movement). Though a financial burden and a humiliation, this tax helped define who possessed the "right" to live as monotheistic Jews and who did not. Within the Roman Empire it was one thing to be a recognized ancient faith with accepted privileges and responsibilities. It was quite another to be a newfangled religious "superstition" urging people to give up their ancestral gods and communal loyalties. Members of the recognized ancient faith were taxed and allowed to practice that faith. Advocates of community-corroding "superstitions" were liable for execution as threats to the Roman peace.

The implications of this distinction became evident during the reign of the emperor Domitian, 81–96 CE, who is said by historian Suetonius to have enforced the Jewish poll tax severely. According to Suetonius, this enforcement involved not only seeking out Jews—practicing or not—who sought somehow to avoid paying the tax. It also included prosecuting "those who, without publicly acknowledging their faith, yet lived as Jews."[25] There is much debate about who was in this latter group. Nevertheless, we have a possible clue in a quotation from another historian, Cassius Dio, who asserts that Domitian executed a prominent Roman, Flavius Clemens, and a number of others who were charged after having "drifted into Jewish ways."[26] This is the time when Romans probably started imposing a "sacrifice test" on non-Jews who were accused of taking on Jewish "atheism." The accused were required to offer a sacrifice to the emperor, anathema to Jews of all kinds, including members of the Jesus movement. Those who offered the sacrifice were considered innocent, while those who refused were executed.

Domitian's "severe" enforcement of the Jewish tax thus had two sides. On the one hand, ethnically Jewish tax evaders liable to the tax were sought out and their property confiscated. On the other hand, non-Jews, like gentile Christians, who had converted somehow to "Jewish ways" were liable to prosecution and execution. On the former side was legalized atheism with its attendant tax. On the other side was the illegal pseudo-Judaism of converts and possible death.[27]

Finally, Domitian's successor, Nerva, added a further reform to the Jewish poll tax that was to have global implications for defining Christianity and Judaism. Upon acceding to the emperorship in 96 CE, Nerva issued coins proclaiming the end to "wrongful accusation of the Jewish poll tax," and Cassius Dio reports that he released those whom Domitian put on trial for atheism. From here on out the only Jews liable for the poll tax would be those "who continued to observe their ancestral customs."[28] They paid the tax, and they enjoyed protection as Jews who were recognized by Rome. Meanwhile, non-Torah-observant Christians, whether ethnically Jewish or not, fell outside the Jewish poll tax and its implied protection.[29]

In this sense Rome now defined Christianity as non-Jewish. This probably had little effect on how Christians were actually treated. There was no widespread persecution of Christians until 250 CE, and it now appears that real incidents of local persecution of Christians were fewer than is often supposed.[30]

More important for our purposes is what Nerva's reform of the Jewish poll tax meant in redefining both Judaism and Christianity in a way that they stood as separate religions. Previously "Judaism" had been an ethnic designation, albeit one with a significant religious component. If you were a Judean—in Palestine or outside it—you were "Jewish," and that counted also for many Jewish followers of Jesus.[31] Now, however, it was not enough to be ethnically Jewish. Being "Jewish" after Nerva's reform meant following ancestral Jewish/Judean customs, Torah, with those Torah customs increasingly defined by rabbinic Judaism. Most churches of the Jesus movement fell outside this definition, since most Jesus followers by this point did not follow basic Jewish practices—circumcision of males, Sabbath, dietary rules, and so on—let alone the Torah rulings of the rabbinic academy.

So if Jesus followers were not "Jewish," what were they? Right around this time, the late first century, we first see the word "Christian" appear in written sources. This designation seems to start as an apparent term of derision used by pagans to link Jesus followers to their insurrectionist founder, Jesus Christ. Tacitus writes of how "the crowd" styled Jesus followers as "Christians," and he then mentions the reputation of "Christus" as a convicted and executed anti-Roman rebel.[32]

1 Peter 4:16 stresses that "if any one of you suffers as a Christian, do not consider it a disgrace, but glorify God because you bear this name."[33] This late-first-century comment seems to counter a presupposition in the churches that there might be "disgrace" in bearing the name of Christ.

We see a concrete example of what "the name" Christian meant in a letter exchange between Pliny, the governor of Roman provinces near the Black Sea, and emperor Trajan. Pliny asks Trajan "whether it is the name of being a Christian itself untainted with crimes, or only the crimes which cling to the name which should be punished?" Apparently Christianity had spread rapidly in his province, and Pliny had to deal with a flood of suspects accused of being "Christian," which he saw as a "debased and boundless superstition." Asking the emperor's approval, Pliny describes a process under which he gave Christians three chances to deny Christ and offer incense to the emperor. Those who refused were imprisoned and executed. Through killing those who stood by "the name" of Christ, Pliny believed he was halting "the infection of this superstition" which had spread through the towns in his district and had led to a desertion of the local temples and collapse in the market for sacrificial animals.[34] Trajan approved.

Around the time of Pliny's writings, Ignatius, the bishop of Antioch, wrote letters to churches that are among the first texts to boldly claim the name Christian and oppose that title to "Judaism." Like the accused mentioned by Pliny, Ignatius likewise had been condemned "for the name."[35] He asked prayers from the churches that he might have the fortitude to face execution and thus "not only be called a Christian, but be found one."[36] For him being Christian meant willingness to face death at the hands of the Romans rather than renounce Christ and worship the emperor.

The world, for Ignatius, had only two "coinages," or types of people. The unbelievers bear "the stamp of the world," while those "faithful in love" are willing of their own free choice "to die unto Christ's passion."[37] The prophets, Paul, and Ignatius were in the latter group, the "faithful in love," the true "Christians." They were defined as such by their willingness to proudly bear "the name" and die in following Jesus. The Romans found this willingness to be criminal "obstinacy."[38] Ignatius called this obstinacy Christian faith.

Ignatius contrasted this Christian faith with Judaism, saying, "It is ridiculous to profess Jesus Christ and practice Judaism" (Ephesians 10:3). Though conscious that Christianity had grown out of Judaism, Ignatius stressed that the church was now something different. His opposition between Christianity and Judaism reflects a new development in the church. The Jesus movement had been drifting away from the rest of Judaism for some time, especially as its membership grew more and more gentile. But Ignatius is among the first to emphatically embrace the outsider label, Christianity, and contrast this Christianity with Judaism, understood as a separate religion.

Ignatius is an important figure because he embodies two interlocked trends in the emergence of Christianity as a religion—an embrace of martyrdom as a Christian attribute and an understanding of Christianity as a religion distinct from Judaism. Just years before Ignatius's letters, Nerva's empire-wide reform of the Jewish poll tax had legally distinguished Jews who "continue to follow the customs of their forefathers" from others, particularly Christians, who did not. This empire-wide definition of true Judaism, combined with the growing pagan identification of the Jesus movement as non-Jewish Christianity, encouraged a global separation of Judaism from Christianity that would have taken longer to occur by purely local dynamics.[39] And the more Christianity was separated from Rome-sanctioned Judaism, the more Christian believers like Ignatius were exposed to potential prosecution. Taking up the cross of Christ, many like Ignatius embraced and even sought out this specifically Christian risk of execution.

Thus we see two religions emerge from the early Judaism that preceded Roman trauma: rabbinic Judaism and an increasingly gentile Christianity. Rabbinic Judaism is built on concepts of holy peoplehood that originated in Judah's earlier, exilic trauma. It proved amazingly resilient, not just in the face of Roman trauma, but in helping the Jewish people confront and survive centuries of later gentile persecution of Judaism. Meanwhile, the gentile church proved incredibly successful in its missionary efforts. Initially, just a tiny, messianic movement in Judaism, Christians eventually formed a substantial part of the population of the late Roman Empire, significantly larger than rabbinic Judaism and any other forms of Judaism that survived the Jewish wars. In this sense the

Romans were right to fear that Christianity might end up replacing traditional local and imperial religion. In time, it did. Though there were some last-ditch attempts by the Roman Empire to stamp out Christianity once and for all in 249–51, 257, and especially 303–11 CE, they all failed. The edict of Galerius in 311 established official toleration of Christianity by the Roman Empire. Constantine, the emperor of the Roman Empire from 306 to 337, converted to Christianity and helped issue the Edict of Milan in 313, which returned Christian property confiscated in earlier persecution. By 380 Christianity was declared the official religion of the Roman Empire. Now the power of the Roman state, once used to try to eliminate Christian "atheism," was turned against the non-Christian cults that Christian monotheism rejected. Judaism, as before, enjoyed an uneasy protection of its status as a tolerated religion in the empire, even as Jews remained vulnerable to local disturbances.

Reasonable questions can be raised about whether Christianity at this or other points truly was "monotheistic." It recognized a trinity of aspects in its godhead—Father, Son, and Holy Ghost—not to mention the cult of the Virgin Mary and numerous other saints, martyrs, and other holy figures. But Christianity was monotheistic in the main sense that mattered in the ancient world: it emphatically rejected worship of gods other than its own. This was no mere disagreement with another ethnic group, rejecting that group's gods as part of inner-group conflict. No, this was the church's inheritance from the Hosean revolution, in which the Israelite prophet, Hosea, responding to Assyrian trauma, urged his people to worship Yahweh alone and reject all other deities. Judah took over this revolution under Josiah's reform, and the exiles in Babylon took it a step farther—believing that there was no other real god in the universe to worship than Yahweh.

This monotheism took different forms in the different religions that survived the destruction of Second Temple Judaism. Some forms of Judaism in the diaspora seem to have come to some kind of accommodation with other people's worship of God, even adopting a Greek translation of the command in Exodus 22:27 "not to revile God" as "you shall not revile the gods"—now understood as a command to respect deities worshiped by other peoples.[40] As a generally nonproselytizing religion, rabbinic Judaism developed its own forms of acceptance of non-Jewish forms of life and worship. Christianity, however, ended up enforcing a harder version of god-rejecting monotheism. Not only did it insist that its converts disassociate themselves from anyone else's idol worship, but when it became the religion of the Roman Empire, it began to suppress all forms of non-Jewish religion. This suppression was not immediately successful, and it only affected areas covered by the severely reduced late Roman Empire.

Rome turned out to be right in its fears of Christianity. Early on Romans had criticized and even prosecuted Jesus followers like Ignatius for promoting a "debased superstition," an "infection," a form of "atheism" that threatened worship of traditional gods. Unlike Judaism, which kept to itself, Christianity thus represented a particularly virulent form of monotheism, one with potential to infect the rest of the Empire. And, as it turned out, the infection did spread. Local executions of Christians like Pliny's, and more global persecutions, like Diocletian's Great Persecution in 303–11, could not stem the tide of Christian expansion. By 313, less than three hundred years after Jesus' crucifixion, Christian "atheism" was triumphant and Roman "paganism" was on the decline.

The religious world we now see in the West is the product of these massive shifts. The Romans thought they could end the Jesus movement by crucifying its founder. They thought they had permanently neutralized Judaism by destroying Jerusalem, removing Jews from Judah and making Judaism an example of a failed rebellion. Later, individual governors like Pliny and emperors like Diocletian executed Christians as representatives of a dangerous, malignant form of monotheistic "atheism." All these efforts, all the bloodshed and communities destroyed, did the opposite of what Rome intended. Out of all this trauma came two religions, rabbinic Judaism and Christianity, that would outlast Roman imperial rule by fifteen hundred years. Rome, at least initially, had superior powers of violence on its side, powers that it used to put down Jewish revolts and suppress Christianity. Judaism and Christianity, in contrast, could build on a heritage of centuries of survival of trauma—Assyrian, Babylonian, and

Hellenistic. It was Judaism and Christianity that continued into the millennia that followed, with Christianity eventually becoming the religion of the empire and acquiring powers of state violence for itself. The Romans ultimately did not stand a chance.

CHAPTER TWELVE

The Posttraumatic Gospel

THE NEW TESTAMENT GOSPELS show how the story of Jesus was reshaped in the decades after the Roman destruction of Jerusalem, during the very time that the church was increasingly seen by Rome as a criminal form of Judaism.

This perspective requires a reorientation in how many view the Christian gospels. According to tradition, they were written by eyewitnesses to Jesus' life, his own apostles and associates—Matthew, Mark, Luke, and John. Yet biblical scholars concluded more than a century ago that this is unlikely. Though these gospels definitely include early traditions, they look back on Jesus' life from the perspective of the later, postapostolic church. They tell his story through the lens of the destruction of the Jerusalem Temple, Christians' alienation from other forms of Judaism, and pagan targeting of Christians as an unusually dangerous form of missionary monotheism. They rewrite the story of Jesus, in other words, in the wake of Roman trauma.

To be sure, some believe that we have access to pretraumatic narratives about Jesus. Scholars have long known of ancient Christian gospels excluded from the Bible, and this awareness was expanded by the find in the 1970s of a library of noncanonical texts in the Egyptian desert town of Nag Hammadi, texts written in Coptic (a late form of Egyptian written with Greek letters). Some have argued that these texts, though copied centuries after Jesus, preserve earlier traditions about him than the biblical gospels do. In some cases, such as the Gospel of Thomas (which is also partially preserved in early Greek copies), a good case can be made that noncanonical texts occasionally preserve earlier traditions than those in the Bible. Nevertheless, the present form of these excluded gospels is generally later than the gospels preserved in the New Testament. Overall, the biblical gospels represent our earliest complete examples of how Jesus followers came to write down the story of Jesus—his life, crucifixion, and resurrection.

Of those biblical gospels, the Gospel of Mark is generally agreed to be the earliest.[1] It is the shortest of the biblical gospels, and it is dominated by Roman trauma. In the Gospel of Mark we can see early stages of the Jesus movement's grappling with the reality of Jesus' crucifixion, along with the Roman destruction of Jerusalem and increasing violence against Christians. As the earliest complete gospel, Mark establishes models for dealing with these traumas that appear in other New Testament gospels as well.

THE TRAUMA OF CRUCIFIXION

To start, as previously mentioned, Mark's gospel preserves an earlier "crucifixion narrative" that describes Jesus' end in a relatively raw, unprocessed way: Jesus pleads in the garden of Gethsemane for God to let him avoid death, his disciples abandon and betray him, he is tried by Jewish leaders and the Roman governor, flogged, and crucified. We cannot know the exact scope of this pre-Markan crucifixion narrative, but one thing is clear: it depicts Jesus as an ambivalent victim of betrayal, trial, flogging, and death. Unlike the heroic victims seen in other tales of noble death, this Jesus is silent when interrogated by the Romans. Instead of offering an elevated speech as he dies, Jesus in this "crucifixion narrative" cries out, "My God, my God why have you forsaken me?"

Mark's gospel prefaces this early account of the trauma of Jesus' death with a new story of his earlier life, a story in which Jesus anticipates and fully accepts his crucifixion. As one scholar famously said, "The Gospel of Mark is a passion narrative [crucifixion narrative] with prologue."[2] Though Mark preserves the earlier crucifixion narrative, in which Jesus is an ambivalent victim, it now features a lead-up to that narrative, chapters 1–13, which portray Jesus as a powerful hero who willingly accepts death for others. According to this new Markan "prologue," Jesus' disciples and the surrounding crowds were mistaken in believing that Jesus was on a straight path to messianic kingship. Instead, Jesus himself knew from the outset that he could enjoy divine glory only on the other side of dying for others. He chose and embraced that destiny.

Mark's picture of Jesus as a misunderstood hero begins with chapters focused on Jesus' divine power. This starts with the announcement of Jesus' arrival by John the Baptist, a prophet-like figure who predicts the coming of someone "more powerful than I" (Mark 1:1–8). Jesus then appears on the scene, John baptizes him with water, and God's voice from heaven booms out to Jesus, "You are my Son, the Beloved, with you I am well pleased" (1:9–11). Thus starts a series of stories in which Jesus battles demons, heals sick people, and announces the coming "kingdom of God"(1:12–3:6). At every stage he is victorious and proves that he is the "stronger man" (*isxuroteros*) predicted by John the Baptist. Yet even this early in the gospel we see a foreshadowing of Jesus' ultimate destiny of trial and death. After Jesus heals a man with a withered hand on the Sabbath, Mark's gospel tells us, "The Pharisees went out and conspired with the Herodians against him, how to destroy him" (3:6). This quotation anticipates stories later in Mark's gospel of Jewish leaders' plotting to have Jesus killed through Roman execution.

The specific Jewish leaders whom this quotation blames for Jesus' death, the Pharisees, are the scholar-founders of later rabbinic Judaism. This is another clue to the vantage point from which Mark's gospel was written. The Pharisees were a popular group in Jesus' time, but they were not as dominant as Mark's gospel makes them appear. In the Gospel of Mark—except for the early crucifixion narrative—they are Jesus' constant opponents, trying to trip him up with questions and planning for his death (Mark 2:16, 18, 24; 3:1–6; 7:1–5; 8:11, 15; 10:2; 12:13–15). In this way the late-first-century author of the Markan prologue to the crucifixion narrative anticipates his later situation—after the destruction of the Second Temple—in which Jesus' followers and the former Pharisee leaders of rabbinic Judaism are competing with each other for the claim to be the true heirs of Second Temple Judaism. The author injects the opponents of the church in his time—Pharisees—into the story leading up to Jesus' crucifixion.

By chapters 8–10 of Mark's gospel Jesus himself begins predicting his impending death. He still performs great miracles and offers teachings. But he baffles his disciples by announcing, three times, that he will be crucified. His final prediction occurs just as he is about to enter Jerusalem. Jesus tells his disciples, "See, we are going up to Jerusalem, and the Son of Man will be handed over to the chief priests and the scribes, and they will condemn him to death; then they will hand him over to the Gentiles [Romans]; they will mock him, and spit upon him, and flog him, and kill him; and after three days he will rise again." By this point Jesus, as depicted in Mark, has predicted virtually every element of the coming crucifixion narrative—including betrayal, flogging, mocking, and crucifixion. Yet at every stage Jesus' disciples—as depicted in Mark—still see Jesus as a king-to-be, on a straight path to heavenly glory.

On one level this just looks like a story about Jesus and his confused disciples. It is hard not to read it as a simple historical account. Yet a closer look reveals the gospel's deeper agenda. Its author aims to counter what he sees as misconceptions about Jesus and his true glory. Yes, the crowds flocked to Jesus for healing and teaching. Yes, Jesus' disciples themselves thought him to be a Messiah figure destined to defeat the Romans. Yet the gospel depicts both groups as fundamentally misunderstanding Jesus' real identity and destiny. According to Mark's gospel, Jesus himself long anticipated his death on a cross. His was no traumatic ending of a life. It was a voluntary death suffered by a divinely empowered hero.

In this way the Gospel of Mark offers a distinctive, late-first-century perspective on Jesus' death. It is built, to be sure, on earlier traditions. The gospel's author apparently knew older sayings and stories about Jesus. Nevertheless, he selected and expanded on those traditions to reframe the story of Jesus' crucifixion. The result is the first extended story of Jesus preserved in the New Testament, the first written "gospel," the biblical book of Mark.

This book reframed and countered the traumatic event of the cross, mostly by presenting a powerful Jesus who anticipated and accepted his crucifixion, with his disciples confused by his predictions of resurrection. The earliest version of the book, however, ended suddenly—with an empty tomb, the angel's prediction that the disciples would see Jesus back home in Galilee, and three women too frightened to report this prediction to anyone else. This ending only faintly anticipated the resurrection, still preserving some of the sting of the traumatic loss of Jesus. The gospels of Matthew, Luke, and John remedied this ending by adding stories about disciples actually seeing the resurrected Jesus, from Matthew's and Luke's reports of the disciples' meetings with Jesus to John's account of Jesus meeting Mary at his tomb and later allowing the disciple Thomas to touch his wounds.[3] By including these resurrection stories, these later gospels countered the shame of crucifixion with the glory of triumph over death.[4]

In saying this, I am not suggesting that these authors invented the story of Jesus' resurrection to lessen the impact of crucifixion. References to the resurrection in Paul and other early writings indicate that Jesus Jews talked from an early point about encounters with Jesus on the other side of crucifixion. What is different here is that such (earlier) traditions were added to the end of an early crucifixion narrative that lacked them. As such, these additions reflect the ongoing struggle of Jesus followers to place the trauma of Jesus' crucifixion into a broader framework.

Eventually, some later Christians even added parts of these resurrection stories to the gospel of Mark itself, producing expanded versions of Mark that ended with resurrection scenes rather than an empty tomb. These versions of Mark—like the gospels of Matthew, Luke, and John—moved farther and farther away from confrontation with the trauma of crucifixion. Perhaps because of this, copies of expanded versions of Mark eventually outnumbered copies of the shorter version.

All this is an oblique testimony to the abiding trauma of Jesus' crucifixion. Mark adds an extended prologue to the story of Jesus' death, and later gospels (and editions of Mark) expand on the ending. But the crucifixion remains, and its power is reflected in the efforts of later Christians to reframe it. In the very process of trying to deal with the reality of Jesus' death, the authors of Mark and later gospels revealed its lingering force.

THE TRAUMA OF JERUSALEM'S DESTRUCTION

Even as the Gospel of Mark grapples with the trauma of Jesus' death decades earlier, it preserves echoes of more recent trauma as well—the Roman destruction of Jerusalem. In the story world of Mark, that destruction lies in the future for Jesus and the disciples. We read that Jesus came to Jerusalem, went to its Temple, and argued with its leadership. Yet here again we must remind ourselves that the book of Mark was written decades after Jesus' death. Its author could look back on the destruction of Jerusalem and relate it to the death of Jesus. Writing from this later perspective, the author of Mark depicted a Jesus who opposed the Temple and predicted its destruction in the days leading up to his own crucifixion.

This depiction starts in chapter 11 of Mark. We read here that Jesus visited the Temple and overturned the tables of the moneychangers and those who sold doves to poor people for sacrifice (Mark 11:15–17). The author of Mark did not invent this tradition, which is preserved in another form in the Gospel of John (2:13–22).[5] Nevertheless, he uses this story in a unique way. He places it at the outset of Jesus' final visit to Jerusalem, making it the first stage of Jesus' confrontation with Jerusalem's leadership. In addition, Mark's account of this episode concludes with Jesus accusing the moneychangers and dove sellers of having turned God's Temple into a "den of bandits." According to the author of Mark, this is what prompted "the chief priests and scribes" to start trying to "destroy" Jesus. Having heard of what he did at the Temple, these Jewish authorities were worried that Jesus' anti-Temple teaching was too appealing to the crowds surrounding him (Mark 11:17–18).

Chapters 12 and 13 in Mark then describe the unfolding conflict between Jesus and Jerusalem's authorities. This starts as Jesus tells a "parable of the vineyard" that predicts the end of the priests and scribes who oppose him. Building on an Old Testament prophecy in which Isaiah predicted God's destruction of Jerusalem's leadership for poorly tending God's vineyard/people (Isaiah 5:1–7), Mark's Jesus implies that the current leadership of Jerusalem is equally guilty of mistreating God's vineyard. In veiled language he implicitly describes the Temple leadership as evil "servants" who take over God's vineyard and kill those whom God sends to the vineyard, including Jesus. This, the gospel implies, is why these Temple leaders were to be destroyed by the Romans decades later. Its Jesus announces that God, the vineyard owner, "will destroy the servants and give the vineyard to another." Next, at the outset of chapter 13, Jesus predicts the destruction of Jerusalem's Temple. The disciples are exclaiming over the greatness of the Temple complex, saying to Jesus, "Teacher, look at the size of the stones, what huge buildings!" To this Mark's Jesus responds, "See these great buildings? Not one of their stones will be left on top of another. They all will be pulled down."

This is how the Gospel of Mark anticipates the signal trauma of Second Temple Judaism: the destruction of the Jerusalem Temple and its leadership. Before that destruction, various forms of Judaism, the Jesus movement included, were joined by having some kind of link to the Temple. To be sure, some groups, such as the church or the Qumran community, were critical of the Jerusalem Temple. Nevertheless, even these Jews were joined to others by having an orientation, positive or negative, to an existing Temple in Jerusalem.

When the Temple was destroyed, that common orientation point was lost, and these chapters in Mark reflect that loss. They show Christians beginning to drift apart from the rest of Judaism. For them, the Temple's destruction was no tragedy to be mourned. It was God's just punishment of the corrupt leadership of Jerusalem. And the book of Mark projects this perspective back into the Jesus story. According to it, Jerusalem was destroyed for one main reason: because Jewish leaders (the evil "tenants") killed Jesus (the vineyard owner's son).

Thus, at least for the author of this text, Judaism's trauma at the hands of the Romans was not Christianity's trauma. This differential impact of trauma is a major mark of an emergent split between followers of Jesus and other parts of Judaism. Rabbinic Judaism, for example, never lost its deep bond with the Jerusalem Temple.[6] Not so for Christianity. These stories in Mark of Jesus are just the first of numerous Christian polemics against the Temple. As mentioned before, later Christian theologians used the Temple's destruction as proof of God's rejection of Judaism and embrace of the Christian church as God's true people, a new "Israel."

In this way Mark stands as a founding document for a post-Jewish Christian church. When the authors of Matthew and of Luke–Acts adapted Mark's story, they took up that book's critical attitude toward Temple leadership and prediction of the Temple's destruction. On the one hand, they emphasized even more the links between Jesus and the Old Testament, undergirding the church's claim to be the true heir of Israel's heritage. On the other hand, they stigmatized other Jews even more, with Matthew's Jesus accusing scribes and Pharisees of being "snakes," "a brood of vipers," and John's Jesus calling Jews "children of the devil" (John 8:44). In all four gospels, Jesus and his disciples' destiny is *not* the destiny of Jerusalem or that of the Pharisaic leadership of rabbinic Judaism.

THE TRAUMA OF PERSECUTION OF JESUS FOLLOWERS

The destiny of Jesus' disciples, however, is hardly one of immediate glory. Instead, much of Mark's gospel anticipates ways that Jesus' later followers would suffer rejection and even death. This message comes early and is repeated every time Jesus predicts his crucifixion. In the very first such announcement, Jesus rebukes Peter for having resisted Jesus' prediction of his own crucifixion and then goes on to predict that Peter and the other disciples will suffer a similar end:

> If any want to become my followers, let them deny themselves and take up their cross and follow me. For those who want to save their life will lose it, and those who lose their life for my sake, and for the sake of the gospel, will save it. (Mark 8:34–35, paralleled in Matthew 16:24–25 and Luke 9:23–24)[7]

Harsh words, anticipating a harsh time. But his disciples don't seem to get the idea. Mark repeatedly shows the disciples anticipating glory for Jesus and themselves. Each time Jesus predicts his own crucifixion and announces that his followers must be ready to suffer the same. Finally, in chapter 13 of Mark, Jesus specifically predicts that his followers will be condemned and flogged in synagogues for their proselytizing ("They will hand you over to Jewish councils and you will be beaten in synagogues"), and will be tried in provincial Roman courts ("And you will stand before governors and kings because of me as a testimony [Greek *martyrion*] to them" [Mark 13:9]). Mark's Jesus even predicts how his later followers will be condemned because of Jesus' "name" (recall Pliny and Ignatius in the last chapter), saying, "You will be hated by all because of my name," reassuring them that "the one who endures to the end will be saved" (Mark 13:13).

Though traditionalists attribute sayings like Mark 13:13 to the Jesus of history, the passage contains clear clues to its later authorship. The Jewish Jesus who lived in first-century Palestine would not have described Roman prosecution of "Christians" as being "hated by all on account of my name." In Jewish Palestine, his name was Jesus, and his title was Messiah. It is only in gentile Christianity that Jesus comes to be known as Christ, the Greek translation of Messiah. Only in later Gentile Christianity would Christ/Christian become the "name" on account of which Jesus followers would be "hated."

In this way and others Jesus' speech in Mark 13 is a post-Jesus statement developed by Mark's author to reinterpret violence against Christians in his own time. Synagogue beatings were a way Jewish communities (like other Greco-Roman groups) undermined the honor of those they judged. Christians of Mark's time faced societal exclusion at the least ("You will be hated by all because of my name") and Roman death-penalty prosecution at the most ("You will stand before governors and kings for my sake"). Some later Christians facing these troubles might have doubted themselves and their movement. But Mark's picture of Jesus, a picture possibly informed by Paul's earlier adoption of the cross as a model for Jesus followers, reassures later Christians that their suffering was anticipated by Jesus. Jesus was crucified, but was risen. So also, they need not fear. Though they suffer in following Jesus' path to the cross, they will be rewarded. Jesus will return "in power and glory" as "the son of Man" to gather his chosen ones (Mark 13:26–27).

Mark's gospel, then, set the pattern for other gospel depictions of the disciples' destiny to take up Jesus' cross and die for the sake of his name. In this respect, Matthew and Luke adapted and expanded on Mark's gospel, though Luke implicitly softens Jesus' command from a potential literal "taking of a cross" to a metaphorical "take up your cross daily"(Luke 9:23). This theme of self-sacrifice is present as well in the Gospel of John, where Jesus calls on his disciples to "lay down one's life for one's friends" (John 15:13).

This became the authorized version of the Christian story, the written gospel. Not only did Jesus—as depicted in these gospels—anticipate his own death on the cross, but he called on his followers to share his fate, to "lay down [their lives] for [their] friends," to "take up [their] cross[es]." The rest of the New Testament reinforces this message. The history of the early church in the book of Acts starts with a story of the killing of Stephen and continues with accounts of the imprisonment and whipping of Paul and others for preaching the gospel. Paul in his letters speaks of how Christians "are handed over to death, on account of Jesus, so that the life of Jesus may also be visible in our body" (2 Corinthians 4:11, NJV adapted). A later writer in the name of Peter tells churches that "this is a credit to you if . . . you endure pain while suffering unjustly . . . because Christ also suffered for you, leaving you an example, so that you should follow in his footsteps" (1 Peter 2:19, 21).

The New Testament thus starts and ends with suffering. It begins with four gospel stories of Jesus focused on his cross and resurrection, and on the destiny of his disciples to follow him. It continues with Paul's and others' letters, many of which call on Jesus' followers to embody his crucifixion in their lives. And it concludes with the apocalyptic vision of the book of Revelation. If there is any book in the New Testament that both reflects trauma and enjoins Christians to endure it, it is the book of Revelation. Its author writes from island banishment to communities dealing with death and rejection. He presents a gruesome vision of God's devastating destruction of Rome ("the great whore Babylon") and God's reward of the Christian righteous. Reading this vision, Jesus followers could trust that any suffering they faced was temporary. Rome might seem triumphant, but its victory—according to Revelation—was illusory. Revelation predicts God's imminent victory over all any forces threatening contemporary Christians.[8]

REPEATING THE CROSS

This was powerful medicine for the early church. Nothing could keep them down. Punishment would not discourage them, but would spur them on. Martyrdom was the greatest form of love.

Though Christians dealt only with sporadic violence from opponents in Judaism and the Roman authorities, all dealt with the endemic suffering characteristic of life in the Roman world. Epitaphs and magical spells from the time chronicle the frequent struggles of people with sickness, starvation, and loss. Even more than today, everyday people yearned for "salvation" from basic threats to their lives, health, and livelihood. Christians told a story about a founder who had suffered the worst form of Roman execution and survived it. Not only that, but this founder called on his followers to follow his path through crucifixion to resurrection. In Mark, Jesus says, "Those who lose their life for my sake and for the sake of the gospel will save it" (8:35). Later he says, "The one who endures to the end will be saved" (13:13). Salvation, for this Jesus, comes not by running from suffering but by moving through it. The New Testament gospels are not explicit on how this happens. They just insist that it does. Jesus' cross and resurrection is contagious for his followers. This message had and has a lasting relevance. In an ancient world of widespread suffering and trauma, Jesus' path through trauma represented a powerful vision of salvation.

Yet though the message of Jesus' cross and resurrection has helped many, many people, I also find myself thinking of studies that describe traumatized survivors who must compulsively repeat their traumatizing event. Adult survivors of sexual abuse find themselves seeking out abusive lovers. War veterans come home and are drawn to occupations that expose them to more violence. Might there be some ways that Christians, from the beginning, sometimes have taken this crucifixion tradition to excess? Actually seeking out, and not just enduring, various forms of violence? What about contexts in which one does not just reinterpret violence but inflicts extra violence on oneself?

Over time, some church leaders strongly encouraged their followers to seek out martyrdom, and early Christianity was plagued with movements (for example, Donatists and Circumcellions) that rejected church leaders who had avoided martyrdom through collaboration. Neither other Jewish groups nor the Romans systematically persecuted Christian groups in the first two centuries of Christian existence, but that did not stop militant Christians from seeking out chances to "take up their cross" and die on behalf of their faith. Already toward the end of the first century, we find a bishop, Clement, objecting to the glee with which some Christians were seeking out chances to die for the faith:

> We . . . say that those who have rushed on death (for there are some, not belonging to us, but sharing the name merely, who are in haste to give themselves up, the poor wretches dying through hatred to the Creator)—these, we say, banish themselves without being martyrs, even though they are punished publicly.[9]

This enthusiasm for martyrdom, however, did not go away. In later centuries we see the flowering of a whole Christian literature of martyrdom, with story after story celebrating earlier martyrs as examples to be emulated: the Martyrdom of Polycarp, the Martyrs of Lyons, the Passion of Perpetua and Felicity, and the like. Many such stories, to be sure, were fabricated or embellished to build a picture of heroic sacrifice. Yet their effect on subsequent Christianity was nonetheless real.

These martyrdom legends described Christians who did not just endure but sought out and welcomed persecution. They subjected themselves to horrific violence that could have been avoided. In this way, the trauma of Jesus' crucifixion repeated itself across the history of Christian tradition, so that some among his followers almost compulsively subjected themselves to the sort of violence that had killed Christianity's founder.

I raise this because I think some such dynamics continue today. To be sure, Christians are not subject to bodily abuse in most parts of the contemporary world, though there certainly are some locations where Christians face serious suffering for openly practicing their religion. Nevertheless, there are a lot of subtle ways in which the scriptural tradition around the cross still encourages Christians to embrace and even seek out suffering that otherwise would be avoidable. Women suffering abuse by their spouses are told by pastors that the abuse is "their cross to bear." And Christians under fire for their politics readily portray themselves as suffering for their faith, even in cases where they wield substantial power over the political process. For example, Rush Limbaugh's younger brother, David Limbaugh, wrote a 2003 book, *Persecution: How Liberals Are Waging War Against Christianity*, and Rick Santorum portrayed himself as persecuted when facing liberal criticism during his 2011 campaign for comments that he had made about homosexuality.[10]

This ongoing "martyr complex" in Christianity takes us back, I argue, to the traumatic origins of the Christian crucifixion tradition. Yes, the Christian transformation of Jesus' crucifixion helped ensure the community's survival. But there may also be ways that Christian crucifixion fixation can have pathological dimensions to it, leading to traumalike compulsive repetition of suffering. In individuals, a first step in guarding against such compulsive repetition is in seeing its origins more clearly. I suggest that Christians would benefit from taking a closer look at the origins of the Christian tradition of martyrdom. Rather than just being a "given" in the Christian tradition, the tradition of martyrdom could be seen as a way that the Jesus movement, from its very outset, has been and is haunted by Roman-inflicted trauma.

The point here is that Jesus' crucifixion is not over. Not everywhere. Not forever. Even as some try to turn it into triumph, there are others who repeat it, in some form, over again. The Christian martyr tradition diminished after the early centuries, especially after Christianity became the religion of Rome, but it never died out completely. And the martyr tradition has continued across Judaism and especially Islam in subsequent centuries. Sometimes, of course, the idea of "taking up one's cross" has provided crucial comfort to suffering people. For them, it is reassuring to think that their loss was anticipated in some way by Jesus' suffering. To feel as if in experiencing life's worst agony, Jesus has walked before them and they are following his path and will find a way forward like he did. At the same time, the martyr tradition, nurtured in part by Christian traditions around Jesus, has led to more suffering. Today we see particularly virulent forms of the martyr tradition in Muslim suicide bombers, "martyred" in the process of killing many others.

The constant, once again, is trauma.

Epilogue

SO WHERE DOES THIS LEAVE US? At the end of a course on Bible and Trauma, one of my students said, "I feel after this course like someone who grew up in a town where all the buildings were knocked down by an earthquake and thought that is the way all buildings were supposed to look." We take a lot of things for granted in a culture dominated by what is often called the Judeo-Christian tradition. Many dimensions of our culture, ones many of us assume are "normal," were formed by ancient communal traumas.

More specifically, Western culture carries ideas and symbols that helped ancient communities survive their traumas. If there is anything like "survival of the fittest" culture, the religions of Judaism and Christianity would qualify as among the religions that have won that competition. Where more glorious myths of more powerful nations faded away with those empires, the Jewish concept of a holy people persisted into the present and also became a founding element of the Christian church.

All three major religions that emerged out of early Judaism—rabbinic Judaism, Christianity, and Islam, all of them—are focused in a unique way on a clearly bounded scripture and unusually affected by trauma through the traumatic formation of that scripture and later tradition. Like Judaism and Christianity, Islam was shaped by its own traumas, whether the forced and yet formative move of Mohammed from Mecca to Medina, the series of traumas that are founding moments of Shia Islam, or other parts of the Muslim martyrological tradition. Of course, every religion relates in some way to trauma. It is a part of human experience. Nevertheless, when I have consulted experts in other religious traditions, the feedback from them so far has been that Judaism, Christianity, and Islam are unusual in the extent to which they were founded on trauma and survival of it.

Throughout this book I've trod a fine line in talking about this dimension of religion. On the one hand, my work can come off as mere religious self-promotion if I emphasize only the positive: how the traumatic background of Jewish and Christian scriptures enables them to help people suffering from traumas of their own. On the other hand, especially given the long history of Christian anti-Semitism, it is all too easy for a book about traumatic origins of Western religion to sound like one more Christian attempt to paint Judaism as pathological.

In particular, one thing I've often heard in response to my work is an attempt to use it to criticize contemporary Zionism. When I have presented this work to some progressive Christian audiences, they often argue that the state of Israel exemplifies how a community reacts to its trauma through becoming a perpetrator and imposing trauma on others. And this tendency is not confined to Christian audiences.[1]

As I have continued to think about this work, I certainly agree that there are ways that both Judaism and Christianity may be negatively shaped by trauma. This can include ways in which Judaism and Israeli politics (which are related, but not identical) have been negatively affected. But I think Christians like me need to be especially careful to work closely with Jewish counterparts in shaping our thought about such issues and preventing a recurrence of age-old Christian polemics against Jewish election, legal observance, attachment to the land of Israel, and other core elements of Judaism.

Meanwhile, the impact of trauma on Christianity is not necessarily all to the good. My last chapter includes discussion of how the Christian institutionalization of trauma sometimes has contributed to more suffering. So also, in the chapter on Paul I discuss ways that Christianity's displaced traumatic identity has contributed to its centuries-long antipathy toward Judaism, an antipathy that has led to the deaths and suffering of millions of Jews. And there is certainly more that could be said on this topic.

I do not want to end on that note. After all, especially in an ever more secularized West, it is all too easy to caricature and critique religion. Fewer people than ever attend church regularly. Belief in God is on the decline. And traditional religions like Judaism and Christianity are particularly prone to societal ridicule. There is little revolutionary any more about attacking the Bible, Judaism, or Christianity. Certainly not in contexts like my own in New York City, or in the broader media environment.

Yet this work on Bible and trauma has given me new appreciation for ancient wisdom in Judaism and Christianity. Trauma can lead to deeper wisdom about the actual character of the world and life in it. A number of studies have shown that people who have a more pessimistic view of the world often prove more accurate in predicting actual outcomes than people who have an optimistic view.[2] Pessimism is not exactly survival of trauma, but trauma can teach awareness of the fact that life involves random suffering. Those who have survived trauma have learned how their assumptions about the world can break apart and how they can suddenly experience a totally unexpected reality.

As we have seen here, authors of Jewish and Christian scriptures sometimes even called that other, trauma-producing reality "God." And here is the most revolutionary element: this traumatizing God they encountered was not just some evil deity in a broader pantheon including good gods. Jewish and Christian scriptures testify that the God who caused the community's deepest suffering was the very same God who loved them and would eventually lead them out of suffering. The God of the wilderness wandering and disaster is also the

God who will lead the people into the land. The God who demands crucifixion also brings resurrection. This kind of devotion to a devastating God does not appeal to many people now, especially in a religious marketplace with more comforting pictures of God and/or limited ideas of how God affects reality. But this idea has persisted and remains compelling to many now because of the way it helps them interpret the worst experiences life has to offer. Those inclined to ridicule the idea of a powerful, violent God—whether Jewish or Christian—might well defer their disdain until they encounter someone for whom that idea is the only thing giving him or her a sense of control over an otherwise overwhelming chaos.

There are more brittle assumptions about the world and more durable ones. Furthermore, the core elements of the Jewish and Christian scriptural traditions are there because those elements proved more durable amidst awful communal (and individual) catastrophes. In life, of course, there are all kinds of places where we're tempted to mold our image of God to fit our wishes, to make God in our (best) image. Then life happens. Such gods prove empty. They provide no answers. Ancient Judah knew this problem. When the nation was on the verge of destruction by Babylon, the most popular prophets proclaimed that disaster could be averted. Or if it did come, any exile would be short-lived. Those prophets turned out to be "false." Instead, doomsday, violent prophets like Jeremiah—who was almost killed and spent the last days of the war imprisoned—those prophets ended up having the last word. Biblical religion was founded on the often harsh words of Jeremiah, Ezekiel, and the anonymous writers of the Torah. Later, Christianity was founded on the powerfully ambivalent and brilliant theology of Paul, the dark vision of the gospel of Mark, and other traditions flowing out of the brutal, shameful Roman execution of Jesus of Nazareth. These are the traditions that had proven staying power.

Let us recall one more time just how unusual are the Bibles of Judaism and Christianity. In particular, Judaism's Bible is hardly triumphant. The Torah could have (and once may have) ended with Joshua's powerful conquest of the land, fulfilling the promises once given to Abraham and the intent of Moses' exodus. But instead, the Torah ends on the edge of the land, before conquest. Moses dies before he can enter. And if one follows the story farther, we hear of Israel's tribes and kings only to conclude with Jerusalem's destruction and the Babylonian exile.

The founding story of Christianity is only a bit more upbeat. Despite the progressive addition of resurrection traditions to the story of Jesus, the writings of the New Testament still return again and again to the crucifixion. So much focuses on processing Jesus' painful, humiliating, community-shattering death. The New Testament eventually ends, in the book of Revelation, with a terrorizing vision of God's violent intervention in world politics.

Throughout, whether in depiction of the faults of Israel or of the misunderstandings of the apostles, these Jewish and Christian scriptures do not whitewash or glorify God's people and its leadership. Instead, the Bibles of both Judaism and Christianity have eyes wide open to both the violence of the world and human shortcomings. Moreover, they speak of a God, whether Jewish or Christian, who chooses, loves, and perseveres with such fallible people, no matter what. Where more triumphal texts have faded with the empires they celebrated, these scriptural texts abide. Their vision of the world and of humans has proven staying power in a chaotic, often randomly traumatic cosmos.

I am profoundly impressed with how the Bible is saturated with trauma and survival of it. If the Bible were a person, it would be a person bearing the scars, plated broken bones, muscle tears, and other wounds of prolonged suffering. It would be a person whose identity, perhaps average at one time, was now profoundly shaped by trauma. This person would certainly have known joys and everyday life, but she or he also would bear, in body and heart, the wisdom of centuries of trauma. He or she would know the truth of trauma and survival of it. Just like the suffering servant of Isaiah or the crucified Christ, that person would not be pretty to look at. We might be tempted to avert our eyes. But for most of us, there will be a time in our lives when we need that person's wisdom.

I had read these texts for years, indeed decades, and I had written books on the formation of these biblical texts in the crucible of history. But I did not know, not on this level, how much these books were infused with trauma.

This work has changed me. I have had plenty of struggles with biblical religion. I still do. Yet my work on trauma in the wake of my near-encounter with death has deepened my appreciation of the Bible. If there is a purpose to my survival, some way in which I was "chosen" to make something of the fact I did not die on October 10, 2010, perhaps part of it is being able to share these reflections.

APPENDIX

Contemporary Study of Trauma and Ancient Trauma

Trauma is a fashionable topic. It is not just the province of psychologists; scholars in numerous other fields of the humanities and social sciences are now writing on trauma in their respective disciplines. This trend has hit biblical studies too. Once psychologically inclined biblical scholars diagnosed Ezekiel or the apostle Paul with hysteria, epilepsy, schizophrenia, and other conditions. Now scholars have begun to propose that Ezekiel, Paul, and some other troubled biblical figures (such as the prophet Jeremiah) suffered from posttraumatic stress disorder (PTSD).[1] But the trauma concept has proven fertile beyond the typical bounds of psychological analysis of biblical characters. Other approaches have emerged, such as Frechette's ongoing work on the "internalized perpetrator" in biblical psalms of lament, Janzen's study of traumatic disruption of the "master narrative" in Deuteronomy through 2 Kings, or Rambo's reading of the gospel of John in relation to themes of trauma and witness.[2] Fall 2013 marked the first meeting of a special consultation in the Society of Biblical Literature on "Biblical Literature and the Hermeneutics of Trauma," gathering an increasing number of scholars relating trauma and Bible in diverse ways.

As these trends gain force, it is important to remember how contemporary concepts of trauma are time- and culture-bound. After all, there was no concept of posttraumatic stress disorder in the biblical period, and there is increasing debate about the applicability of PTSD concepts to contemporary non-Western cultures.[3] Where contemporary cultures are ever more inclined to see trauma as a certification of the legitimacy of an individual or group's suffering, ancient cultures tended to see catastrophic suffering as a clear mark of an individual or group's cursedness, abandonment by their god, or sin. This is important to bear in mind, particularly as the recent wave of trauma studies of the Bible (this book included) ride the wave of contemporary fascination with and legitimation of trauma. Within our world, highly diverse groups—from combat soldiers inflicting violence on others, to abused children, to Palestinian refugees, to victims of industrial accidents—can gain broader recognition of their pain by having the label "trauma" applied to it. In contrast, identity-shredding catastrophe was no badge of brave victimhood in antiquity, there was no broadly recognized and certified cultural concept of trauma, and there certainly was no Western-style psychotherapeutic approach to treating it.[4]

Trauma Studies Before PTSD

We can gain perspective on present views of trauma and PTSD by backing up a bit and looking at the origins of medical study of trauma. Most discussions of the origins of contemporary concepts of trauma start with John Eric Erichsen's foundational medical work on railway trauma, where he found that victims of railway accidents suffered similar symptoms of debilitating memory disturbance, flashbacks, repetition compulsions, and the like. He argued that the effects started soon after the patient returns home. "A revulsion of feeling takes place. He bursts into tears, becomes unusually talkative, and is excited. He cannot sleep, or if he does, he wakes up suddenly with a vague sense of alarm. The next day he complains of feeling shaken or bruised all over."[5] Erichsen's work provided a medical basis for railway companies to be sued by passengers for injuries suffered, and soon the railway companies could cite in their defense countertreatments by other doctors who argued that the suffering passengers had been made vulnerable to injury by prior mental problems. Much turned at this point on whether the trauma was physical from the accident, caused by lesions on the brain, or merely mental, caused by fear or surprise in the accident. The former physical injuries were seen as grounds for suit, while the latter mental problems were seen as the patients' problems. Despite the best efforts of some doctors like Erichsen, the predisposition of many was to see claims of "railway spine" as selfish attempts to gain compensation.[6]

Meanwhile, in the late nineteenth century there was a virtual arms race among psychiatrists to find a cure for hysteria, an ailment attributed at the time virtually exclusively to women and involving a mix of mental and behavioral symptoms that partially overlap with contemporary diagnoses of PTSD. In particular, while working with a senior colleague, Josef Breuer, on female patients between 1892 and 1896, a young Sigmund Freud developed a hypothesis that trauma was caused when their patients suffered from an event that somehow could not be absorbed. The memories of the traumatic event could not be comprehended by the conscious mind, were not discharged, and thus entered a second consciousness. Thus, for Freud and Breuer, "hysterics suffer mainly from reminiscences." Trauma was a suffering from memory. Freud went on to argue early on that the particular type of incomprehensible memory that many of his female patients could not absorb were experiences of early childhood sexual incest. Furthermore, Freud, linked these findings in his famous hysteria lecture to studies of railway spine, and saw analogies between the mental disruptions that he saw in his hysterical female patients and the symptoms Erichsen had diagnosed as "railway spine."[7]

As is well known, Freud abandoned this trauma-related (early) "seduction hypothesis" in 1905, mainly because he found some of the testimonies of his patients impossible to believe and because he found his alternative theory about primal fantasy of seduction explanatory of more phenomena. But studies of hysteria and trauma continued. One of the most notable was Jean-Martin Charcot's research published in 1889, based on his work at the Salpêtrière infirmary and later, where he identified symptoms of "male hysteria" among male patients. For him this happened among patients unusually susceptible to hypnosis or suggestion, and the traumatic symptoms came from intense fright. Distinctive about his approach was his resolute argument that trauma was a more general phenomenon, not limited to railway accidents, childhood abuse, or the like. And though he resisted the notion of a biological basis to the ailment, he also argued against those who dismissed traumatic symptoms as the result of fraud to secure reparations. Still, by basing his work on patients at Saltpêtrière, Charcot maintained the tradition of diagnosing relatively marginalized people with trauma, since the patients there were working-class, not elite men. Whether for Freud or Charcot, mental trauma was something typically suffered by people who were not their own masters. The trauma diagnosis did not validate people's suffering but further stigmatized them as lower-class individuals.[8]

The next major stop of most histories of trauma usually is World War I and the oft-discussed phenomenon of "shell shock." Again, the initial theory was that the physical violence of explosions on the brain could explain the debilitating mental disruptions suffered by many soldiers. This condition was understood to be a form of "hysteria," and typically noncomissioned officers and enlisted men were diagnosed with it. These "lesser" soldiers could not handle the fear and inability to flee, and therefore their brains developed forms of hysteria or a related diagnosis of "neuroasthenia" (defined as the effects of prolonged mental and/or physical strain, resulting in nerve exhaustion). The battle trauma did not really cause the functional disorders but was just the last straw for a particular soldier's brain that was already weakened from other neurotic disorders. According to this approach, the lower-level traumatized soldier was really a neurotic, and his symptoms were evidence of his inability to deal with stresses that others could handle. His trauma marked his cowardice, and brutal treatments were prescribed to push him back into the patriotic effort as fast as possible.[9]

The Birth of the PTSD Diagnosis

Studies of war trauma were revived in the midst of World War II, but this war added a new dimension to twentieth-century trauma studies: analysis of trauma suffered by noncombatants, starting with victims of Nazi concentration camps. Again, as in case of railway spine, this study was prompted in part by the question of legal reparations for harm. Scandinavian doctors in the 1950s started to find common mental problems among survivors of German concentration camps, and these findings came to play a role in discussions of West German reparations to concentration camp victims. By 1961 the psychologist William Niederland had coined the term "survivor syndrome" to describe the sorts of mental disturbances caused by exposure to extreme suffering. Just a few years later, in 1968, Robert Lifton found similar symptoms among survivors of the Hiroshima bombing.

Both Niederland's and Lifton's work played important roles in the decisive establishment of the PTSD diagnosis in the 1970s, mainly as an outgrowth of a struggle among progressive psychiatrists to chronicle the debilitating effect of the Vietnam War on recently returned veterans. Amidst much societal hostility to returned Vietnam veterans and in the matrix of the late 1960s, these returned vets formed "rap groups," where they shared their experiences, often finding that they all struggled with flashbacks, memory gaps, compulsions, and other symptoms now associated with PTSD. One psychiatrist, Chaim Shatan, in an editorial page essay in the *New York Times* written in 1972, coined a variation of Niederland's "survivor syndrome" in arguing that Vietnam vets suffered from "post-Vietnam Syndrome." Lifton himself joined the effort to add this sort of designation to the standard diagnostic manual used by psychiatrists, psychologists, and other mental health professionals, the DSM or Diagnostic and Statistical Manual. This manual was crucial for providing not only societal recognition of the suffering of Vietnam vets but also specific financial support for treatment through the Veterans Administration and private insurance companies. Lifton and Shaton approached those responsible for revising that manual in 1975 to form a subcommittee to consider adding post-Vietnam syndrome to the third edition, DSM III.

There was much debate about this, and the ultimate compromise was to define the condition not narrowly as as post-Vietnam syndrome, but more generally as posttraumatic stress syndrome. DSM III, published in 1980, included for the first time a diagnosis that specifically located the cause of various disturbances of memory and behavior to experience of prior trauma.[10]

Once it was established as a general diagnosis, PTSD started to be applied to numerous other experiences of trauma. The late-twentieth-century wave of the women's movement, emergent about the same time as the antiwar and Vietnam vet movements, took up language of PTSD to secure societal recognition and medical support for treatment of raped, battered, and otherwise assaulted women and girls. In this sense, the discourse about trauma returned to some of its origins earlier on, in the diagnosis and treatment of specifically female problems. Trauma was genderized.

Trauma, however, entered ever more into broader societal and political vocabulary. At first, the concept of trauma was broadcast society-wide in such popular treatments of the Vietnam War as *Rambo* or *The Deer Hunter*. Trauma lost its stigma and became part of common vocabulary. In the 1980s more and more women and men were diagnosed with PTSD, whether combat veterans, raped women, abused spouses, or others. Increasing numbers of men and women came to the belief that they were suffering in the present for childhood abuse either not remembered or recently recovered through hypnosis or other therapeutic techniques.

The explosion of trauma recollections and accusations of abuse during the 1980s led to significant debate about trauma and memory. Many questioned the techniques by which traumatic memories were "recovered," and some argued against the idea that memories might lie completely dormant before being accessed through therapeutic processes.[11] Again, as in the cases of railway spine, survivors of Nazism, Vietnam vets, and others, this debate took place in a societal context in which the results had concrete implications for the acknowledgment of suffering, legal proceedings, and insurance compensation. Again, though men were included in the debate, females were the more frequent protagonists in such discussions of trauma, both as victims and as advocates.

The more PTSD has come to be understood to be a universal diagnosis of a general psychological problem in the wake of trauma, the more it has infiltrated the practices and discourse around response to war and other disaster by nongovernmental agencies. The theory has been that surely men, women, and particularly children in war-torn countries or areas hit by natural disasters are vulnerable to PTSD. Psychologists and social workers were dispatched to help survivors of disasters such as the tsunami that afflicted Sri Lanka and other Southeast Asian countries in 2004. PTSD checklists came to play an increasing role in determining which people did or did not receive aid in Haiti, Rwanda, and other areas afflicted by collective suffering. As Erica James has argued, PTSD has come to serve as a sort of "currency" by which victims obtained assistance and the organizations who were helping them justified requests for funding.[12] Yet others have argued that there are numerous signs that the PTSD diagnosis is culture-specific. Some maintain that the Western imposition of the diagnosis in Sri Lanka and elsewhere has failed to recognize the local shape of suffering in those countries, devalued local forms of response to such suffering, and imposed individualistic Western categories and medicalized treatment on people disempowered in numerous other ways as well. In other words, Western diagnosis and treatment of "trauma" in developing nations seemed all too much like a new form of Western colonialism.[13]

Meanwhile, scholars in the humanities have raised basic questions about the conceptualization of traumatic stress syndrome and the increasing popularity of study of it. For example, Laura Brown argued in a trenchant article "Not Outside the Range" that the early DSM III definition of trauma as caused by an event "outside the range" of normal human experience subtly reinforced the false idea that the extraordinary suffering of women, minorities, and other marginalized people was somehow not normal and enshrined the experience of privileged, relatively nontraumatized people as the norm.[14] Susanna Radstone raised the question in an essay on trauma theory whether it has gained popularity because of the way it so easily situates blame outside the one who suffers. Where earlier psychological theories like Freud's later system located mental illness in ungovernable processes inside a person, trauma theory could be used to locate a victim's suffering in an event inflicted *on* them.[15] Finally, even as literary studies of trauma built on the major studies by Cathy Caruth, Shoshana Felman, and Dori Laub have expanded, other scholars have criticized these studies as based on fundamental misconceptions about the character of memory and as uncritically celebrating the redemptive effect of therapeutic "witness."[16]

Finally, partly in response to such critiques, the definition of PTSD itself has continued to evolve. The fourth edition of DSM removed the problematic definition of trauma as "outside the range" of normal experience and broadened the definition of PTSD to include a greater variety of responses to trauma. The fifth edition, published in 2012, added two new criteria for trauma (among other changes): "persistent and distorted blame of self or others; and, persistent negative emotional state" and "reckless or destructive behavior." Meanwhile, it removed the reaction of the trauma victim from the list of diagnostically significant criteria, and it added subtypes of PTSD relating to dissociative disorder and to preschool-age children.

From Individual to Collective Trauma

Meanwhile, the concept of trauma has been applied to communities in addition to individuals. Again, as in the case of railway spine and veterans benefits, political and legal interests have played an important role. For example, some of the most influential studies of community trauma were done by anthropologist Kai Erikson, when he was hired as part of legal suits to document injury done to communities by disasters such as the Buffalo Creek flood or the Three Mile Island Nuclear meltdown.[17] The concept of collective or cultural trauma also has been used to support political claims for redress. Activists for American Indians have argued that the Amerindian population has been afflicted with centuries of group trauma, and the trauma concept has been applied to numerous other oppressed, exiled, and persecuted groups—Australian Aboriginal peoples, African Americans, Jews under the Nazis, the German people in the wake of Nazism and the Second World War, various groups in diaspora, and citizens of South American and other countries that have undergone periods of severe political repression.[18] In these cases, the concept of trauma has validated long-standing suffering by these groups.

As such discussion of collective trauma has expanded, some have argued for care in distinguishing dynamics of group trauma from dynamics of individual trauma. For example, Jeffrey Alexander in a 2004 essay argues for the importance of developing an "empirical scientific concept of cultural trauma" that looks at the concrete social processes by which a given group explicitly identifies itself as collective victim of a certain trauma and creates a group identity built in part around that common recognition.[19] Another essay published the same year by Hudnall Stamm argues for a theory of "cultural trauma" that focuses specifically on injury to a group's culture, such as the systematic disruption, repression, and denigration of American Indian culture by

Euro-American people and practices.[20] Other work, such as a 2004 series of essays on the traumatic impact of the September 11, 2001 attacks, have focused instead on psychological dynamics afflicting entire groups. For example, a suggestive essay by Michael Rustin on the military response by the United States to the September 11 attack argues that groups are even more prone than individuals to react to collective trauma through aggressive feelings and behavior toward others.[21] These works are important in reflecting on where group trauma—whether characterized as "cultural," "collective," or otherwise—is both different from and similar to forms of trauma afflicting individuals.

Some, however, argue that the concept of trauma is fundamentally misapplied when it is extended to groups. After all, groups are not persons, and most of the central ideas surrounding trauma were developed in diagnosing and treating individuals. These questions about individual versus group trauma are particularly acute when it comes to theories about groups repressing traumatic memories in a way analogous to individuals who have undergone trauma. Walter Benn Michaels has questioned the racial presuppositions required for a claim that groups might forget and then remember events belonging particularly to them, and Neil Smelser concludes, "It seems inadvisable to seek any precise sociocultural analogy for the psychological repression of trauma."[22]

Others, however, resolutely maintain that collective amnesia is, if anything, more typical of groups dealing with trauma than is trauma-induced amnesia in individuals. As one cross-cultural study of recollection of political events concludes, "Forgetting is one of the main processes found in collective memory."[23] In particular, several studies have found a time lag in collective discussion of traumatic events, with a delay of approximately two decades before widespread public discourse about the causes and impact of painful events such as the American Civil War or the Vietnam War. And in other cases, such as the Turkish genocide of Armenians in the early twentieth century, one could argue that some societies can maintain a collective amnesia or "silent collective memory" about shameful or painful events far longer than a few decades.[24]

Sometimes a society can focus on one set of collective memories as a balance to recollection of traumatic memories. For example, numerous studies have chronicled an approximate twenty-year period after World War II in which there was little discussion of the Nazi genocide of Jews, even in the state of Israel and diaspora Jewish communities. Such memories of victimization undermined the ethos of self-defense carefully developed in Israel, an ethos formed in response to both nearby Arab threats and memories of Jewish persecution by the Nazis and others. Meanwhile, in place of such painful memories of victimization, the nation of Israel collectively focused on events seen to exhibit resolute resistance, such as the story of Jewish rebels at Masada choosing suicide over surrender to the Romans in 70 CE. This national commemoration of resistance at Masada served, at least for some decades, as an antidote to memories of exile and genocide that both generated and yet conflicted with the emerging Israeli national identity.[25]

From Contemporary Trauma Studies to Study of Ancient Trauma

The outcome of this brief and all too approximate survey of the development of the concept of trauma in Western academic discourse highlights several things to keep in mind in doing studies of the kind attempted in this book.

First, study of trauma, however scientific it sounds, is always linked to the social context of the researcher. Despite the fact that PTSD is an established psychological diagnosis, it is ever more clear that contemporary discourses about trauma are thoroughly rooted in the legal, political, gender, and other struggles of the age in which they take place. And that applies to contemporary scholars like me. We must be careful how our discourses about trauma are braided with our own gender, class, and other aspects of our social location. Specifically, one thing that is risky for Christian scholars like myself is the risk of perpetuating historic, Christian anti-Judaism in ways that might pathologize Old Testament texts and Judaism. It would be easy for trauma studies to become a way to dress up old and pernicious Christian tendencies to denigrate Judaism and texts associated with it. On the other side, it is possible to view this book and studies like it as using contemporary concepts of trauma and victimhood as a way to promote ancient religions like Judaism and Christianity, often embattled in the current context. No study of trauma is exempt from questions about its embeddedness in its own cultural context, but this study's significance should not be reduced to its potential context either.

Second, trauma manifests itself in culturally specific ways. PTSD distinguishes itself as Western in the way it is a medical diagnosis focused on individuals' mental condition. Non-Western societies, ancient and contemporary, have known explosive trauma of their own, but have viewed it in other ways, ways only beginning to be studied. For example, many non-Western societies lack the mind-body dichotomy so prominent across much of Western culture. When they discuss intense suffering, it is generally located in a part of the body. There is no exclusively "mental" trauma.[26] And this is only one example among many of ways that both the concept of trauma and the valorization of it in contemporary contexts is foreign to the ancient contexts studied in this book. Though people certainly experienced explosive, identity-destroying events long before contemporary research on trauma began, present concepts of trauma always must be evaluated for their ethno- and chronocentrism, especially amidst the expansion of academic talk about trauma as if its character is self-evident.

Indeed, the whole individualistic focus of much contemporary discussion of trauma may be misleading—for study of both ancient trauma and contemporary trauma. As Patrick Bracken's critique of trauma discourse has emphasized, individual psyches are always structured by common cultural assumptions. As a result, any individual's trauma is deeply shaped by who and where someone is suffering.[27] Trauma, which comes from a Greek word for "wound," takes different forms depending on what mental elements are broken apart. This means in particular that the traumas standing behind the Bible are probably distinct from many that afflict contemporary trauma victims, that the traumas behind the Bible may be more social than individual, and that the particular interplay of social and individual may be quite distinct.

This leads to a third and final set of considerations surrounding analysis of trauma afflicting groups. As discussed above, it can be misleading to reapply dynamics of individual trauma—already quite culturally specific—to groups. Collective/group/cultural trauma has its own dynamics. Therefore, insofar as biblical scholars are focused on how collective suffering was processed and reflected in scriptural texts intended for communities, this biblical scholarship is best informed by anthropological and historical studies of how groups and their collective memories have been affected by intensely painful events. That is why, for example, I find social-psychological study of collective amnesia, rather than debates about individual memory, particularly helpful in analysis of ancient Judean gaps and indirection in recollection of Babylonian exile.

In conclusion, scholars like me must engage in this study in the full knowledge that we do so amidst a wave of recent studies of trauma from diverse angles. As some have pointed out, this fascination with trauma is not necessarily all good.

When someone is running pell-mell in one direction, it is often good to glance back and see what that person is running away from. Might the current preoccupation with trauma mask a disinclination for people to own up to their own role in some of their suffering and an effort to gain sympathy and/or compensation from others? Is it part of a more general trend in Western society toward loss of agency and attribution of behavior to forces beyond anyone's control? What sorts of discourses does language about trauma fit, and are these discourses ones that promote long-term agency and communal development? The answers to these questions are not yet clear, but we need to acknowledge the potentially sinister side of the contemporary preoccupation with trauma even as we explore evocative potential of such studies to illuminate the Bible and how we might use it in our communities and lives.

NOTES

Items appearing in the select bibliography that follows are cited by author's last name and short title.

Abbreviations

LCL	Loeb Classical Library, Cambridge, Mass; Harvard University Press
NJV	New Jerusalem Version, 1985 New York; Doubleday
NRSV	New Revised Standard Version, 1989 National Council of the Churches of Christ
//	Citations of passages that are parallel to each other

Introduction

1. Published as "Refractions of Trauma in Biblical Prophecy," in *Interpreting Exile: Interdisciplinary Studies of Displacement and Deportation in Biblical and Modern Contexts*, ed. Brad Kelle, Frank Ames, and Jacob Wright (Atlanta: SBL, 2011), 295–308.

2. Islam represents a closely related world religious tradition that also features a prominent focus on community and on suffering. Since I lack particular expertise in Islam, I leave discussion of it to others.

3. This part of the answer, of course, pertains only to how the character of the Jewish and Christian scriptures played a role in their ongoing use. The other part of the answer about the flourishing of the Jewish and Christian scriptures focuses on the postbiblical history of Judaism and Christianity, how each religious movement persisted into the present and used scriptures along the way. That postbiblical history lies outside the scope of this book.

4. This quotation of Agamemnon 176–83 is found in Janzen, *The Violent Gift*, 3; Janzen takes the name of his book, one of the most extensive studies of trauma and Bible to date, from this poem.

5. Such "posttraumatic growth" is an increasing focus of research into trauma and recovery. For a survey through the mid-1990s, see Tedeschi and Calhoun, "Posttraumatic Growth."

6. Quotations from Herman, *Trauma and Recovery*, 32, and Caruth, *Trauma*, 153. The description from Carole Beebe Tarantelli is from "Life Within Death," 918–21.

7. Examples of discussions focused on culturally recognized "shared trauma" include Volkan, *Bloodlines* (especially 34–49), and Jeffrey Alexander, "Toward a Theory of Trauma," in *Cultural Trauma and Collective Identity*, ed. Jeffrey Alexander (Berkeley: University of California Press, 2004), 1–30. This book's focus on oblique effects of trauma is one way I avoid the charge of projecting late-twentieth-century victim culture into a time when trauma was viewed quite differently. I discuss this problem at more length in the appendix.

8. For accessible surveys of past work on monotheism, see Robert Gnuse, *No Other Gods: Emergent Monotheism in Israel* (Sheffield: Sheffield Academic Press, 1997), 62–128, and Mark S. Smith, *The Origins of Biblical Monotheism: Israel's Polythe-*

istic Background and the Ugaritic Texts (New York: Oxford University Press, 2001).

CHAPTER 1
Israel, Judah, and the Birth of Scripture

1. Translation from Victor Matthews and Don Benjamin, *Old Testament Parallels*, Fully Revised and Expanded ed. (New York: Paulist, 2006), 98. This dating of the Mernephtah stele roughly corresponds to when a large number of small settlements appear across the highlands of ancient Canaan, settlements identified by many scholars as early "Israelite."

2. Jack Goody, *The Interface Between the Written and the Oral* (Cambridge: Cambridge University Press, 1987), 86–105.

3. Carr, *Writing on the Tablet of the Heart*, 47–61, 84–90.

4. 1 Chronicles 18:16, 2 Samuel 8:17, 1 Kings 4:3, and 2 Samuel 20:25, respectively. For discussion, see T. Mettinger, *Solomonic State Officials: A Study of the Civil Government Officials of the Israelite Monarchy* (Lund, Sweden: Gleerup, 1971), 45–51.

5. Scholars today question how much one can recover the literary heritage of David and Solomon, the proposal here regarding Song of Songs and Ecclesiastes is particularly subject to challenge. For more discussion, see my *Formation of the Hebrew Bible*, 355–469.

6. Frank Moore Cross, *Canaanite Myth and Hebrew Epic: Essays in the History of the Religion of Israel* (Cambridge: Harvard University Press, 1973), 198–99.

7. To be sure, some texts now in books associated with Isaiah and Micah do mention the exodus and/or wilderness. Nevertheless, most scholars agree that these mentions (e.g., Isa 63:10–14 or Micah 7:15) were added to the books of Isaiah and Micah by exilic or postexilic scribes.

CHAPTER 2
The Birth of Monotheism

1. A. Kirk Grayson, "Assyrian Rule of Conquered Territory in Ancient Western Asia," in *Civilizations of the Ancient Near East*, ed. Jack Sasson (New York: Scribner, 1995), 959–68.

2. Erikson, "Notes on Trauma and Community," 194 (emphasis in original).

3. Herman, *Trauma and Recovery*, 53–54; Janoff-Bulman, *Shattered Assumptions*, 123–32.

4. For more on trauma and theology from Serene Jones, see her book *Trauma and Grace: Theology in a Ruptured World* (Louisville, Ky.: Westminster John Knox, 2009).

5. Jan Assmann, "Monotheism, Memory, and Trauma: Reflections on Freud's Book on Moses," in *Religion and Cultural Memory: Ten Studies*, trans. Rodney Livingstone (Stanford: Stanford University Press, 2005), 56–57.

6. Assmann, *The Price of Monotheism*. Assmann calls the renunciation of other gods "the Mosaic distinction." Given the fact that Hosea is the first datable example of such ideas, perhaps we should speak instead of "the Hosean distinction."

7. Some scholars, perhaps because of prior assumptions regarding the dating of covenant themes in the Bible, attribute this whole verse or its reference to covenant as an addition by later scribes. One can never rule this out, but the occurrence of "covenant" (Hebrew *berit*) in a Hosean prophecy of the Assyrian period is probably not a coincidence.

8. Cynthia Chapman, *The Gendered Language of Warfare in the Israelite-Assyrian Encounter* (Winona Lake, Ind.: Eisenbrauns, 2004), 20–59.

9. Janoff-Bulman, *Shattered Assumptions*, 5–21.

CHAPTER 3
Judah's Survival

1. Bob Becking, "Two Neo-Assyrian Documents from Gezer in Their Historical Context," *Jaarbericht van her Vooraziatisch-Egyptisch Genootschap "Ex Orient Lux"* 27 (1981–1902): 76–89.

2. William Schniedewind, *A Social History of Hebrew: Its Origins Through the Rabbinic Period* (New Haven: Yale University Press, 2013), 88–89. See pages 89–90 of the same study for some additional proposals about the pro-Israelite policies of Hezekiah and his successors. For another perspective on the growth of Jerusalem, see Philippe Guillaume, "Jerusalem 720–705 BCE: No Flood of Israelite Refugees," *SJOT* 22 (2008): 195–211.

3. This time of Judean incorporation of remnants of the Northern Kingdom may also be the period when Aaronide priests, formerly associated with the royal sanctuary of Israel at Bethel, moved south and rose to dominance within Judah. This development is then reflected in one of the sources of the Pentateuch, usually termed the Priestly strand, which projects back into Israel's wilderness origins a God-ordained dominance of Aaron's descendants over the priesthood and even over Israel as a whole (note, for example, Exodus 29, Leviticus 8–9, and Numbers 16–18). This does not mean that the Priestly strand as a whole was created in Hezekiah's time, but it suggests that the late eighth century is a likely time for the beginnings of developments leading to the creation of that document.

4. See also a similar taunt by the Assyrians in 2 Kings 19:10–13// Isaiah 37:10–13. Many scholars think these originally were two separate, parallel accounts of the siege before they were combined into the present text.

5. Additional biblical mentions of this covenant with David's house appear in 2 Samuel 23:5; Jeremiah 33:17, 20–22; Psalm 89:3–4, 19–37.

6. Another Zion psalm states that "God's shelter is in Salem [a shortened form of Jerusalem], his dwelling place in Zion. There God broke the flashing arrows, shield, sword and weapon of war" (Psalm 76:2–3).

7. This often appears in English translations as "Yahweh of hosts," but the Hebrew word translated as "host" clearly means "army." The "host" translation dates from a time when "host" meant "army" in older English.

8. Assmann, *Religion and Cultural Memory*.

9. Jan Assmann, *Moses the Egyptian: The Memory of Egypt in Western Monotheism* (Cambridge: Harvard University Press, 1997), 217.

10. Many translations of Deuteronomy 27 have the altar built at "Mount Ebal," not "Mount Gerizim." This, however, probably is a later scribal modification. For discussion, see my *Formation of the Hebrew Bible*, 167–68. Even if Mount Ebal is the original reading, the point made here, about the originally northern referents of Deuteronomy, would still hold, since Mount Ebal is likewise a northern mountain.

11. For discussion and literature, see my *Formation of the Hebrew Bible*, 307–9.

12. A classic argument for this basic idea remains Richard D. Nelson, *The Double Redaction of the Deuteronomistic History* (Sheffield: Sheffield Academic Press, 1981). These arguments are countered in one of the most extensive treatments of 1–2 Kings from the perspective of trauma, David Janzen's *Violent Gift*, 7–25. This is not the context for detailed response to Janzen's arguments. I note only that many of Janzen's most compelling points about traumatic disjunctures in 1–2 Kings and other historical books—such as his repeated note that parts of the last chapters of 2 Kings (2 Kings 21–25) contradict assertions elsewhere in Joshua–2 Kings about divine justice (e.g., pp. 45–46, 110, 115–16, 142, 212, 218–19, 226–29, 233, 235)—coincide quite well with places where other scholars have seen later, exilic additions being made to an earlier, pre-exilic version of the books of Kings.

13. Daniel Fleming, *The Legacy of Israel in Judah's Bible: History, Politics, and the Reinscribing of Tradition* (Cambridge: Cambridge University Press, 2011). See pp. 13–16 of that work for a judicious survey of earlier theories about the relationship of ancient Judah and Israel.

CHAPTER 4
Jerusalem's Destruction and Babylonian Exile

1. Jeremiah 52:30 gives a report of yet a third Babylonian deportation in 582 BCE, but it is not clear exactly what prompted this deportation.

2. For a nuanced picture of areas left relatively unaffected by the Babylonian onslaught see Oded Lipschits, "Shedding New Light on the Dark Years of the 'Exilic Period': New Studies, Further Elucidations, and Some Questions Regarding the Archaeology of Judah as an 'Empty Land,' " in *Interpreting Exile: Interdisciplinary Studies of Displacement and Deportation in Biblical and Modern Contexts*, ed. Brad Kelle, Frank Ames, and Jacob Wright (Atlanta: SBL, 2011), 57–90.

3. For discussion of how the "shattering" of such core beliefs is a central aspect of trauma, see Janoff-Bulman, *Shattered Assumptions*. For critique of the way Janoff-Bulman depicts such shattering, see especially Patrick Bracken, *Trauma: Culture, Meaning, and Philosophy* (London: Whurr, 2002).

4. Tel Aviv is a Babylonian settlement of Judeans mentioned in Ezekiel 3:22. The "city of Judah" is another settlement of Judeans, in Babylon, that is mentioned in several cuneiform legal documents of Judean exiles that were recently discovered. Preliminary description of these finds is in Laurie Pearce, "New Evidence for Judeans in Babylon," in *Judah and the Judeans in the Persian Period*, ed. Oded Lipschits and Manfred Oeming (Winona Lake, Ind.:

Eisenbrauns, 2007), 399–412, but more extensive publication of them is imminent.

5. For more discussion of literature regarding collective "forgetting" of traumatic events see the appendix of this book.

6. See Janzen, *Violent Gift*, which traces these and other ripples found in Deuteronomy–2 Kings, some of which can be traced back (contra Janzen) to exilic attempts to augment these books with explanations of exile, augmentations that only partially conform to the contexts in which they occur and sometimes disagree with one another.

7. David Garber, "Traumatizing Ezekiel: Psychoanalytic Approaches to the Biblical Prophet," in *Psychology and the Bible: A New Way to Read the Scriptures*, ed. J. Harold Ellens and Wayne G. Rollins (Westport, Conn.: Praeger, 2004), 215–20.

8. I was first pointed to this text by a student paper, Karenna Gore, "Ezekiel and Exile: A Study in Individual and Community Trauma," unpublished paper (2013) for a Trauma and the Bible class taught in fall 2012 at Union Theological Seminary. Cited with permission. See also Paul Joyce, *Ezekiel: A Commentary* (New York: T and T Clark, 2008), 168, who is among those interpreting the book of Ezekiel as reflecting communal trauma (3, 80).

9. This expression "death in life" comes from an older, classic study of trauma in the wake of the Hiroshima bombing, Lifton, *Death in Life*. See in particular Lifton's paraphrase on p. 207 of the feelings of death in life by survivors of that bombing. Kai Erikson provides some quotations along these lines from survivors of communal catastrophe in his "Notes on Trauma and Community," 186.

10. A survey of studies of collective trauma in multiple contemporary cultures finds "retaining hope" to be one of the "five essential elements" for group recovery from mass trauma; S. E. Hobfoll et al., "Five Essential Elements of Immediate and Mid-Term Mass Trauma Intervention: Empirical Evidence," *Psychiatry* 70, no. 4 (2007): 298–300. Though this conclusion results from study of contemporary

traumas, it has implications, I believe, for hypotheses about ancient trauma and recovery from it.

11. As one specialist in communal trauma, Kai Erikson, puts it, one of the "hardest earned and fragile accomplishments of childhood is basic trust—and this can be damaged beyond repair by trauma"; "Notes on Trauma and Community," 197.

12. For discussion see Smith, *Origins of Biblical Monotheism*, 153–54 and 179–93.

13. For discussion of the problem of dissociation and healing reintegration, see Cathy Caruth, "An Interview with Robert J. Lifton," in Caruth, *Trauma*, 137.

14. "The Traumatized Self as Suffering Servant: Aftershocks of Trauma in Isaiah 52:13–53:1," Unpublished Student Paper (2013) for Bible and Trauma course, Fall 2012. Perry argues in this paper that the individual cast of the servant allowed a community to safely reflect on its own trauma and restoration. Cited with permission.

CHAPTER 5
Abraham and Exile

1. There are two possible oblique connections to Jerusalem in the Abraham story of Genesis. Genesis 14:18 says that the "king of Salem, Melkizedeq" came to meet Abraham after Abraham had rescued his nephew Lot. "Salem" could be seen as a shortened form of "Jerusalem," and "Melkizedeq" is mentioned in connection with Jerusalem/Zion in Psalm 110:4. In addition, the story of Abraham's near-sacrifice of Isaac takes place on a mountain in "Moriah" (Genesis 22:2), a place mentioned elsewhere in the Bible as the site for Solomon's building of the Jerusalem Temple (2 Chronicles 3:1). Both of these potential references to Jerusalem in the Pentateuch are complicated and indirect. Finally, the song of Moses in Exodus 15 features two

references to places in the land that can be taken as being to Jerusalem (though Jerusalem is not mentioned specifically): "your holy dwelling" (15:13) and "the mountain of your inheritance, the place which you, Yahweh, have made your dwelling, the sanctuary, my lord, prepared by your hands" (15:17).

2. The dating of the monarchy has become particularly controversial in recent decades, with many reputable scholars concluding that a real monarchy did not develop until the 800s BCE or later. I discuss these issues at more length in my *Formation of the Hebrew Bible*, 355–85, concluding that there is good evidence for an initial emergence of a monarchy centered in Jerusalem around 1000, with yet greater centralization in northern Israel around a century later.

3. The years given across this section are approximate. Aside from Mernephtah's brief mention of "Israel" in the Mernephtah stela (dated to 1207 BCE), we have no contemporary mentions of early Israelite kings in datable ancient Near Eastern documents to add precision to dating. For discussion of limited, craft literacy in this prestate period, see Ryan Byrne, "The Refuge of Scribalism in Iron I Palestine," *BASOR* 345 (2007): 1–31.

4. It should be noted that there is some controversy about the dating and formation of the Pentateuch's earliest sources. Some scholars, particularly in Europe, have argued that virtually the entire Pentateuch was written down after the exile, perhaps well into the Hellenistic period. In contrast, I remain convinced that the Pentateuch contains some writings about the primeval history, ancestors, and Moses that could date as early as the ninth or tenth century. My most recent arguments to this effect can be found in *The Formation of the Hebrew Bible*, 456–83. Despite this possible early dating of biblical stories about Abraham and others, however, I am arguing in this chapter that those stories were reread in a new light during exile, revised and expanded (for a recent statement see *The Formation of the Hebrew Bible*, 252–303). This model of ongoing revision of early texts diverges from

a documentary approach in Pentateuchal scholarship, revived in new form in the self-designated "Neo-Documentarian" school, that argues instead that the Pentateuch was created out of the interweaving of four sources (J, E, D and P) with relatively little editorial intervention or expansion. A recent, accessible introduction to this approach can be found in Joel Baden, *The Composition of the Pentateuch: Renewing the Documentary Hypothesis* (New Haven: Yale University Press, 2012).

5. The term "screen memory" is taken from Freud's classic essay on this topic, "Screen Memories," in *Sigmund Freud: The Collected Papers*, vol. 6, ed. Alix Strachey and James Strachey (London: Hogarth, 1899), 43–63. The dynamic of collective avoidance of traumatic memory (of Nazi genocide) and refocus on a group form of "screen memory" (Jewish resistance at Masada) is beautifully described for modern Israel in Zerubabel, *Recovered Roots*, 57–76.

6. This and the other quotations in this paragraph exemplify what Hilde Nelson, in *Damaged Identities and Narrative Repair* (21), calls "infiltrated consciousness." This is where individuals or groups internalize others' negative views of them. These negative depictions impinge on a group's consciousness of itself, and people within such groups often find themselves suffering from their own affirmation of others' bad opinions of them. In response, groups affected by such "infiltrated consciousness" often develop some form of what Nelson calls "counterstories," stories that offer a positive spin on their identity. On similar processes of development of group counterstories in opposition to how others see them, see the brilliant discussion in Malkki, *Purity and Exile*, 245–46.

7. For more on this translation and citation of scholarly discussion, see my *Reading the Fractures of Genesis*, 186–88.

8. Early Christian literature considered Abraham a paradigm of Christian faith. He is mentioned twice, for example, in the hymn to faith in Hebrews 11. Judaism, however, also has focused on Abraham as a model, this time of faithful Torah obedience.

9. A central task for traumatized communities in Erikson, "Notes on Trauma and Community," 197.

10. The close connection between these texts is just one of the many reasons I find implausible the theory that Genesis 22 originated as part of an Elohistic document that was independent of Genesis 12. For more discussion of this link and other considerations weighing against the traditional source approach to the Abraham story, see my *Reading the Fractures*, 196–202.

11. In my *Reading the Fractures*, 153–59, I discuss in more detail the distinction between this promise in Genesis 22:15–18 and that found in Genesis 12. Like numerous other scholars, I am inclined to see these promises as different, but related, stages in the development of the tradition about Abraham.

12. Translations are from Shalom Spiegel, *The Last Trial: On the Legends and Lore of the Command to Abraham to Offer Isaac as a Sacrifice: The Akedah* (New York: Schocken, 1967), 20–21.

13. In my *Reading the Fractures*, 203–17, I discuss these links of Abraham to the Pentateuch. I also summarize (248–53) previous scholarship that argues persuasively, in my view, that the stories in Genesis about Jacob (25–35) and Joseph (37–50) were revised by Judean scribes from their originally northern Israelite form into their present form that feature Judah more prominently.

CHAPTER 6
The Story of Moses

1. I review major points of disagreement in "The Formation of the Moses Story: Literary-Historical Reflections," *Journal of Hebrew Bible and Ancient Israel* 1 (2012): 7–36.

2. Translation is from Daniel Smith-Christopher, "The Politics of Ezra: Sociological Indicators of Postexilic Judaean Society," in *Second*

Temple Studies 1: Persian Period, ed. Philip R. Davies (Sheffield: Sheffield Academic Press, 1991), 79.

3. A brief reference to plagues also appears in Amos 4:10: "I sent a plague among you in the manner of Egypt and killed your young men by the sword." Most scholars agree, however, that "in the manner of Egypt" is a gloss added to connect this verse with the Egypt account. It breaks up the poetic line, and it was common for scribes to link different texts with such brief coordinating comments.

4. Jeremiah 28, for example, tells of Jeremiah's confrontation with another prophet, Hananiah, in the time between the first Babylonian deportation of Judah's king and elite, but before Jerusalem's destruction and the second wave of exiles. Where Jeremiah was predicting that Babylon's domination of Judah would last, Hananiah predicted that Judah's king and temple would be restored within two years (Jeremiah 28:3–4).

5. Though there are questions about the list of returnees in Ezra 2, it initially features a descendant of David, Zerubbabel, and his retinue (Ezra 2:2), and is particularly dominated by lists of various priestly personnel (Ezra 2:36–58).

6. Two more ancient texts that describe these festivals are Exodus 23:14–17 and Deuteronomy 16:1–17.

7. Caruth, *Unclaimed Experience*, 64 (emphasis is in the original).

8. Ibid., 71.

9. See Malkki, *Purity and Exile*, 230 specifically and 197–230 more generally for discussion of an analogous development of concepts of separateness and purity among Hutus living in exile in Tanzania.

CHAPTER 7
The Return Home

1. Amelie Kuhrt, "The Cyrus Cylinder and Achamenid Royal Ideology," *JSOT* 25 (1983): 83–97.

2. "Exiles" in Ezra 1:11, 6:21, 9:4, 10:6; "captive exiles," Ezra 2:1// Nehemiah 7:6; "the sons of the exile," Ezra 4:1, 6:19–20, 8:35, 10:7, 16; "the assembly of exiles," Ezra 10:8.

3. This corresponds to the way trauma often accentuates prior fault lines in groups that experience trauma. See Erikson, "Notes on Trauma and Community," 185–86.

4. The expression "peoples of the land" occurs in Ezra 9:1–2, 11; 10:2, 11; Nehemiah 9:24, 30; 10:29, 30, 31.

5. For similar lists of (to be) conquered peoples, see also Exodus 3:8, 17; 13:5; Deuteronomy 20:17; Joshua 3:10.

6. See Katherine Southwood, *Ethnicity and the Mixed Marriage Crisis in Ezra 9–10: An Anthropological Approach* (New York: Oxford University Press, 2012), especially 41–56 and 203–8, for a nuanced discussion of the phenomenon of "reverse migration" on how anthropological studies of reverse migration can inform understanding of the conflict of exiles with homeland people now perceived as "foreign."

7. The question of dating Ezra relates particularly to the problem of whether he was roughly contemporaneous with Nehemiah (as described in the Bible) or whether he long postdated Nehemiah. The Bible places Ezra's arrival in Judah in the seventh year of the reign of "Artaxerxes" (Ezra 7:1, 8), while Nehemiah's trip to Judah is linked with the twentieth year of "Artaxerses" (Nehemiah 2:1). What the compilers of Ezra-Nehemiah may not have realized is that the Artaxerses in the case of Nehemiah may have been a different king from the Artaxerses associated with Ezra. Especially when one more closely examines the manuscript tradition for Ezra, there are indicators that the Judah that Ezra encounters postdates the work of Nehemiah. See on this particularly Dieter Böhler, *Die heilige Stadt in Esdras a und Esra-Nehemia: Zwei Konzeptionen der Wiederherstellung Israels* (Göttingen: Vandenhoeck and Ruprecht, 1997), which is summarized in English in "On the Relationship Between Textual and Literary

Criticism: The Two Recensions of the Book of Ezra: Ezra-Neh (MT) and 1 Esdras (LXX)," in *The Earliest Text of the Hebrew Bible*, ed. Adrian Schenker (Atlanta: Society of Biblical Literature, 2003), 35–50. I briefly engage some additional literature in *Formation of the Hebrew Bible*, 207–8.

8. The first reference in the book of Ezra to return, Ezra 1:5, mentions only Judeans and Benjaminites, alongside priests and Levites, among the returnees. Nevertheless, subsequent references, such as Ezra 2:2 and 3:1, routinely refer to this group of returnees as the "sons of Israel."

9. See Levy and Lemma, *The Perversion of Loss*, particularly the essay by Michael Rustin, "Why Are We More Afraid Than Ever? The Politics of Anxiety After Nine Eleven," 21–36, on the particular tendency of traumatized groups to project their pain outward.

CHAPTER 8
Traumatic Crystallization of Scripture

1. I provide an overview of the major data for this idea in "Canonization in the Context of Community: An Outline of the Formation of the Tanakh and the Christian Bible," in *A Gift of God in Due Season: Essays on Scripture and Community in Honor of James A. Sanders*, ed. Richard D. Weis and David M. Carr (Sheffield: JSOT Press, 1996), 34–49.

2. For more extensive arguments on this point, see my *Writing on the Tablet of the Heart*, 260–71, and *Formation of the Hebrew Bible*, 158–66.

3. Here I am informed by arguments about "invented tradition" in Eric Hobsbawm, "Introduction: Inventing Traditions," in Hobsbawm and Ranger, *The Invention of Tradition*, 1–14.

4. Benjamin Sommer, "Did Prophecy Cease? Evaluating a Reevaluation," *JBL* 115 (1996): 31–47.

5. Carr, *Writing on the Tablet of the Heart*, 107.

6. Again, I am influenced here by Eric Hobsbawm (*The Invention of Tradition*), though without adopting his term "invented" for the reappropriation of older traditions.

CHAPTER 9
Christianity's Founding Trauma

1. Cicero, *Verrine Orations*, 2.5.66 (§170 in Greenwood, LCL).

2. Josephus, *Jewish Wars*, 7.6.4 (§ 203 in Thackeray, LCL).

3. See Martin Hengel, *Crucifixion in the Ancient World and the Message of the Cross*, trans. John Bowden (1976; Philadelphia: Fortress, 1977), 22–32, for a judicious survey of evidence. Gunnar Samuelsson offers a more comprehensive survey of mentions of crucifixion (*Crucifixion in Antiquity* [Tübingen: Mohr Siebeck, 2011]), arguing that there was virtually no common ancient understanding of what crucifixion entailed. This contribution is a welcome balance to often elaborate step-by-step descriptions of the crucifixion process often repeated in various books and articles (some of which Samuelsson quotes), but his study suffers, in my view, from an underreading of the New Testament evidence and an unbalanced attempt to require nonbiblical mentions of such execution to provide a full and identical account of the crucifixion process. For a more extensive response to Samuelsson's argument, see Brian Pound's review of the book, "Review of Samuelsson, *Crucifixion in Antiquity*," *JSNT* 33 (2011): 398–405.

4. Attempts to identify earlier nonbiblical Christian texts about Jesus' crucifixion have proven unsuccessful. The most prominent such attempt was John Dominic Crossan's argument that the noncanonical Gospel of Peter preserves an earlier form of the story of Jesus' crucifixion than the biblical gospels. See his *The Cross That Spoke: The Origin of the Passion Narratives* (San Francisco: Harper and Row,

1988). This theory has not fared well in subsequent debate. For a summary of considerations against it, see Raymond Brown, "The Gospel of Peter and Canonical Gospel Priority," *NTS* 33 (1987): 321–43, and Raymond Brown, *The Death of the Messiah: From Gethsemane to the Grave—A Commentary on the Passion Narratives in the Four Gospels* (New York: Doubleday, 1994), 1318–36.

5. For a useful table surveying these parallels see Clifton Black, *Mark*, Abingdon New Testament Commentaries (Nashville: Abingdon, 2011), 277–81. Notably, where Mark and John agree outside the Passion narrative, it generally concerns traditions about Jesus in Jerusalem—for example, his "cleansing of the temple" or entry into the city—traditions, in other words, that could well have been part of an early crucifixion narrative. Note that though both gospels seem to reflect some early crucifixion narrative, most scholars presume that it is more faithfully preserved in Mark than John. One good discussion of the overlapping traditions about Jesus' death in Mark and John is Wolfgang Reinbold, *Der älteste Bericht über den Tod Jesus* (Berlin: De Gruyter, 1994), 227–82.

Some may wonder about Matthew and Luke's crucifixion narratives. These gospels overlap even more with Mark's passion narrative than does John's, but most scholars explain that overlap as part of a broader dependence of Matthew and Luke on (some form of) the gospel of Mark as a whole. Unlike John, they overlap with large portions of Mark's earlier story of Jesus as well.

6. Where the rest of Mark is built around brief stories about Jesus only vaguely located in time and place, the crucifixion narrative in Mark 14–16 precisely chronicles the place and time of each episode (Adela Yarbro Collins, *The Beginning of the Gospel: Probings of Mark in Context*. [Minneapolis: Fortress, 1992], 92–93), and where Jesus appears as a strong, decisive teacher in Mark 1–13, anticipating and almost welcoming his crucifixion (Mark 8:27–33, 9:30–32, 10:32–34), the picture in Mark 14–16 is quite different: he prays at Gethsemane

to be spared execution and is largely silent when interrogated by Jewish and Roman authorities (Eugene M. Boring, *Mark: A Commentary* [Louisville: Westminster John Knox, 2006], 378–79). In addition, Judas is reintroduced as "one of the twelve" in this early crucifixion narrative (Mark 14:43), even though he has already been introduced as part of the twelve apostles in two earlier gospel scenes (Mark 3:19, 14:10), as emphasized in Marion Soard's initial discussion in appendix 9 of Brown, *Death of the Messiah*, 1522.

7. For a useful survey, see the overview by Marion Soards of different ways this crucifixion narrative has been identified in studies up through the early 1990s in Brown, *Death of the Messiah*, 1492–524.

8. The following walk-through of potential parts of the pre-Markan crucifixion narrative follows Reinbold, *Älteste Bericht*, in particular in using overlaps of Mark and John as an external control for identifying potential parts of that narrative. I diverge, however, from Reinbold (esp. pp. 97–106) in using this overlap method—also important in his analysis—to include Mark 16:1–8//John 20:1–18) as a probable part of the early crucifixion narrative.

9. Some have suggested that Jesus' muteness here is prompted by the suffering servant model, in which the servant does not respond when abused, but this early crucifixion narrative nowhere explicitly links to the wording of Isaiah 53. If anything, its primary links are to Psalm 22 instead, both Jesus' quotation of the outset of the psalm in his dying and the earlier reference to soldiers dividing up his clothes (cf. Psalm 22:18).

10. Origen, *Contra Celsum*, 6.10 (translation Henry Chadwick, *Origen: Contra Celsum* [Cambridge: Cambridge University Press, 1953], 324).

11. Here I am informed by an article on Palestinian reinterpretation of a (reported) Israeli policy of attempting to suppress Palestinian resistance by imposing humiliating beatings on Arab men accused of illegal activities; Julie Peteet, "Male Gender

and Rituals of Resistance," *Am. Ethnol.* 21 (1994): 31–49. Though Peteet's article, like any treatment of Israeli-Palestinian relations, has a bias, it presents evocative ideas about how symbols can be interpreted differently by different parties, especially when those parties have very different levels of power and are embedded in situations of conflict.

12. These are the letters which most scholars agree were written by Paul. One good brief recent discussion is Bart D. Ehrman, *The New Testament: A Historical Introduction to the Early Christian Writings*, 4th ed. (New York: Oxford University Press, 2008), 380–401.

13. In the past, links of Isaiah 53 with expressions of "dying for" in the New Testament have been tied up in arguments that the New Testament is dependent exclusively on inner-Jewish models, and attempts to establish an early origin for later Christian ideas that Jesus' death was an atoning sacrifice for his people. I do not share this agenda. Second Temple Judaism was Hellenistic in all its forms, and therefore attempts to establish exclusively inner-Jewish origins for this and other New Testament ideas are doomed to failure. Moreover, I am not arguing for an early origin for Christian atonement theology. For a thorough argument (and citation of earlier literature) regarding Greek, non-Jewish parallels to the idea and terminology of vicarious "dying for" others, see particularly Henk S. Versnel, "Making Sense of Jesus's Death: The Pagan Contribution," in *Deutungen des Todes Jesus im Neuen Testament*, ed. Jörg Frey and Jens Schröter (Tubingen: Mohr Siebeck, 2005), 213–94.

14. Some have argued recently that the scrolls found near the Dead Sea site at Qumran contain references to a suffering Messiah modeled on Isaiah 53. For review and rebuttal of these arguments, see especially John J. Collins, "A Messiah Before Jesus?" in *Christian Beginnings and the Dead Sea Scrolls*, ed. John J. Collins and Craig Evans (Grand Rapids, Mich.: Baker, 2006), 15–35.

15. Versnel, "Making Sense of Jesus's Death."

16. For more on the centrality of Moses as a model for Jesus in the gospels of Matthew and John, see Michael P. Theophilos, *Jesus as the New Moses in Matthew 8–9: Jewish Typology in First Century Greek Literature* (Piscataway, N.J.: Gorgias, 2011), 1–19; Norman R. Petersen, *The Gospel of John and the Sociology of Light: Language and Characterization in the Fourth Gospel* (Valley Forge, Pa.: Trinity Press International, 1993), 80–109.

17. Klaus Baltzer, *Deutero-Isaiah: A Commentary on Isaiah 40–55* (Minneapolis: Fortress, 2001), especially 125 ff.

18. Aitken, *Jesus' Death in Early Christian Memory*, 69–71.

19. Ibid., 170.

20. James Cone, *The Cross and the Lynching Tree* (Maryknoll, N.Y.: Orbis, 2011), 22.

CHAPTER 10
The Traumatized Apostle

1. For summary of the data that lead most scholars to separate these events, see James B. Wallace, *Snatched into Paradise (2 Cor 12:1–10): Paul's Heavenly Journey in the Context of Early Christianity* (Berlin: De Gruyter, 2011), 251–52, note 57. See Dennis C. Duling, *The New Testament: History, Literature, and Social Context* (Belmont, Calif.: Wadsworth, 2003), 365–67, for a brief overview of some problems with depending excessively on the book of Acts for historical specifics about Paul.

2. Alan Segal, *Paul the Convert: The Apostolate and Apostasy of Saul the Pharisee* (New Haven: Yale Univ. Press, 1990), 36–37.

3. Some older examples of psychological studies of Paul include Arthur A. Holmes, *The Mind of St. Paul: A Psychological Study* (New York: Macmillan, 1929), Carl T. Healer, *Freud and St. Paul*

(Philadelphia: Dorrance, 1970), and Gerd Theissen, *Psychological Aspects of Pauline Theology* (1983; Philadelphia: Fortress, 1987). Some recent essays include Anthony Bash, "A Psychodynamic Approach to 2 Corinthians 10–13," in *Psychology and the Bible: A New Way to Read the Scriptures*, vol. 3, ed. J. Harold Ellens and Wayne G. Rollins (Westport, Conn.: Praeger, 2004), 149–63; Terrance Callan, "Psychological Perspectives on the Life of Paul," in *Psychological Insight into the Bible: Texts and Readings*, ed. Wayne G. Rollins and Andrew Kille (Grand Rapids, Mich.: Eerdmans, 2007), 127–37; and (with a focus on trauma) Sandra Hack Polaski, "2 Corinthians 12:1–10: Paul's Trauma," *Review and Expositor* 105 (2008): 279–84.

4. Though the link to Damascus appears only in Acts, I use the term "Damascus event" here as a shorthand way to refer to Paul's experience and avoid prejudging the character of his experience as a "conversion," "call," "epiphany," or the like.

5. Here I side with those who maintain that the frequent translation of *pisteo Christou* as "faith in Christ" is mistaken, and that this phrase refers instead to "faith of Christ." For arguments for this translation, see particularly Richard Hays, *The Faith of Jesus Christ: The Narrative Substructure of Galatians 3:1–4:1* (1983; Grand Rapids, Mich.: Eerdmans, 2002), 119–62.

6. In this and several other respects, I have been influenced by the position in Stanley Stowers, *A Rereading of Romans: Justice, Jews, and Gentiles* (New Haven: Yale University Press, 1994), on this point particularly 213–36.

7. In so emphasizing Paul's complicated relationship with his prechurch past and his conflicted consciousness, I should note that my account of Paul here runs counter to some aspects of what has come to be called the "alternative perspective" on Paul developed by numerous scholars over the past fifty years, partly in the wake of the classic article by Krister Stendahl, "The Apostle Paul and the Introspective Conscience of the West," *Harvard Theological*

Review 56 (1963): 199–215. Though I agree with Stendahl and others in affirming Paul's continued Jewish identity, I resist tendencies among some to arrive at a new simplicity about the complex figure of Paul. I am anticipated in this emphasis on some sort of discontinuity in Paul by Segal, *Paul the Convert*, especially 5–7.

8. In trauma studies there is discussion of distinctions between those traumatized exclusively by ways they were acted upon by perpetrators and those haunted not only by violence to themselves but also by horrific acts of violence they have inflicted by others. The latter type of trauma, the trauma of the perpetrator, is experienced more often by war veterans. See the appendix to this book for more discussion of how contemporary trauma studies developed in large part as a response to the trauma of war veterans, particularly veterans of the Vietnam War.

9. I am informed throughout this discussion by a dissertation recently completed by Asha Moorthy, "A Seal of Faith."

10. Of course, Judaism is not immune from tendencies—also seen in Christianity and other religions—toward overfocus on external practices. Indeed, some of Judaism's greatest figures (for example, Hillel, Akiba) fought these tendencies and are celebrated in Jewish tradition for doing so.

11. See also 1 Thessalonians 2:14 and 2 Corinthians 13:4: "For he was crucified in weakness, but lives by the power of God. For we are weak with him, but in dealing with you we will live with him by the power of God."

CHAPTER 11
The Traumatic Origins of Judaism and Christianity

1. Martin Goodman, "Diaspora Reactions to the Destruction of the Temple," in *Jews and Christians: The Parting of the Ways, A.D. 70 to 135*, ed. James D. G. Dunn (Tübingen: Mohr, 1992), 27.

2. Josephus, *Jewish Wars*, 6.414–20; 7.118, 216 (Thackeray, LCL). For a good brief summary of the impact of the Roman assault, see Stephen G. Wilson, *Related Strangers: Jews and Christians 70–170 CE* (Minneapolis: Fortress, 1995), 3–4, and Ekkahard Stegemann and Wolfgang Stegemann, *The Jesus Movement: A Social History of Its First Century*, trans. O. C. Dean (Minneapolis: Fortress, 1994), 221.

3. Heemstra, *Fiscus Judaicus*, 9–23.

4. Wilson, *Related Strangers*, 3–8.

5. Tessa Rajak, "The Jewish Community and Its Boundaries," in *The Jews Among Pagans and Christians in the Roman Empire*, ed. Judith Lieu, John North, and Tessa Rajak (London: Routledge, 1992), 9–11.

6. Ibid., 11–14.

7. Josephus, *Jewish Wars*, 4.3.2 (§ 130 in Thackeray, LCL) and 4.8.1 (§444).

8. Shaye Cohen, "The Significance of Yavneh: Pharisees, Rabbis, and the End of Jewish Sectarianism," *Hebrew Union College Annual* 55 (1984): 27–53.

9. Wilson, *Related Strangers*, 23.

10. David M. Carr, "Canonization in Community: An Outline of the Formation of the Tanakh and the Christian Bible," in *A Gift of God in Due Season: Essays on Scripture and Community in Honor of James A. Sanders*, ed. Richard D. Weis and David M. Carr (Sheffield: JSOT Press, 1996), 49–58.

11. Tacitus, *Historiae*, 5.5 (Moore, LCL).

12. Josephus, *Antiquities*, 19.287–91; the reported edict for Alexandria is in *Antiquities*, 19.280–85, and the back-reference to the Claudius edict in 19.303–11. On these reports, see Miriam Pucci Ben-Zeev, *Jewish Rights in the Roman World* (Tübingen: Mohr Siebeck, 1998), 328–42, 344–56.

13. Josephus, *Jewish Wars*, 2.462–65 (Thackeray, LCL).

14. Ibid., 7.420–35 (Thackeray, LCL).

15. Josephus, *Jewish Wars*, 7.437–50 (Thackeray, LCL).

16. Tacitus, *Annales*, 15.44 (Jackson, LCL).

17. L. F. Janssen, " 'Superstitio' and the Persecution of the Christians," *Vigiliae christiannae* 33 (1979): 131–59.

18. Stegemann and Stegemann, *Jesus Movement*, 244–46.

19. Philip S. Alexander, " 'The Parting of the Ways' from the Perspective of Rabbinic Judaism," in *Jews and Christians: The Parting of the Ways A.D. 70 to 135*, ed. James D. G. Dunn (Tübingen: Mohr, 1992), 1–25.

20. Zetterholm, *The Formation of Christianity in Antioch*, 218–22.

21. Ignatius, Magnesians 8:1–2, translation adapted from Zetterholm, *Formation of Christianity at Antioch*, 220.

22. Zetterholm, *Formation of Christianity at Antioch*, 219–22.

23. In older scholarship, there was a tendency to think that Jewish communities in the diaspora sometimes had significant proportions of "God fearers," attracted to Judaism but not ready to take the full step of conversion. For a critique of this approach, see Judith Lieu, "Do God-Fearers Make Good Christians" (31–47) and "The Race of the God-Fearers" (49–68) in *Neither Jew nor Greek? Constructing Early Christianity* (London: Continuum, 2002).

24. Goodman, "Diaspora Reactions," 36–37.

25. Suetonius, *Domitian*, 12.2 (Rolfe, LCL).

26. Cassius Dio, *Roman History*, 67.14.1–2 (Cary, LCL).

27. Heemstra, *Fiscus Judaicus*, 24–66 and passim, and Zetterholm, *Formation of Christianity at Antioch*, 186–89. Some have expressed skepticism about the extent of persecution under Domitian, particularly given the lack of specific reports in Christian sources of deaths during his reign. Nevertheless, Pliny 10.96 refers in passing to Christians he interrogated who experienced persecution around the time of Domitian. Moreover, as Wilson points out (*Related Strangers*,

17), Pliny himself claims to have executed Christians, but we have no Christian sources commemorating these martyrdoms.

28. Cassius Dio, *Roman History* 65.7.2 (Cary, LCL).

29. Heemstra, *Fiscus Judaicus*, 67–84, 174–76.

30. Moss, *The Myth of Christian Persecution.*

31. Anders Runesson, "Inventing Christian Identity: Paul, Ignatius, and Theodosius I," in *Exploring Early Christian Identity*, ed. Bengt Holmberg (Tübingen: Mohr Siebeck, 2008), 64–70.

32. Tacitus, *Annales*, 15.44 (Jackson, LCL).

33. Note also Acts 11:26, where the emphasis is on when others in Antioch first started calling Jesus followers "Christians."

34. Pliny, *Epistles*, Trajan, 10.96. Translation here is from P. G. Walsh, *The Complete Letters: Pliny the Younger* (New York: Oxford University Press, 2006), 278–79.

35. Expressions about "the name" appear in Ignatius's letter to the Ephesians, both in 1:2 and 3:1.

36. Ignatius, Romans 3:2, translation here from William R. Schoedel, *Ignatius of Antioch: A Commentary on the Letters of Ignatius of Antioch*, ed. Helmut Koester, Hermeneia (Minneapolis: Fortress, 1985), 170.

37. Magnesians 5:2. The translation of Ignatius here is from Maxwell Staniforth and Andrew Louth, *Early Christian Writings: The Apostolic Fathers* (New York: Penguin, 1987), 72.

38. For emphasis on "obstinacy" as a factor in Christian persecution, see particularly the classic article G. E. M. Ste. Croix, "Why Were the Early Christians Persecuted?" *Past and Present* 26 (1963): 6–38. Moss argues that this factor merely contributed to a negative image of Christians by others, an image founded primarily on fears on other grounds (*Myth of Christian Persecution*, 176). For another perspective, A. N. Sherwin-White, *The Letters of Pliny: A Historical and Social Commentary* (Oxford: Clarendon, 1966), 783–87 on *contumacia* (disobedience of an official order) as the main charge against Christians.

39. A major strand of recent scholarship on the emergence and self-definition of Judaism and Christianity has argued that the two were inextricably intertwined into a relatively late period. For discussion and review of earlier scholarship see the essays in Adam Becker and Annetee Yoshiko Reed, eds., *The Ways That Never Parted: Jews and Christians in Late Antiquity and the Early Middle Ages* (Tübingen: Mohr Siebeck, 2003), and (extending earlier work) Daniel Boyarin, *Border Lines: The Partition of Judaism and Christianity* (Philadelphia: University of Pennsylvania Press, 2004). This body of scholarship has rightly balanced anachronistic tendencies in some earlier scholarship yet has some shortcomings as well. For other perspectives see Thomas Robinson, *Ignatius of Antioch and the Parting of the Ways: Early Jewish-Christian Relations* (Peabody, Mass.: Hendrickson, 2009), 203–40, and Heemstra, *Fiscus Judaicus*, 67–84.

40. Note also, similar injunctions found in Josephus, *Antiquities*, 4.207 (Thackeray, LCL; paraphrasing the Torah), and Philo, *Special Laws*, 1.53 (LCL, Colson), emphasizing that gentile worship of other gods should be tolerated.

CHAPTER 12
The Posttraumatic Gospel

1. The gospel of Matthew, to be sure, comes first in the New Testament and is best known by many Christians, but it represents an expansion of Mark's gospel. The same is true for the gospel of Luke. The gospel of John, though preserving a different set of traditions from those seen in the other biblical gospels, seems to have been written as late as or later than Matthew and Luke. This represents the general consensus of most contemporary international scholarship.

2. Martin Kähler, *Der sogenannte historische Jesus und der geschichtliche, biblische Christus*, 2nd expanded and rev. ed. (Leipzig: Deichert, 1896), 80, note 11.

3. The original ending is in John 20:30–31, while chapter 21 is generally agreed to be a later extension of the gospel, one featuring a similar conclusion (21:25).

4. Colleen Conway, *Behold the Man: Jesus and Greco-Roman Masculinity* (New York: Oxford University Press, 2008), 120–22, 145–49.

5. The setting of the story in Jerusalem, its preservation in John 2 (including a reference to the Passover in John 2:13), and the possible back-reference to the original story in Mark 14:58 (which refers back to a saying preserved only in John 2:19, but not in Mark's version of this episode in Mark 11:15–19 [//Matthew 21:12–17, Luke 19:45–48) suggest that it probably was a part of the early "crucifixion narrative" I have discussed in chapter 8. Yet the authors of Mark and John each used this story of Jesus' attack on the Temple marketplace for his own purposes. While the author of Mark used it as the introduction to his account of Jesus' stay in Jerusalem, the author of John placed it toward the very beginning of his gospel as an explanation of Jesus' conflict with Jewish leaders.

6. The earliest core of the first main rabbinic text, the Mishnah, consists of Temple regulations, and much of Jewish life revolves around laws regarding purity. Jacob Neusner, *Method and Meaning in Ancient Judaism* (Missoula, Mont.: Scholars Press, 1979), 133–53.

7. This is the version found in Mark and parallels. There is another source used by the gospels of Matthew and Luke, usually referred to as the "Q source," that had related sayings, including Matthew 10:38//Luke 14:27 ("whoever does not bear his own cross and come after me, may not be my disciple") and Matthew 10:39//Luke 17:33 ("whoever seeks to gain his life will lose it, but whoever loses his life will keep it"). There is some evidence that this last version, without a reference to the cross, originates with the historical Jesus. For brief comments along these lines, see Robert Funk, *The Gospel of Mark: The Red Letter Edition* (Sonoma, Calif.: Polebridge, 1991), 139.

8. Adele Reinhartz, "The Destruction of the Jerusalem Temple as a Trauma for Proto-Christian," in *Trauma and Traumatization in Individual and Collective Dimensions: Insights from Biblical Studies and Beyond*, ed. Eva Marie Becker and Else Kragelund Holt, Studia Aarhusiensis no. 2 (Göttingen: Vandenhoeck and Ruprecht, 2014), 285.

9. Miscellanies 4.16–17, as quoted in Moss, *Myth of Christian Persecution*, 194.

10. Moss, *Myth of Christian Persecution*, 10–11.

Epilogue

1. In a provocative study of "the abusing God" written during the Palestinian Intifada (*Facing the Abusing God*, 203), David Blumenthal criticized Jewish policies that confused a rock-throwing Palestinian teenager with the Nazis who had tormented earlier generations.

2. Janoff-Bulman, *Shattered Assumptions*, 5–21.

Appendix

1. A good survey and response to earlier studies of Ezekiel is Garber, "Traumatizing Ezekiel" and this now is supplemented with the review on pp. 11–35 of Ruth Poser, *Das Ezechielbuch als Trauma-Literature* (Leiden: Brill, 2012). For Jeremiah, see O'Connor, *Jeremiah: Pain and Promise*. Early in my work, I was particularly informed by Smith-Christopher, *A Biblical Theology of Exile*.

2. Rambo, *Spirit and Trauma*; Janzen, *Violent Gift*. Christopher Frechette's study, "Destroying the Internalized Perpetrator," will be published (along with a number of other excellent studies on Bible and trauma) in Eva Marie Becker and Else Kragelund Holt, eds., *Trauma and Traumatization in Individual and Collective Dimensions*.

In addition, Ruth Poser's lengthy 2011 dissertation "Ezechielbuch" represents a multidimensional approach to interpreting Ezekiel in relation to studies of both individual and collective trauma.

3. See, for example, the account of application of Western PTSD ideas to treatment of survivors of the 2004 tsunami in Sri Lanka in Watters, *Crazy Like Us*, 65–125, and the study of nightmares in the same area in J. Grayman and B. Good, "Conflict Nightmares and Trauma in Aceh," *Culture, Medicine, and Psychiatry* 33 (2009): 290–312. For broader discussion see Summerfield, "A Critique of Seven Assumptions" and "The Invention of Post-Traumatic Stress Disorder." One response to these critiques is Derek Silove, Zachary Steel, and Adrian Bauman, "Mass Psychological Trauma and PTSD: Epidemic or Cultural Illusion," in *Cross Cultural Assessment of Psychological Trauma and PTSD*, 319–36, particularly table 1 on 320–23.

4. Here I am particularly informed by Fassin and Rechtman, *Empire of Trauma.*

5. John Eric Erichsen, *On Railway and Other Injuries of the Nervous System* (London: Walton and Maberly, 1866), 96.

6. For further discussion, Ralph Harrington, "The Railway Accident: Trains, Trauma, and Technological Crises in Nineteenth Century Britain" (31–55) and Eric Caplan, "Trains and Trauma in the American Gilded Age" (56–77), both in *Traumatic Pasts: History, Psychiatry, and Trauma in the Modern Age, 1870–1930*, ed. Mark S. Micale and Paul Lerner (Cambridge: Cambridge University Press, 2001).

7. Caroline Garland, "Thinking About Trauma," in *Understanding Trauma: A Psychoanalytical Approach*, ed. C. Garland (London: Karnac, 1998), 9–31. For a subtle discussion of different elements in Freud's understanding of trauma, elements that had different trajectories in subsequent study of trauma, see Leys, *Trauma*, 21–35.

8. Mark S. Micale, "Jean-Martin Charcot and les névroses traumatiques: From Medicine to Culture in French Trauma Theory of

the Late Nineteenth Century," in Micale and Lerner, *Traumatic Pasts*, 115–39.

9. Young, *Harmony of Illusions*; Shephard, *War of Nerves*; Leys, *Trauma*; and Fassin and Rechtman, *Empire of Trauma*, 40–57.

10. Shephard, *War of Nerves*, 355–66.

11. Richard J. McNally, *Remembering Trauma* (Cambridge: Belknap Press of Harvard University Press, 2003).

12. See particularly Erica James, "The Political Economy of 'Trauma' in Haiti in the Democratic Era of Insecurity," *Culture, Medicine, and Psychiatry* 28 (2004): 127–49, but also her longer work *Democratic Insecurities.*

13. On this, see the studies cited above in note 3, along with the essays in Warwick Anderson, Deborah Jenson, and Richard Keller, eds., *Unconscious Dominions: Psychoanalysis, Colonial Trauma, and Global Sovereignties* (Durham: Duke University Press, 2011).

14. Laura S. Brown, "Not Outside the Range: One Feminist Perspective on Psychic Trauma," in Caruth, *Trauma*, 100–112.

15. Radstone, "Trauma Theory." Note also the thoughtful introduction in the same issue of *Paragraph* by Nerea Arruti, "Trauma, Therapy, and Representation: Theory and Critical Reflection," *Paragraph* 30 (2007): 1–8. For a broader critique of politics oriented around injury see Wendy Brown, *States of Injury* (Princeton: Princeton University Press, 1995), especially 64–74.

16. Caruth's work (e.g., *Unclaimed Experience*) and Felman and Laub's (especially *Testimony: Crises of Witnessing in Literature, Psychoanalysis, and History* [New York: Routledge, 1992]) form something of a foundational canon for studies of trauma in the humanities. Just to pick two examples, the theory of memory in Caruth (and Van der Kolk before her) is criticized by Ruth Leys in particular (*Trauma*, esp. 229–97 and 304–5), while Felman and Laub's ideas about witnessing are reviewed in 53–59 of Kali Tal, *Worlds of Hurt: Reading Literatures of Trauma* (Cambridge: Cambridge University Press, 1996).

17. Insights summarized in Erikson, "Notes on Trauma and Community."

18. Essays related to collective memory of political events, especially in Spanish-speaking countries, can be found in James Pennebaker, Dario Paez, and Bernard Rime, eds., *Collective Memory of Political Events: Social Psychological Perspectives* (Mahwah, N.J.: Erlbaum, 1997). For examples of application of trauma to numerous other groups, see Yael Danieli, ed., *International Handbook of Multigenerational Legacies of Trauma* (New York: Plenum, 1998).

19. Jeffrey Alexander, "Toward a Theory of Cultural Trauma," in *Cultural Trauma and Collective Identity*, ed. Jeffrey Alexander (Berkeley: University of California Press, 2004), 1–30. As noted in the introduction to this book, this position resembles the concept of "chosen trauma" in Vamik Volkan's work, *Bloodlines: From Ethnic Pride to Ethnic Terrorism* (New York: Farrar, Straus and Giroux, 1997). On this topic, see as well Neil J. Smelser, "Psychological Trauma and Cultural Trauma," in Alexander, *Cultural Trauma and Collective Identity*, 31–59.

20. R. Hudnall Stamm et al., "Considering a Theory of Cultural Trauma and Loss," *Journal of Trauma and Loss* 9 (2004): 89–111.

21. Michael Rustin, "Why Are We More Afraid Than Ever? The Politics of Anxiety After Nine Eleven," in Levy and Lemma, *The Perversion of Loss*, 21–36.

22. Walter Benn Michaels, "Race into Culture: A Critical Genealoogy of Cultural Identity," *Critical Inquiry* 18 (1992): 655–85; Walter Benn Michaels, "The No Drop Rule," *Critical Inquiry* 20 (1994): 758–69; Smelser, "Psychological Trauma and Cultural Trauma," 50.

23. Dario Paez, Nekane Basabe, and Jose Luis Gonzalez, "Social Processes and Collective Memory: A Cross-Cultural Approach to Remembering Political Events," in *Collective Memory of Political Events: Social Psychological Perspectives*, ed. James Pennebaker, Dario Paez, and Bernard Rime (Mahwah, N.J.: Erlbaum, 1997), 147.

24. The expression "silent collective memory" comes from page 256 of Jose Marques, Dario Paez, and Alexandra Serra, "Social Sharing, Emotional Climate, and the Transgenerational Transmission of Memories: The Portuguese Colonial War," in Pennebaker, Paez, and Rime *Collective Memory of Political Events*, 253–75; the authors document several examples of communal forgetting of difficult events.

25. For a beautifully nuanced study of this and other dynamics in the formation of Israeli national memory, see Zerubavel, *Recovered Roots*.

26. See, for example, the classic early article Byron J. Good, "The Heart of What's the Matter: The Semantics of Illness in Iran," *Culture, Medicine, and Psychiatry* 1 (1977): 25–58, and a more recent example, E. Coker, " 'Traveling Pains': Embodied Metaphors of Suffering Among Southern Sudanese Refugees in Cairo," *Culture, Medicine, and Psychiatry* 28 (2004): 15–39.

27. Patrick Bracken, *Trauma: Culture, Meaning, and Philosophy* (London: Whurr, 2002).

SELECT BIBLIOGRAPHY ON BIBLE AND TRAUMA

A more complete bibliography of works cited in this book can be found on the Web at http://dx.doi.org/10.7916/D8H41PJW.

Aitken, Ellen. *Jesus' Death in Early Christian Memory: The Poetics of the Passion.* Göttingen: Vandenhoeck and Ruprecht; Fribourg: Academic Press, 2004.

Assmann, Jan. *The Price of Monotheism.* Trans. Robert Savage. 2003; Stanford: Stanford University Press, 2010.

Becker, Eva Marie, and Else Kragelund Holt, eds. *Trauma and Traumatization in Individual and Collective Dimensions: Insights from Biblical Studies and Beyond.* Göttingen: Vandenhoeck and Ruprecht, 2014.

Blumenthal, David. *Facing the Abusing God: A Theology of Protest.* Louisville, Ky.: Westminster John Knox, 1993.

Carr, David M. *The Formation of the Hebrew Bible: A New Reconstruction.* New York: Oxford University Press, 2011.

———. *Reading the Fractures of Genesis: Historical and Literary Approaches.* Louisville, KY: Westminster John Knox, 1996.

———. *Writing on the Tablet of the Heart: Origins of Scripture and Literature*. New York: Oxford University Press, 2005.

Caruth, Cathy. *Unclaimed Experience: Trauma, Narrative, and History*. Baltimore: Johns Hopkins University Press, 1996.

———, ed. *Trauma: Explorations in Memory*. Baltimore: Johns Hopkins University Press, 1995.

Daniel, E. Valentine, and John Chr. Knudsen, eds., *Mistrusting Refugees*. Berkeley: University of California Press, 1995.

Erikson, Kai. "Notes on Trauma and Community." Pp. 183–99 in Caruth, *Trauma*.

Fassin, Didier, and Richard Rechtman. *The Empire of Trauma: An Inquiry into the Condition of Victimhood*. Trans. Rachel Gomme. 2007; Princeton: Princeton University Press, 2009.

Freud, Sigmund. *Moses and Monotheism*. Trans. Katherine Jones. New York: Vintage, 1939.

Garber, David. "Trauma Studies." In *Oxford Encyclopedia of Biblical Interpretation*. Vol. 2, ed. Steven McKenzie, 421–28. New York: Oxford University Press, 2013.

Gutiérrez, Gustavo. *On Job: Suffering and God Talk*. Maryknoll, NY: Orbis, 1987.

Heemstra, Marius. *The* Fiscus Judaicus *and the Parting of the Ways*. Tübingen: Mohr, 2010.

Herman, Judith Lewis. *Trauma and Recovery*. New York: Basic, 1992.

Hobsbawm, Eric, and Terence Ranger, eds. *The Invention of Tradition*. New York: Cambridge University Press, 1983.

James, Erica. *Democratic Insecurities: Violence, Trauma, and Intervention in Haiti*. Berkeley: University of California Press, 2003.

Janoff-Bulman, Ronnie. *Shattered Assumptions: Towards a New Psychology of Trauma*. New York: Free Press, 1992.

Janzen, David. *The Violent Gift: Trauma's Subversion of the Deuteronomistic History's Narrative*. New York: T and T Clark, 2012.

Levy, Susan, and Alessandra Lemma, eds. *The Perversion of Loss: Psychoanalytic Perspectives on Trauma*. London: Whurr, 2004.

Leys, Ruth. *Trauma: A Genealogy*. Chicago: University of Chicago Press, 2000.

Lifton, Robert J. *Death in Life: Survivors of Hiroshima*. New York: Basic, 1967.

Linafelt, Tod. *Surviving Lamentations: Catastrophe, Lament, and Protest in the Afterlife of a Biblical Book*. Chicago: University of Chicago, 2000.

Malkki, Liisa. *Purity and Exile: Violence, Memory, and National Cosmology Among Hutu Refugees in Tanzania*. Chicago: University of Chicago Press, 1995.

Moorthy, Asha. "A Seal of Faith: Rereading Paul on Circumcision, Torah and the Gentiles." Ph.D. diss. Columbia University, 2013.

Moss, Candida. *The Myth of Christian Persecution: How Early Christians Invented a Myth of Martyrdom*. New York: HarperOne, 2013.

Nelson, Hilde L. *Damaged Identities: Narrative Repair*. Ithaca, NY: Cornell University Press, 2001.

O'Connor, Kathleen. *Jeremiah: Pain and Promise*. Minneapolis: Fortress, 2011.

Pennebaker, James, Dario Paez, and Bernard Rime, eds. *Collective Memory of Political Events: Social Psychological Perspectives*. Mahwah, NJ: Erlbaum, 1997.

Peteet, Julie. "Male Gender and Rituals of Resistance." *American Ethnologist* 21 (1994): 31–49.

Radstone, Susanna. "Trauma Theory: Contexts, Politics, Ethics." *Paragraph* 30 (2007): 9–29.

Rambo, Shelly. *Spirit and Trauma: A Theology of Remaining*. Louisville, Ky.: Westminster John Knox, 2010.

Segal, Alan. *Paul the Convert: The Apostolate and Apostasy of Saul the Pharisee*. New Haven: Yale University Press, 1990.

Shephard, B. *A War of Nerves: Soldiers and Psychiatrists in the Twentieth Century*. Cambridge: Harvard University Press, 2000.

Smith-Christopher, Daniel. *A Biblical Theology of Exile*. Minneapolis: Fortress, 2002.

Summerfield, Derek. "A Critique of Seven Assumptions Behind Psychological Trauma Programmes in War-Affected Areas." *Social Science and Medicine* 48 (1999): 1449–62.

———. "The Invention of Post-Traumatic Stress Disorder and the Social Usefulness of a Psychiatric Category." *British Medical Journal* 322 (2001): 95–98.

Tarantelli, Carole Beebe. "Life Within Death: Toward a Metapsychology of Catastrophic Psychic Trauma." *International Journal of Psychoanalysis* 84 (2003): 915–28.

Tedeschi, R., and L. Calhoun. "Posttraumatic Growth: Conceptual Foundations and Empirical Evidence." *Psychological Inquiry* 15 (2004): 1–18.

Volkan, Vamik. *Bloodlines: From Ethnic Pride to Ethnic Terrorism*. New York: Farrar, Straus and Giroux, 1997.

Watters, Ethan. *Crazy Like Us: The Globalization of the American Psyche*. New York: Free Press, 2010.

Young, Alan. *The Harmony of Illusions: Inventing Post-Traumatic Stress Disorder*. Princeton: Princeton University Press, 1995.

Zerubavel, Yael. *Recovered Roots: Collective Memory and the Making of Israeli National Tradition*. Chicago: University of Chicago Press, 1996.

Zetterholm, Magnus. *The Formation of Christianity at Antioch: A Social-Scientific Approach to the Separation of Judaism and Christianity*. London: Routledge, 2003.

ACKNOWLEDGEMENTS

As I conclude this book, I want to offer special thanks to those who have helped me conceive, research, and write it. To Don Fehr, literary agent at Trident Media, who helped me develop the idea for this book and found an excellent publishing home for it. To Karen Seeley, who allowed me into her superb seminar on trauma at Columbia University, and the students of that seminar as well. To New York City–area therapists and psychiatrists with special expertise on trauma who gave generously of their time and expertise to me, particularly Debbie Rothschild, Joseph Napoli, Nina Short, and Ghislaine Boulanger. To the students of two seminars on Bible and Trauma that I offered at Union Theological Seminary and taught me so much: Rachel Lonberg, Janelle Stanley, Anna Grunner, Shadi Halabi, Sara Cairatti, Amy Meverden, Will Owen, Caroline Perry, Rosalind Gnatt, Rix Thorsell, C. B. Stewart, Nathaniel Mahlberg, Tristan Brennan-Torell, John Allen, Karenna Gore, Jeff Grant, Leslie Culbertson, and

Carolyn Klassen. To colleagues who generously gave me advance copies of research that enriched my thinking on Bible and trauma, especially Daniel Smith-Christopher and Else Kragelund Holt. To the audiences of lectures in which I developed and tested the material for this book at Union Theological Seminary, the Exile/Forced Migrations and Biblical Literature Consultation in the Society of Biblical Literature, the University of Oslo, St. Andrews Seminary in Saskatoon, the Catholic University of America, the Columbia University Faculty Seminars on Hebrew Bible and on New Testament, the Engaging the Powers Project at Union Theological Seminary, and Presbyterian Churches in Ramsey, Hackensack, and Englewood, New Jersey. Throughout this project I have greatly benefited from the superlative collections and gifted staffs of the Burke Library at Union Theological Seminary and other libraries in the Columbia University system. I also am very grateful to my employer, Union Theological Seminary in New York, for its substantial support of my research through its provision of a research leave and overall support for my research while teaching.

Finally, this book is much better for the efforts of family, colleagues, and dear friends who read and commented on drafts of chapters, so I thank Robbie Harris, Marc Mauceri, Nadeleen Tempelman-Kluit, J. P. Partland, David Beriss, Debbie Rothschild, Christopher Frechette, Esther Hamori, and my father, John Carr, for their help. I thank my editor, Jennifer Banks, for immense aid in revising the manuscript, and thanks as well to Kellie Anderson Picallo, who provided expert assistance in helping me envision how to present the book to others. In closing, I cannot offer enough gratitude to my wife, Colleen Conway, expert in both New Testament and in writing, who read each chapter and pushed me to make each one better.

INDEX

Illustrations indicated by **boldface**.